SCREEN WORLD

edited by

JOHN WILLIS

1966

Volume 17

CROWN PUBLISHERS, INC.

New York

In Memoriam

DANIEL BLUM

1899 - 1965

FOUNDER and EDITOR

of

SCREEN WORLD

4　　　Julie Christie, Laurence Harvey
in
"DARLING"

TABLE OF CONTENTS

Editorial Assistants: Harold Stephens,
Aileen Carter, Carl Raymund, Stanley Reeves

Oskar Werner

Capucine

Warren Beatty

Leslie Caron

Simone Signoret

Marlon Brando

Lana Turner

Louis Jourdan

James Fox

Lilia Kedrova

Cliff Robertson

Brigitte Bardot

Vivien Leigh

Lee Marvin

Bette Davis

George Segal

6

Charles Boyer

Barbara Stanwyck

Rock Hudson

Jane Fonda

Olivia De Havilland

Terence Stamp

Gina Lollobrigida

Sidney Poitier

1965 RELEASES

George Maharis

Jeanne Moreau

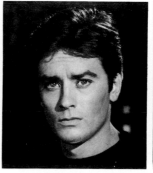

Alain Delon

Elizabeth Ashley

Cindy Carol, Billy Mumy, Fabian, Glynis Johns,
James Stewart, John Williams

Cindy Carol, Glynis Johns, James Stewart

DEAR BRIGITTE

(20th CENTURY-FOX) Producer-Director, Henry Koster; Screenplay, Hal Kanter; Based on Novel "Erasmus With Freckles" by John Haase; Music, George Duning; Director of Photography, Lucien Ballard; Assistant Director, Fred R. Simpson; Costumes, Moss Mabry; A Fred Kohlmar Production in CinemaScope and DeLuxe Color. January release.

CAST

Prof. Robert Leaf	James Stewart
Kenneth	Fabian
Vina Leaf	Glynis Johns
Pandora Leaf	Cindy Carol
Erasmus Leaf	Billy Mumy
Peregrine Upjohn	John Williams
Dr. Volker	Jack Kruschen
George	Charles Robinson
Dean Sawyer	Howard Freeman
Terry	Jane Wald
Unemployment Clerk	Alice Pearce
Argyle	Jesse White
Lt. Rink	Gene O'Donnell
The Captain	Ed Wynn

and Brigitte Bardot

James Stewart, Billy Mumy, Brigitte Bardot
Above: Ed Wynn, Glynis Johns, James Stewart
Left: Cindy Carol, Fabian, James Stewart

8

Don Murray, Steve McQueen, Lee Remick

Lee Remick, Steve McQueen

Kimberly Block, Lee Remick, Steve McQueen,
Estelle Hemsley. Above: Steve McQueen,
Lee Remick, Kimberly Block. (R) Don Murray,
Ruth White

BABY, THE RAIN MUST FALL

(COLUMBIA) Producer, Alan Pakula; Director, Robert Mulligan; Screenplay, Horton Foote; Based on his Play "The Traveling Lady"; Music, Elmer Bernstein; Director of Photography, Ernest Laszlo; Song Lyrics, Ernest Sheldon; Assistant Director, Joseph E. Kenny; A Park Place-Solar Productions Picture. January release.

CAST

Georgette Thomas	Lee Remick
Henry Thomas	Steve McQueen
Slim	Don Murray
Judge Ewing	Paul Fix
Mrs. Ewing	Josephine Hutchinson
Miss Clara	Ruth White
Mr. Tillman	Charles Watts
Mrs. Tillman	Carol Veazie
Catherine	Estelle Hemsley
Margaret Rose	Kimberly Block
Mrs. T. V. Smith	Zamah Cunningham
Counterman	George Dunn

9

QUICK, BEFORE IT MELTS

(M-G-M) Producers, Douglas Laurence, Delbert Mann; Director, Delbert Mann; Screenplay, Dale Wasserman; Based on Novel by Philip Benjamin; Music, David Rose; Director of Photography, Russell Harlan; Assistant Director, Erich Von Stroheim, Jr.; In Panavision and Metrocolor. January release.

CAST

Peter Santelli	George Maharis
Oliver Cromwell Cannon	Robert Morse
Tiare Marshall	Anjanette Comer
Vice Admiral	James Gregory
Harvey T. Sweigert	Howard St. John
Mikhail Drozhensky	Michael Constantine
George Snell	Norman Fell
Diana Grenville-Wells	Janine Gray
Sharon Sweigert	Yvonne Craig
Leslie Folliott	Bernard Fox
Orville Bayleaf	Conlan Carter
Ben Livingston	Richard Lepore
Milton Fox	Milton Fox
Prison Guard	Hal Baylor
Ham Operator	Doodles Weaver
Shaggy Type	Frank London
Scientist	Nelson Olmstead
Military Men	Tom Vize, John Dennis, Hugh "Slim" Langtry, Fletcher Allen, Davis Roberts, Dale Malone
Bar Maids	Marjorie Bennett, Karen Scott

Left: Yvonne Craig, Robert Morse, Anjanette Comer, George Maharis. Below Right: Robert Morse, George Maharis

Parley Baer, Connie Stevens, Cesar Romero
Above: Virginia Gregg, Dean Jones

TWO ON A GUILLOTINE

(WARNER BROS.) Producer-Director, William Conrad; Screenplay, Henry Slesar, John Kneubuhl; Story, Henry Slesar; Director of Photography, Sam Leavitt; Music, Max Steiner; Assistant Director, Phil Rawlins; In Panavision. February release.

CAST

Melinda and Cassie Duquesne	Connie Stevens
Val Henderson	Dean Jones
"Duke" Duquesne	Cesar Romero
"Buzz" Sheridan	Parley Baer
Dolly Bast	Virginia Gregg
Ramona Ryerdon	Connie Gilchrist
Carl Vickers	John Hoyt
Carmichael	Russell Thorson

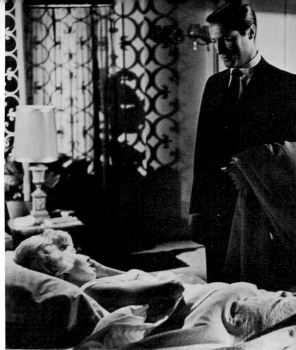

THE NIGHT WALKER

(UNIVERSAL) Producer-Director, William Castle; Screenplay, Robert Bloch; Director of Photography, Harold Stine; Assistant Directors, Terry Nelson, Bill Gilmore; Associate Producer, Dona Hollway. February release.

CAST

Irene Trent	Barbara Stanwyck
Barry Morland	Robert Taylor
Howard Trent	Hayden Rorke
Dream	Lloyd Bochner
Joyce	Judith Meredith
Hilda	Rochelle Hudson
Manager	Marjorie Bennett
Malone	Jess Barker
Gardener	Tetsu Komai
Narrator	Ted Durant

Robert Taylor, Barbara Stanwyck. Top: Rochelle Hudson, Robert Taylor

Barbara Stanwyck, Hayden Rorke. Top: Barbara Stanwyck, Lloyd Bochner

11

36 HOURS

(M-G-M) Producer, William Perlberg; Director, George Seaton; Screenplay, George Seaton; Based on "Beware of The Dog" by Roald Dahl, and a Story by Clark K. Hittleman and Luis H. Vance; Music, Dimitri Tiomkin; Director of Photography, Philip H. Lathrop; Assistant Director, Donald Roberts; A Perlberg-Seaton Production in Panavision. February release.

CAST

Major Jefferson Pike	James Garner
Anna Hedler	Eva Marie Saint
Major Walter Gerber	Rod Taylor
Otto Schack	Werner Peters
Ernst	John Banner
General Allison	Russell Thorson
Colonel Peter MacLean	Alan Napier
Lt. Colonel Osterman	Oscar Beregi
Captain Abbott	Ed Gilbert
German Guard	Sig Ruman
Elsa	Celia Lovsky
Corporal Kenter	Karl Held
Kraatz	Martin Kosleck
Charwoman	Marjorie Bennett
German Soldiers	Henry Rowland, Otto Reichow
German Agent	Hilda Plowright
Denker	Walter Friedel
Lemke	Joseph Mell

James Garner, Eva Marie Saint, Rod Taylor

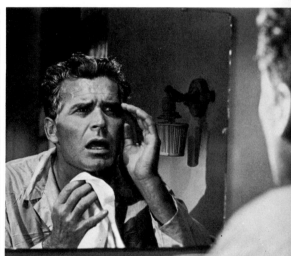

Rod Taylor, James Garner, Eva Marie Saint
Above: James Garner, Eva Marie Saint

Eva Marie Saint, James Garner (also above)

12

James Garner, Eva Marie Saint

Eva Marie Saint, James Garner

Rod Taylor, James Garner, Eva Marie Saint
Above: Eva Marie Saint, Rod Taylor

Eva Marie Saint, James Garner
Above: Rod Taylor, Oscar Beregi

Jack Lemmon, Terry-Thomas. Right: Virna Lisi,
Jack Lemmon

HOW TO MURDER YOUR WIFE

(UNITED ARTISTS) Produced and Written by
George Axelrod; Executive Producer, Gordon
Carroll; Director, Richard Quine; Music, Neal
Hefti; Director of Photography, Harry Strad-
ling; Assistant Director, Carter DeHaven;
Choreographer, Robert Sidney; In Technicolor.
February release.

CAST

Stanley Ford	Jack Lemmon
Mrs. Ford	Virna Lisi
Charles	Terry-Thomas
Harold Lampson	Eddie Mayehoff
Edna	Claire Trevor
Judge Blackstone	Sidney Blackmer
Tobey Rowlins	Max Showalter
Dr. Bentley	Jack Albertson
District Attorney	Alan Hewitt
Harold's Secretary	Mary Wickes

Virna Lisi

Jack Lemmon, Eddie Mayehoff

14

Virna Lisi, Jack Lemmon

Virna Lisi, Claire Trevor, Jack Lemmon,
Eddie Mayehoff

Terry-Thomas, Jack Lemmon

Terry-Thomas, Jack Lemmon, Virna Lisi

Murvyn Vye (L), Ann Wedgeworth,
Norman Alden

Sudi Bond, Norman Alden

ANDY

(UNIVERSAL) Produced, Directed and Written
by Richard C. Sarafian; Director of Photography, Ernesto Capparos; Assistant Directors,
Larry Sturhahn, Paul Leaf. February release.

CAST

Andy	Norman Alden
Mrs. Cliadakis	Tamara Daykarhonova
Mr. Cliadakis	Zvee Scooler
Margie	Ann Wedgeworth
Bartender	Murvyn Vye
Sommerville	Al Nesor
Simovich	Warren Finnerty

Norman Alden. Left: Tamara Daykarhonova,
Norman Alden, Zvee Scooler. Above: Norman
Alden, Cynthia Grover

16

SYLVIA

(PARAMOUNT) Producer, Martin Poll; Director, Gordon Douglas; Assistant Producer, Shirley Mellner; Screenplay, Sydney Boehm; Based on Novel by E. V. Cunningham; Cinematographer, Joseph Ruttenberg; Assistant Director, Dick Moder; Costumes, Edith Head; Music, David Raksin. February release.

CAST

Sylvia West	Carroll Baker
Alan Macklin	George Maharis
Jane Phillips	Joanne Dru
Frederick Summers	Peter Lawford
Irma Olanski	Viveca Lindfors
Oscar Stewart	Edmond O'Brien
Jonas Karoki	Aldo Ray
Mrs. Argona	Ann Sothern
Bruce Stamford III	Lloyd Bochner
Lola Diamond	Paul Gilbert
Big Shirley	Nancy Kovack
Peter Memel	Paul Wexler
Father Gonzales	Jay Novello
Molly Banter	Connie Gilchrist

and Alan Carney, Shirley O'Hara, Anthony Caruso, Gene Lyons, Bob Random, Val Avery, Manuel Padilla

Right: Shirley O'Hara, Carroll Baker, Aldo Ray

George Maharis, Viveca Lindfors. Above: Ann Sothern, Carroll Baker

Carroll Baker, George Maharis. Above Carroll Baker, Anthony Caruso, Edmond O'Brien

Clint Walker, Frank Sinatra, Richard Bakalyan,
Tommy Sands, Sammy Jackson

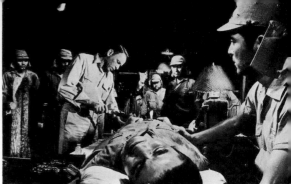

Frank Sinatra, Susumu Kurobe, Tatsuya Mihashi

Tony Bill, Clint Walker. Above: Frank Sinatra
(R) Clint Walker, Laraine Stephens

NONE BUT THE BRAVE

(WARNER BROS.) Producer-Director, Frank Sinatra; Executive Producer, Howard W. Koch; Associate Producer, William H. Daniels; Screenplay, John Twist and Katsuya Susaki; Story, Kikumaru Okuda; Director of Photography, Harold Lipstein; Assistant Director, David Salven; Music, Johnny Williams; A Co-Production of Tokyo Eiga Co., Toho Film and Artanis Productions, and Sinatra Enterprises Productions; In Technicolor and Panavision. February release.

CAST

Maloney	Frank Sinatra
Capt. Bourke	Clint Walker
Lt. Blair	Tommy Sands
Sgt. Bleeker	Brad Dexter
Keller	Tony Bill
Lt. Kuroki	Tatsuya Mihashi
Sgt. Tamura	Takeshi Kato
Cpl. Craddock	Sammy Jackson
Cpl. Ruffino	Richard Bakalyan
Pvt. Johnson	Rafer Johnson
Pvt. Dexter	Jimmy Griffin
Pvt. Searcy	Christopher Dark
Pvt. Hoxie	Don Dorrell
Pvt. Magee	Phil Crosby
Pvt. Waller	John H. Young
Pvt. Swensholm	Roger Ewing
Hirano	H. Suguro
Cpl. Fujimoto	K. Sahara

Don Derrell, Roger Ewing, Rafer Johnson

Clint Walker, Frank Sinatra, Brad Dexter,
Tommy Sands

Frank Sinatra, Tommy Sands, Clint Walker
Above: Frank Sinatra, Tommy Sands,
Tony Bill, Clint Walker

Frank Sinatra, Clint Walker, Richard Bakalyan,
Phil Crosby. Above: Clint Walker, Frank Sinatra

SIGNPOST TO MURDER

(M-G-M) Producer, Lawrence Weingarten; Director, George Englund; Screenplay, Sally Benson; Based on Play by Monte Doyle; Music, Lyn Murray; Director of Photography, Paul C. Vogel; Gowns by William Travilla; Assistant Director, Wallace Worsley; A Marten Picture in Panavision. February release.

CAST

Molly Thomas	Joanne Woodward
Alex Forrester	Stuart Whitman
Dr. Mark Fleming	Edward Mulhare
The Vicar	Alan Napier
Mrs. Barnes	Joyce Worsley
Supt. Bickley	Leslie Denison
Dr. Graham	Murray Matheson
Officer Rogers	Hedley Mattingly
Auntie	Carol Veazie

Murray Matheson, Joanne Woodward,
Edward Mulhare, Stuart Whitman
Left: Stuart Whitman, Joanne Woodward

MY BLOOD RUNS COLD

(WARNER BROS.) Producer-Director, William Conrad; Screenplay, John Mantley; Story, John Meredyth Lucas; Director of Photography, Sam Leavitt; Music, George Duning; Assistant Director, Russell Llewellyn; In Panavision. March release.

CAST

Ben Gunther	Troy Donahue
Julie Merriday	Joey Heatherton
Julian Merriday	Barry Sullivan
Harry Lindsay	Nicolas Coster
Aunt Sarah	Jeanette Nolan
Sheriff	Russell Thorson
Lansbury	Ben Wright
Mrs. Courtland	Shirley Mitchell
Henry	Howard McNear
Mayor	Howard Wendell
Mr. Courtland	John Holland
Owen	John McCook

Joey Heatherton, Troy Donahue. Right:
Joey Heatherton, Barry Sullivan

20

Glenn Ford, Henry Fonda, and Right:
with Chill Wills

THE ROUNDERS

(M-G-M) Producer, Richard E. Lyons; Director,
Burt Kennedy; Screenplay, Burt Kennedy; From
a Novel by Max Evans; Music, Jeff Alexander;
Director of Photography, Paul C. Vogel; Assistant Director, Al Jennings; In Panavision
and Metrocolor. March release.

CAST

Ben Jones	Glenn Ford
Howdy Lewis	Henry Fonda
Mary	Sue Ann Langdon
Sister	Hope Holiday
Jim Ed Love	Chill Wills
Vince Moore	Edgar Buchanan
Agatha Moore	Kathleen Freeman
Meg Moore	Joan Freeman
Bull	Denver Pyle
Tanner	Barton MacLane
Arlee	Doodles Weaver
Mrs. Norson	Allegra Varron

Henry Fonda, Hope Holiday, Sue Ann Langdon,
Glenn Ford. Above: Henry Fonda, Edgar
Buchanan, Glenn Ford

Henry Fonda, Denver Pyle, Glenn Ford

THE GREATEST STORY EVER TOLD

(UNITED ARTISTS) Producer-Director, George Stevens; Screenplay, James Lee Barrett, George Stevens; In Creative Association with Carl Sandburg; Music, Alfred Newman; Executive Producer, Frank I. Davis; Associate Producers, George Stevens, Jr., Antonio Vellani; Costumes, Vittorio Nino Novarese; Screenplay based on The Bible, other ancient writings, "The Greatest Story Ever Told" by Fulton Oursler, and writings by Henry Denker; Directors of Photography, William C. Mellor, Loyal Griggs; Assistant Directors, Ridgeway Callow, John Veitch; In Ultra Panavision 70 and Technicolor. March release.

CAST

Jesus	Max Von Sydow
Mary	Dorothy McGuire
Joseph	Robert Loggia
John The Baptist	Charlton Heston
James The Younger	Michael Anderson, Jr.
Simon The Zealot	Robert Blake
Andrew	Burt Brinckerhoff
John	John Considine
Thaddaeus	Jamie Farr
Philip	David Hedison
Nathanael	Peter Mann
Judas Iscariot	David McCallum
Matthew	Roddy McDowall
Peter	Gary Raymond
Thomas	Tom Reese
James The Elder	David Sheiner
Martha of Bethany	Ina Balin
Mary of Bethany	Janet Margolin
Lazarus	Michael Tolan
Simon of Cyrene	Sidney Poitier
Mary Magdalene	Joanna Dunham
Veronica	Carroll Baker
Young Man At The Tomb	Pat Boone
Bar Amand	Van Heflin
Uriah	Sal Mineo
Woman of No Name	Shelley Winters
Old Aram	Ed Wynn
The Centurion	John Wayne
Pontius Pilate	Telly Savalas
Claudia	Angela Lansbury
Pilate's Aide	Johnny Seven
Questor	Paul Stewart
General Varus	Harold J. Stone
Caiaphas	Martin Landau
Shemiah	Nehemiah Persoff
Nicodemus	Joseph Schildkraut
Sorak	Victor Buono
Emissary	Robert Busch
Alexander	John Crawford
Scribe	Russell Johnson
Speaker of Capernaum	John Lupton
Joseph of Arimathaea	Abraham Sofaer
Theophilus	Chet Stratton
Annas	Ron Whelan
Herod Antipas	Jose Ferrer
Herod The Great	Claude Rains
Aben	John Abbott
Captain of Lancers	Rodolfo Acosta
Herod's Commander	Michael Ansara
Chuza	Philip Coolidge
Philip	Dal Jenkins
Archelaus	Joe Perry
Herodias	Marian Seldes
Dark Hermit	Donald Pleasence
Barabbas	Richard Conte
The Tormentor	Frank DeKova
Dumah	Joseph Sirola
Melchior	Cyril Delevanti
Balthazar	Mark Lenard
Caspar	Frank Silvera

and members of the Inbal Dance Theatre of Israel

Left: Max Von Sydow, also above and top right
Top Left: Dorothy McGuire

Max Von Sydow (C) Above: (R): Max Von Sydow, John Wayne
(L) Michael Tolan, Ina Balin, Janet Margolin. Top: (C) Max Von Sydow

Max Von Sydow
in
"THE GREATEST STORY EVER TOLD"

Richard Basehart, George Maharis

George Maharis, John Larkin, Anne Francis,
Richard Bull, Dana Andrews

Frank Sutton, George Maharis, Anne Francis,
Edward Asner. Above: George Maharis (L & R)

THE SATAN BUG

(UNITED ARTISTS) Producer-Director, John Sturges; Screenplay, James Clavell, Edward Anhalt; Based on Novel by Ian Stuart; Music, Jerry Goldsmith; Director of Photography, Robert Surtees; Assistant Director, Jack Reddish; Wardrobe, Wes Jeffries; A Mirisch Corporation presentation of a Mirisch-Kappa Picture in DeLuxe Color. March release.

CAST

Lee Barrett	George Maharis
Dr. Hoffman	Richard Basehart
Ann	Anne Francis
The General	Dana Andrews
Veretti	Edward Asner
Donald	Frank Sutton
Michaelson	John Larkin
Cavanaugh	Richard Bull
Martin	Martin Blaine
Reagan	John Anderson
Mason	Russ Bender
Johnson	Hari Rhodes
Raskin	John Clarke
Tesserly	Simon Oakland
Dr. Baxter	Henry Beckman
Dr. Ostrer	Harold Gould
Dr. Yang	James Hong

STRANGE BEDFELLOWS

(UNIVERSAL) Producer-Director, Melvin Frank; Associate Producer, Hal Kern; Director of Photography, Leo Tover; Story and Screenplay, Norman Panama and Melvin Frank; Assistant Directors, Joe Kenny, Paul Cameron; A Panama-Frank Production in Technicolor. March release.

CAST

Carter Harrison	Rock Hudson
Toni	Gina Lollobrigida
Richard Bramwell	Gig Young
Harry Jones	Edward Judd
J. L. Stevens	Howard St. John
Carter's Taxi Driver	Arthur Haynes
Toni's Taxi Driver	David King
Bagshott	Hedley Mattingly
Mortician	Terry-Thomas

Left: Jack Good, Edward Judd, Gina Lollobrigida, Peggy Rea, Rock Hudson

Gina Lollobrigida

Rock Hudson, Gig Young

Gig Young, Edith Atwater, Howard St. John

Jack Raine, Terry-Thomas, Rock Hudson

Rock Hudson, Edward Judd, Gina Lollobrigida
Above: Gina Lollobrigida

Rock Hudson, Gina Lollobrigida (also above)

Cliff Robertson, Lana Turner　　　　　　Lana Turner, Hugh O'Brian

Lana Turner, Cliff Robertson. Above: Hugh
28　O'Brian, Enrique Lucero, Ron Husmann

Ruth Roman, Hugh O'Brian. Above: Cliff
Robertson, Lana Turner, Stefanie Powers

Stefanie Powers, Cliff Robertson

Hugh O'Brian, Lana Turner

LOVE HAS MANY FACES

(COLUMBIA) Producer, Jerry Bresler; Director, Alexander Singer; Screenplay, Marguerite Roberts; Director of Photography, Joseph Ruttenberg; Music, David Raskin; Wardrobe, Edith Head; Assistant Director, Richard Moder; In color. March release.

CAST

Kit Jordon	Lana Turner
Pete Jordon	Cliff Robertson
Hank Walker	Hugh O'Brian
Margot Elliot	Ruth Roman
Carol Lambert	Stefanie Powers
Irene Talbot	Virginia Grey
Chuck Austin	Ron Husmann
Lt. Riccardo Andrade	Enrique Lucero
Don Julian	Carlos Montalban
Manuel Perez	Jamie Bravo
Maria	Fannie Schiller
Ramos	Rene Dupreyon

Hugh O'Brian, Ruth Roman, Virginia Grey, Ron Husmann. Above: Lana Turner, Cliff Robertson. Left: Lana Turner

Olivia De Havilland, Mary Astor
Left: Bette Davis

HUSH . . . HUSH . . . SWEET CHARLOTTE

(20th CENTURY-FOX) Producer-Director, Robert Aldrich; Screenplay, Henry Farrell, Lukas Heller; Story by Henry Farrell; Associate Producer, Walter Blake; Director of Photography, Joseph Biroc; Music, Frank DeVol; Song Lyrics, Mack David; Assistant Directors, William McGarry, Sam Strangis; Costumes, Norma Koch; Choreography, Alex Ruiz; An Associates and Aldrich Production. March release.

CAST

Charlotte Hollis	Bette Davis
Miriam Deering	Olivia De Havilland
Dr. Drew Bayliss	Joseph Cotten
Velma Cruther	Agnes Moorehead
Harry Willis	Cecil Kellaway
Big Sam Hollis	Victor Buono
Mrs. Jewel Mayhew	Mary Astor
Paul Marchand	William Campbell
Sheriff Luke Standish	Wesley Addy
John Mayhew	Bruce Dern
Foreman	George Kennedy
Taxi Driver	Dave Willock
Boy	John Megna
Gossips	Ellen Corby, Helen Kleeb, Marianne Stewart
Newspaper Editor	Frank Ferguson

Bette Davis, Agnes Moorehead
Above: Victor Buono

Cecil Kellaway, William Campbell,
Wesley Addy. Right: Olivia De Havilland

Olivia De Havilland, Bette Davis

Joseph Cotten, Bette Davis

Ian Bannen, Carroll Baker, Alexander Knox
Right: Robert Mitchum, Carroll Baker

MISTER MOSES

(UNITED ARTISTS) Producer, Frank Ross; Director, Ronald Neame; Screenplay, Charles Beaumont, Monja Danischewsky; Based on Novel by Max Catto; Director of Photography, Oswald Morris; Music, John Barry; Assistant Director, Colin Brewer; In Panavision and Technicolor. April release.

CAST

Joe Moses	Robert Mitchum
Julie Anderson	Carroll Baker
Robert	Ian Bannen
Rev. Anderson	Alexander Knox
Ubi	Raymond St. Jacques
Chief	Orlando Martins
Parkhurst	Reginald Beckwith

Alexander Knox, Orlando Martins, Ian Bannen,
Robert Mitchum (also above C)

Robert Mitchum, Carroll Baker

32

Julie Andrews
in
"THE SOUND OF MUSIC"

Christopher Plummer, Julie Andrews, Eleanor Parker, Richard Haydn, and the
Von Trapp Children. Above: (L & R) Julie Andrews, Peggy Wood, Anna Lee
Top: (L) Julie Andrews, Peggy Wood, (R) Eleanor Parker, Christopher Plummer

THE SOUND OF MUSIC

(20th CENTURY-FOX) Producer-Director, Robert Wise; Associate Producer, Saul Chaplin; Director of Photography, Ted McCord; Screenplay, Ernest Lehman; From the Musical Play by Richard Rodgers and Oscar Hammerstein II; Lyrics, Oscar Hammerstein II; Music and Additional Lyrics, Richard Rodgers; Choreography, Marc Breaux and Dee Dee Wood; Costumes, Dorothy Jeakins; Puppeteers, Bil and Cora Baird, Assistant Director, Ridgeway Callow; In Todd-AO(R) and DeLuxe Color. April release.

CAST

Maria	Julie Andrews
Captain Von Trapp	Christopher Plummer
The Baroness	Eleanor Parker
Max Detweiler	Richard Haydn
Mother Abbess	Peggy Wood
Liesl	Charmian Carr
Louisa	Heather Menzies
Friedrich	Nicolas Hammond
Kurt	Duane Chase
Brigitta	Angela Cartwright
Marta	Debbie Turner
Gretl	Kym Karath
Sister Margaretta	Anna Lee
Sister Berthe	Portia Nelson
Herr Zeller	Ben Wright
Rolfe	Daniel Truhitte
Frau Schmidt	Norma Varden
Franz	Gil Stuart
Sister Sophia	Marni Nixon
Sister Bernice	Evadne Baker
Baroness Ebberfeld	Doris Lloyd

Christopher Plummer, Julie Andrews and the Von Trapp Children (also above and top)
Left: Julie Andrews, Christopher Plummer

35

GIRL HAPPY

(M-G-M) Producer, Joe Pasternak; Director, Boris Sagal; Screenplay, Harvey Bullock, R. S. Allen; Music, George Stoll; Director of Photography, Philip H. Lathrop; Vocal Background, The Jordanaires; Assistant Director, Jack Aldworth; A Euterpe Production in Panavision and Metrocolor. April release.

CAST

Rusty Wells	Elvis Presley
Valerie	Shelley Fabares
Big Frank	Harold J. Stone
Andy	Gary Crosby
Wilbur	Joby Baker
Sunny Daze	Nita Talbot
Deena	Mary Ann Mobley
Romano	Fabrizio Mioni
Sgt. Benson	Jackie Coogan
Doc	Jimmy Hawkins
Brentwood Von Durgenfeld	Peter Brooks
Mr. Penchill	John Fiedler
Betsy	Chris Noel
Laurie	Lyn Edgington
Nancy	Gale Gilmore
Bobbie	Pamela Curran
Linda	Rusty Allen

Elvis Presley, Mary Ann Mobley

Jimmy Hawkins, Shelley Fabares, Elvis Presley

Lynn Edington, Chris Noel, Shelley Fabares, Elvis Presley, John Fiedler. Above: Gary Crosby, Jackie Coogan, Jimmy Hawkins, Elvis Presley, Joby Baker

Ann-Margret, Michael Parks

Ann-Margret, Claire Carlton, Parley Baer,
Michael Parks. Above: Marc Cavell, David
Carradine, Michael Parks. Right: Michael
Parks, Janet Margolin

BUS RILEY'S BACK IN TOWN

(UNIVERSAL) Producer, Elliott Kastner; Director, Harvey Hart; Screenplay, Walter Gage; Based on Story by William Inge; Director of Photography, Russell Metty; Gowns, Jean Louis; Music, Richard Markowitz; Assistant Directors, Terry Nelson, Bill Gilmore; In Color. April release.

CAST

Laurel	Ann-Margret
Bus Riley	Michael Parks
Judy	Janet Margolin
Slocum	Brad Dexter
Mrs. Riley	Jocelyn Brando
Howie	Larry Storch
Spencer	Crahan Denton
Gussie	Kim Darby
Carlotta	Brett Somers
Paula	Mimsy Farmer
Mrs. Nichols	Nan Martin
Joy	Lisabeth Hush
Mrs. Spencer	Ethel Griffies
Woman Customer	Alice Pearce
Benji	Chet Stratton
Stretch	David Carradine
Egg Foo	Marc Cavell
Mr. Griswald	Parley Baer

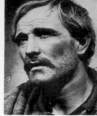

Charlton Heston   **Senta Berger**   **Richard Harris**

MAJOR DUNDEE

(COLUMBIA) Producer, Jerry Bresler; Director, Sam Peckinpah; Screenplay, Harry Julian Fink, Oscar Saul, Sam Peckinpah; Story, Harry Julian Fink; Music, Daniele Amfitheatrof; Lyrics, Ned Washington; Sung by Mitch Miller's Sing Along Gang; Director of Photography, Sam Leavitt; Costumes, Tom Dawson; Assistant Directors, John Veitch, Floyd Joyer, Cliff Lyons; In Panavision and Eastman Color. April release.

CAST

Maj. Amos Charles Dundee	Charlton Heston
Capt. Benjamin Tyreen	Richard Harris
Lt. Graham	Jim Hutton
Samuel Potts	James Coburn
Tim Ryan	Michael Anderson, Jr.
Teresa Santiago	Senta Berger
Sgt Gomez	Mario Adorf
Aesop	Brock Peters
O. W. Hadley	Warren Oates
Sgt. Chillum	Ben Johnson
Rev. Dahlstrom	R. G. Armstrong
Arthur Hadley	L. Q. Jones
Wiley	Slim Pickens
Capt. Waller	Karl Swenson
Sierra Charriba	Michael Pate
Jimmy Lee Benteen	John Davis Chandler
Priam	Dub Taylor
Capt Jacques Tremaine	Albert Carrier
Linda	Begonia Palacios
Dr. Aguilar	Enrique Lucero
Riago	Jose Carlos Ruiz
Melinche	Aurora Clavell

38   **Charlton Heston, Mario Adorf. Above: Richard Harris, Jim Hutton, R. G. Armstrong, Michael Anderson, Jr., Charlton Heston**

Richard Harris, Charlton Heston. Above: Jim Hutton, Charlton Heston, Senta Berger

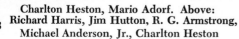

Warren Oates

Mario Adorf

Jim Hutton

Brock Peters

Michael
Anderson, Jr.

James Coburn

Brock Peters, Jim Hutton, R. G. Armstrong,
Dub Taylor. Above: Charlton Heston,
Michael Anderson, Jr., Richard Harris

Charlton Heston, Jim Hutton, Michael Anderson,
Jr. Above: Richard Harris, James Coburn

39

Shirley MacLaine, and above with
Richard Crenna

Richard Crenna (L). Above: Peter Ustinov

JOHN GOLDFARB,
PLEASE COME HOME

(20th CENTURY-FOX) Producer, Steve Parker; Director, J. Lee Thompson; Story and Screenplay, William Peter Blatty; Director of Photography, Leon Shamroy; Music, Johnny Williams; Costumes, Edith Head; Dances Staged by Paul Godkin; Assistant Director, John Flynn; In Cinemascope and DeLuxe Color. April release.

CAST

Jenny Ericson	Shirley MacLaine
King Fawz	Peter Ustinov
John Goldfarb	Richard Crenna
Sakalakis	Scott Brady
Miles Whitepaper	Jim Backus
Editor STRIFE magazine	Charles Lane
Mr. Brinkley	Jerome Cowan
Guz	Wilfrid Hyde White
Deems Sarajevo	Harry Morgan
Subtile Cronkite	David Lewis
Heinous Overreach	Fred Clark
Harem Recruiter	Telly Savalas
Maginot	Richard Deacon
Mandy	Angela Douglas
Samir	Leon Askin
Prince Ammud	Pat Adiarte
Frobish	Richard Wilson
Air Force General	Milton Frome
Father Ryan	Jackie Coogan
Pinkerton	Jerome Orbach

and Nai Bonet, Sultana, Barbara Bouchet, Irene Tsu, Ann Morrell, Shelby Grant, Eve Bruce, Gari Hardy, Jane Wald, Linda Foster

Richard Crenna, Peter Ustinov (also above)
Top: (R) Richard Crenna (L) Shirley MacLaine 41

John Wayne, Burgess Meredith, Tod Andrews,
Tom Tryon. Right: Patricia Neal, Jill Haworth

IN HARM'S WAY

(PARAMOUNT) Producer-Director, Otto Preminger; Screenplay, Wendell Mayes; Based on Novel by James Bassett; Music, Jerry Goldsmith; Director of Photography, Loyal Griggs; Assistant Director, Danny McCauley; In Panavision. April release.

CAST

Capt. Rockwell Torrey	John Wayne
Cmdr. Paul Eddington	Kirk Douglas
Lt. Maggie Haynes	Patricia Neal
Lt./jg William McConnel	Tom Tryon
Bev McConnel	Paula Prentiss
Ens. Jeremiah Torrey	Brandon de Wilde
Ens. Annalee Dorne	Jill Haworth
Admiral "Blackjack" Broderick	Dana Andrews
Clayton Canfil	Stanley Holloway
Cmdr. Egan Powell	Burgess Meredith
Admiral	Franchot Tone
Cmdr. Neal O'Wynn	Patrick O'Neal
Lt. Cmdr. Burke	Carroll O'Connor
C.P.O. Culpepper	Slim Pickens
Liz Eddington	Barbara Bouchet
Airforce Major	Hugh O'Brian
CINCPAC Admiral	Henry Fonda

and James Mitchum, George Kennedy, Bruce Cabot, Tod Andrews

John Wayne, Stanley Holloway. Above: John
Wayne, Brandon DeWilde, Jill Haworth,
Patricia Neal

Tom Tryon, Bruce Cabot

42

Hugh O'Brian, Barbara Bouchet John Wayne, Patricia Neal

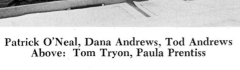

Patrick O'Neal, Dana Andrews, Tod Andrews
Above: Tom Tryon, Paula Prentiss

John Wayne, Brandon DeWilde, Burgess
Meredith, Kirk Douglas. Above: John Wayne,
Burgess Meredith, Henry Fonda

43

Geraldine Fitzgerald, Rod Steiger. Above:
Thelma Oliver, Rod Steiger

Thelma Oliver, Jaime Sanchez. Top: (L)
John McCurry, Raymond St. Jacques, Rod Steiger
(R) Rod Steiger

44

THE PAWNBROKER

(LANDAU) Executive Producer, Worthington Miner; Director, Sidney Lumet; Screenplay, David Friedkin, Morton Fine; Based on Novel by Edward Lewis Wallant; Producers, Roger H. Lewis, Philip Langer; Director of Photography, Boris Kaufman; Music, Quincy Jones; Associate Producer, Joseph Manduke; Costumes, Anna Hill Johnstone; Assistant Director, Dan Eriksen. April release.

CAST

Sol Nazerman	Rod Steiger
Marilyn Birchfield	Geraldine Fitzgerald
Rodriguez	Brock Peters
Jesus Ortiz	Jaime Sanchez
Ortiz' Girl	Thelma Oliver
Tessie	Marketa Kimbrell
Mendel	Baruch Lumet
Mr. Smith	Juano Hernandez
Ruth	Linda Geiser
Bertha	Nancy R. Pollock
Tangee	Raymond St. Jacques
Buck	John McCurry
Robinson	Ed Morehouse
Mrs. Ortiz	Eusebia Cosme
Savarese	Warren Finnerty
Morton	Jack Ader
Papa	E. M. Margolese
Joan	Marianne Kanter

Marketa Kimbrell, Rod Steiger. Top: Juano Hernandez, Rod Steiger. Right: Geraldine Fitzgerald

Jaime Sanchez, Rod Steiger
in
"THE PAWNBROKER"

CLARENCE, THE CROSS-EYED LION

(M-G-M) Producer, Leonard B. Kaufman; Director, Andrew Marton; Screenplay, Alan Caillou; Story, Art Arthur, Marshall Thompson; Associate Producer, Harry Redmond, Jr.; Director of Photography, Lamar Boren; Music, Shelly Manne; Assistant Director, Rex Bailey; An Ivan Tors Production in Metrocolor. April release.

CAST

Dr. Marsh Tracy	Marshall Thompson
Julie Harper	Betsy Drake
Rupert Rowbotham	Richard Haydn
Paula	Cheryl Miller
Carter	Alan Caillou
Juma	Rockne Tarkington
Gregory	Maurice Marsac
Sergeant	Bob Do Qui
Husseini	Albert Amos
Dinny	Dinny Powell
Larson	Mark Allen

and Laurence Conroy, Allyson Daniell, Janee Michele, Naaman Brown, Napoleon Whiting, Chester Jones

Right: Maurice Marsac, Clarence. Above: Cheryl Miller, Betsy Drake, Marshall Thompson, Richard Haydn, Clarence

BRAINSTORM

(WARNER BROS.) Producer-Director, William Conrad; Screenplay, Mann Rubin; Story, Larry Marcus; Director of Photography, Sam Leavitt; Assistant Director, Howard L. Grace, Jr.; Music, George Duning; In Panavision. May release.

CAST

Jim Grayam	Jeff Hunter
Lorrie Benson	Anne Francis
Cort Benson	Dana Andrews
Dr. E. Larstadt	Viveca Lindfors
Josh Reynolds	Stacy Harris
Angie DeWitt	Kathie Brown
Dr. Ames	Phillip Pine
Dr. Mills	Michael Pate
Sgt. Dawes	Robert McQueeney
Mr. Clyde	Strother Martin
Clara	Joan Swift
Butler	George Pelling
Julie	Victoria Meyerink
Judge	Stephen Roberts
Bobby	Pat Cardi

Anne Francis, Jeff Hunter, and above with Dana Andrews. Left: Jeff Hunter, Viveca Lindfors

SYNANON

(**COLUMBIA**) Producer-Director, Richard Quine; Screenplay, Ian Bernard, S. Lee Pogostin; Story, Barry Oringer, S. Lee Pogostin; Director of Photography, Harry Stradling; Music, Neal Hefti; Assistant Producer-Director, Carter De-Haven, Jr. May release.

CAST

Ben	Chuck Connors
Joaney	Stella Stevens
Zankie Albo	Alex Cord
Reid	Richard Conte
Betty Coleman	Eartha Kitt
Chuck Dederich	Edmond O'Brien
Mary	Barbara Luna
Chris	Alejandro Rey
Hopper	Richard Evans
Vince	Gregory Morton
Arline	Chanin Hale
Pruddy	Casey Townsend
Bob Adamic	Larry Kert
Pete	Bernie Hamilton
Joe Mann	Mark Sturges
The Greek	Lawrence Montaigne
Carla	Patricia Huston

and residents of Synanon House

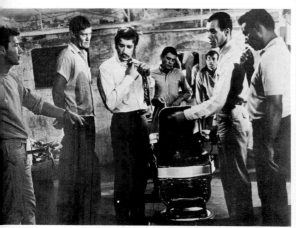

Lawrence Montaigne, Chuck Connors, Alex Cord, Jay Sebring, Alejandro Rey, John Peterson, Bernie Hamilton. Top: Edmond O'Brien Richard Conte, Eartha Kitt

Stella Stevens, Alex Cord
Above: Stella Stevens, Alex Cord, Chuck Connors
Top: Richard Conte (C)

THE SWORD OF ALI BABA

(UNIVERSAL) Producer, Howard Christie; Director, Virgil Vogel; Screenplay, Oscar Brodney; Director of Photography, William Margulies; Assistant Directors, Phil Bowles, Bill Gilmore; In color. May release.

CAST

Ali Baba	Peter Mann
Amara	Jocelyn Lane
Abou	Peter Whitney
Hulagu Khan	Gavin MacLeod
Prince Cassim	Frank Puglia
Pindar	Frank McGrath
Yusuf	Greg Morris
Baba	Frank DeKova
Captain of Guard	Morgan Woodward

Right: (Top) Greg Morris, Jocelyn Lane, Peter Mann

THE WORLD OF ABBOTT AND COSTELLO

(UNIVERSAL) Producers, Max J. Rosenberg, Milton Subotsky; Associate Producer, Norman E. Gluck; Narration, Gene Wood; Editorial Direction, Sidney Meyer; Musical Supervision, Joseph Gershenson. A Vanguard Production. May release.

CAST

Bud Abbott
Lou Costello
Lon Chaney
Tom Ewell
Margaret Hamilton
Bela Lugosi
Marjorie Main
Jack E. Leonard, Narrator
in sequences from Abbott and Costello films.

Right (and above): Bud Abbott, Lou Costello

BLACK SPURS

(PARAMOUNT) Producer, A. C. Lyles; Director, R. G. "Bud" Springsteen; Director of Photography, Ralph Woolsey; Screenplay, Steve Fisher; Assistant Directors, James Rosenberger, Dale Coleman; In Technicolor and Techniscope. May release.

CAST

Santee	Rory Calhoun
Anna	Terry Moore
Sadie	Linda Darnell
Tanner	Scott Brady
Kile	Lon Chaney
Henderson	Bruce Cabot
Pete	Richard Arlen
Clare Grubbs	Patricia Owens
Sheriff Elkins	James Best
Sam Grubbs	Jerome Courtland
First Sheriff	DeForest Kelley
Sheriff Nemo	James Brown
Swifty	Joe Hoover
Manuel	Manuel Padilla
Mrs. Nemo	Jeanne Baird
Norton	Chuck Roberson
Sadie's Girls	Sandra Giles, Sally Nichols, Rusty Allen

Richard Arlen, James Best, Lon Chaney, Bruce Cabot, Linda Darnell, Rory Calhoun, Scott Brady, Terry Moore

I'LL TAKE SWEDEN

(UNITED ARTISTS) Producer, Edward Small; Director, Frederick DeCordova; Screenplay, Nat Perrin, Bob Fisher, Arthur Marx; Story, Nat Perrin; Associate Producer, Alex Gottlieb; Music, Jimmie Haskell, "By" Dunham; Title Song, Diane Lampert, Ken Lauber; Director of Photography, Daniel L. Fapp; Assistant Director, Herbert S. Greene; Costumes, Paula Giokaris; Choreography, Miriam Nelson; In Technicolor. June release.

CAST

Bob Holcomb	Bob Hope
JoJo Holcomb	Tuesday Weld
Kenny Klinger	Frankie Avalon
Karin Grandstedt	Dina Merrill
Erik Carlson	Jeremy Slate
Marti	Rosemarie Frankland
Bjork	Walter Sande
Olaf	John Qualen
Ingemar	Peter Bourne
Hilda	Fay DeWitt
Greta	Alice Frost
Captain	Roy Roberts
Spinster	Maudie Prickett
Electra	Beverly Hills
Inter	Siv Marta Aberg
Musical Group	The Vulcanes

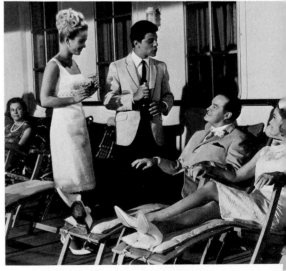

Tuesday Weld, Frankie Avalon, Bob Hope, Dina Merrill. Above: Tuesday Weld, Frankie Avalon (L) Bob Hope, Dina Merrill. Top: (L) Frankie Avalon, Bob Hope, Tuesday Weld, (R) Bob Hope, Tuesday Weld, Jeremy Slate

ohn Dennis, Jocelyn Lane, Elvis Presley. Above:
Jocelyn Lane, Elvis Presley, Jack Mullaney
(R) Elvis Presley, Jocelyn Lane. Top: (L) Elvis
resley (C), Connie Gilchrist (R); (R) Jocelyn Lane,
Elvis Presley

TICKLE ME

(ALLIED ARTISTS) Producer, Ben Schwalb;
Director, Norman Taurog; Story and Screenplay,
Elwood Ullman, Edward Bernds; Music, Walter
Scharf; Director of Photography, Loyal Griggs;
Assistant Director, Artie Jacobson; Choreogra-
phy, David Winters; Costumes, Leah Rhodes;
In Panavision and DeLuxe Color. June release.

CAST

Lonnie Beale	Elvis Presley
Pam Merritt	Jocelyn Lane
Vera Radford	Julie Adams
Stanley Potter	Jack Mullaney
Estelle Penfield	Merry Anders
Hilda	Connie Gilchrist
Brad Bentley	Edward Faulkner
Deputy Sturdivant	Bill Williams
Henry	Louis Elias
Adolph	John Dennis
Janet	Laurie Burton
Clair Kinnamon	Linda Rogers
Sibyl	Ann Morell
Ronnie	Lilyan Chauvin
Evelyn	Jean Ingram
Mildred	Francine York
Pat	Eve Bruce
Gloria	Jackie Russell
Dot	Peggy Ward
Donna	Angela Greene
Polly	Dorian Brown
Ophelia	Inez Pedroza

51

Diane Baker, Gregory Peck

Gregory Peck, Walter Abel

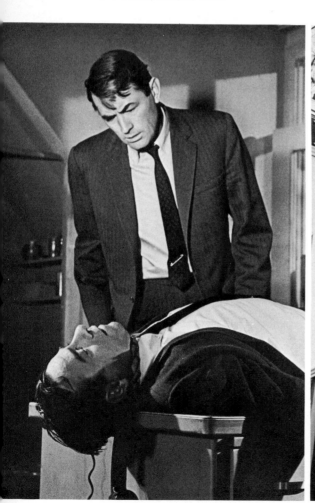

Walter Matthau, Gregory Peck

Gregory Peck

Leif Erickson, Gregory Peck, Diane Baker
Left: Anne Seymour, Gregory Peck

MIRAGE

(**UNIVERSAL**) Producer, Harry Keller; Director, Edward Dmytryk; Screenplay, Peter Stone; Based on Story by Walter Ericson; Director of Photography, Joseph MacDonald; Music, Quincy Jones; Gowns, Jean Louis; Assistant Director, Terence Nelson. June release.

CAST

David	Gregory Peck
Shela	Diane Baker
Ted Caselle	Walter Matthau
Josephson	Kevin McCarthy
Lester	Jack Weston
Major Crawford	Leif Erickson
Calvin	Walter Abel
Willard	George Kennedy
Dr. Broden	Robert H. Harris
Frances	Anne Seymour
Bo	House B. Jameson
Lt. Franken	Hari Rhodes
Benny	Syl Lamont
Irene	Eileen Baral
Joe Turtle	Neil Fitzgerald
Group Leader	Franklin E. Cover

Walter Matthau, Gregory Peck

Gregory Peck, Kevin McCarthy, George Kennedy
Above: Hari Rhodes, Gregory Peck

53

PIE IN THE SKY

(ALLIED ARTISTS) Producers, Merrill Brody, Allen Baron, Dorothy E. Reed; Direction and Screenplay, Allen Baron; Director of Photography, Donald Malkames; Music, Robert Mersey; Associate Producers, James Gealis, Joel Glickman; Assistant Director, Richard Wolf. June release.

CAST

Suzy	Lee Grant
Brill	Richard Bray
Carl	Michael Higgins
Paco	Roberto Marsach
Brill's Father	Robert Allen
Rose	Sylvia Miles
Farmer's Wife	Ruth Attaway
Farmer	Robert Earl Jones
Rick	Jaime Charlamagne
Artificial Inseminator	Charles Jordan
Preacher	Roscoe Browne
Pickpocket	Rick Colitti
Brill's Sisters	Muriel Franklin, Debby Bliss, Susie Dresser
Pitchman	Monroe Arnold
Haberdasher	Boris Marshalov
Doorman	Spencer Davis
Gas Station Attendant	Fred Feldt
Hot Dog Vendor	Bill Da Prato
Delicatessen Man	Joseph Leberman
Bartender	Milton Luchan
Brill's Brother	Danny Dresser
Truck Driver	Mel Brown

Left: Lee Grant, Richard Bray. Above: Roberto Marsach, Richard Bray, Jaime Charlamagne

ZEBRA IN THE KITCHEN

(M-G-M) Producer-Director, Ivan Tors; Associate Producers, Ralph Helfer, Harry Redmond, Jr.; Screenplay, Art Arthur; From a Story by Elgin Ciampi; Music, Warren Barker; Title Song, Hal Hopper; Sung by The Standells; Director of Photography, Lamar Boren; Assistant Director, Eddie Saeta; In Metrocolor. June release.

CAST

Chris Carlyle	Jay North
Dr. Del Hartwood	Martin Milner
Branch Hawksbill	Andy Devine
Isobel Moon	Joyce Meadows
Adam Carlyle	Jim Davis
Anne Carlyle	Dorothy Green
Wilma Carlyle	Karen Green
Councilman Pew	Vaughn Taylor
Sgt. Freebee	John Milford
Councilman Lawrence	Tris Coffin
Chief of Police	Merritt Bohn
Sheriff	Robert Clarke
Mr. Richardson	Percy Helton
Tim	Jimmy Stiles
Kookie	Dal Jenkins
Ribs	Gordon Westcourt
Greenie	Gary Judis
Preston Heston	Robert Lowery
Newscaster	Wayne Thomas
Judge	Jon Lormer
Nearsighted Man	Doodles Weaver
Man in Man-hole	Vince Barnett
Man in Tub	Phil Arnold

Jay North. Above: Andy Devine, Joyce Meadows, Jim Davis, Jay North, Dorothy Green, Karen Green, Martin Milner

FLUFFY

(UNIVERSAL) Producer, Gordon Kay; Director, Earl Bellamy; Director of Photography, Clifford Stine; Costumes, Rosemary O'Dell; Assistant Directors, Phil Bowles, Bob Daley; In Color. June release.

CAST

Daniel Potter	Tony Randall
Janice Claridge	Shirley Jones
Griswald	Edward Andrews
James Claridge	Ernest Truex
Sweeny	Howard Morris
Tommy	Dick Sargent
Sally Brighton	Celia Kaye
Robert Brighton	Adam Roarke
Agnes Claridge	Harriet MacGibbon
Hotel Maid	Connie Gilchrist
Police Captain	Parley Baer
Dr. Braden	Whit Bissell
State Trooper	Stuart Randall

Frank Faylen, Ernest Truex, Jim Bowles
Top: Tony Randall, Shirley Jones

Edward Andrews, Howard Morris, Tony Randall
Above: Edward Andrews, Dick Sargent, Shirley
Jones. Top: Shirley Jones, Fluffy, Tony Randall

55

Nat King Cole, Oscar Blank, Stubby Kaye

Tom Nardini, Jane Fonda, John Marley,
Lee Marvin

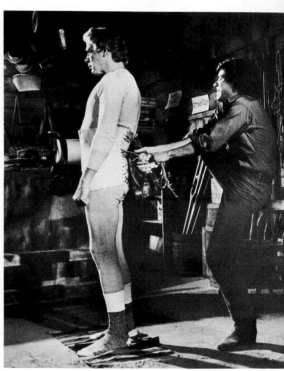

Lee Marvin, Jane Fonda, Michael Callan,
Dwayne Hickman, Tom Nardini. Above: Jane
Fonda, Lee Marvin, (R) Lee Marvin, Tom Nardini

CAT BALLOU

(COLUMBIA) Producer, Harold Hecht; Director, Elliot Silverstein; Screenplay, Walter Newman, Frank R. Pierson; Based on Novel by Roy Chanslor; Music, DeVol; Songs, Mack David, Jerry Livingston; Director of Photography, Jack Marta; Associate Producer, Mitch Lindemann; Gowns, Bill Thomas; Assistant Directors, Lee Lukather, Ray Gosnell; Choreographer, Miriam Nelson; In Eastman Color by Pathe. June release.

CAST

Cat Ballou	Jane Fonda
Kid Shellen and Tim Straun	Lee Marvin
Clay Boone	Michael Callan
Jed	Dwayne Hickman
Shouters	Nat King Cole, Stubby Kaye
Jackson Two-Bear	Tom Nardini
Frankie Ballou	John Marley
Sir Harry Percival	Reginald Denny
Sheriff Cardigan	Jay C. Flippen
Butch Cassidy	Arthur Hunnicutt
Sheriff Maledon	Bruce Cabot
Accuser	Burt Austin
Train Messenger	Paul Gilbert

Lee Marvin, Tom Nardini, Michael Callan,
Jane Fonda, Dwayne Hickman

Reginald Denny, Jane Fonda

Michael Callan, Jane Fonda (above)

Lee Marvin, Michael Callan, Jane Fonda
Above: Jane Fonda, Dwayne Hickman   57

JOY IN THE MORNING

(M-G-M) Producer, Henry T. Weinstein; Director, Alex Segal; Screenplay, Sally Benson, Alfred Hayes, Norman Lessing; Based on Novel by Betty Smith; Music, Bernard Herrmann; Title Song, Sammy Fein, Paul Francis Webster; Sung by Richard Chamberlain; Director of Photography, Ellsworth Fredricks; Assistant Director, Sheldon Schrager; Costumes, Don Feld; In Metrocolor. June release.

CAST

Carl Brown	Richard Chamberlain
Annie McGairy	Yvette Mimieux
Patrick Brown	Arthur Kennedy
Stan Pulaski	Oscar Homolka
Anthony Byrd	Donald Davis
Beverly Karter	Joan Tetzel
Dean James Darwent	Sidney Blackmer
Mrs. Lorgan	Virginia Gregg
Mary Ellen Kincaid	Chris Noel
Prof. Victor Newcole	Bartlett Robinson
Clerk	Ellen Atterbury
Dr. Marson	Harvey Stephens
Dr. Kirkson	Ira Barmak

Right: Richard Chamberlain, Yvette Mimieux, and below with Arthur Kennedy

Richard Chamberlain, Yvette Mimieux

Richard Chamberlain, Arthur Kennedy
Above: Arthur Kennedy, Yvette Mimieux,
Richard Chamberlain

THE FAMILY JEWELS

(PARAMOUNT) Producer-Director, Jerry Lewis; Screenplay, Jerry Lewis, Bill Richmond; Music, Pete King; Assistant Director, Ralph Axness; Director of Photography, W. Wallace Kelley; Costumes, Edith Head; Associate Producer, Arthur P. Schmidt. June release.

CAST

Jerry Lewis as Willard Woodward, Everett Peyton, James Peyton, Capt. Eddie Peyton, Julius Peyton, "Bugs" Peyton, Skylock Peyton
Circus Clown .... Gene Baylos
Pilot .... Milton Frome
Joe .... Herbie Faye
Attorneys .... Jay Adler, Neil Hamilton
Dr. Matson .... Sebastian Cabot
Donna Peyton .... Donna Butterworth
Plane Passengers .... Marjorie Bennett, Frances Lax, Ellen Corby, Renie Riano, Jesslyn Fax
Pool Hall Proprietor .... Robert Strauss
and John Lawrence, Francine York, John Hubbard, Michael Ross, John Macchia, Douglas Deane, Maurice Kelly

Left: Donna Butterworth, Neil Hamilton
Below: Jerry Lewis as the Peyton brothers

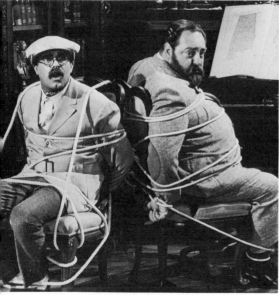

Jerry Lewis, Sebastian Cabot

Donna Butterworth, Jerry Lewis

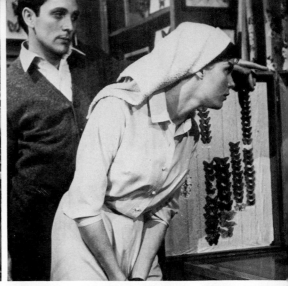

THE COLLECTOR

(COLUMBIA) Producers, Jud Kinberg, John Kohn; Director, William Wyler; Screenplay, Stanley Mann, John Kohn; Based on Novel by John Fowles; Music, Maurice Jarre; Directors of Photography, Robert L. Surtees, Robert Krasker; In Technicolor. June release.

CAST

Freddie Clegg	Terence Stamp
Miranda Grey	Samantha Eggar
Aunt Annie	Mona Washbourne
The Neighbor	Maurice Dallimore

Terence Stamp, Samantha Eggar. Right: Terence Stamp, Maurice Dallimore. Top and Center Left: Terence Stamp with Samantha Eggar; (R) with Mona Washbourne

HARLOW

(PARAMOUNT) Producer, Joseph E. Levine; Director, Gordon Douglas; Screenplay, John Michael Hayes; Based on Book by Irving Shulman in collaboration with Arthur Landau; Director of Photography, Joseph Ruttenberg; Gowns, Edith Head; Assistant Director, Dave Salven; Music, Neal Hefti; In Panavision and Technicolor. June release.

CAST

Jean Harlow	Carroll Baker
Everett Redman	Martin Balsam
Arthur Landau	Red Buttons
Jack Harrison	Michael Connors
Mama Jean Bello	Angela Lansbury
Paul Bern	Peter Lawford
Marino Bello	Raf Vallone
Richard Manley	Leslie Nielsen
Studio Secretary	Mary Murphy
Mrs. Arthur Landau	Hanna Landy
Assistant Director	Peter Hansen
Girl at Pool	Kipp Hamilton
Director of '30's	Peter Leeds

Right: Michael Connors, Martin Balsam, Peter Lawford, Carroll Baker, Hanna Landy, Red Buttons, Raf Vallone, Angela Lansbury

Carroll Baker, Raf Vallone, also above with Red Buttons, Angela Lansbury

Carroll Baker

WHAT'S NEW PUSSYCAT?

(UNITED ARTISTS) Producer, Charles K. Feldman; Executive Producer, John C. Shepridge; Director, Clive Donner; Associate Producer, Richard Sylbert; Screenplay, Woody Allen; Music, Burt Bacharach; Lyrics, Hal David; Director of Photography, Jean Badal; Assistant Director, Enrico Isacco; Costumes, Mia Fonssagrives, Vicki Tiel; In Technicolor; A Production of Famous Artists Productions and Famartists Productions. June release.

CAST

Fritz Fassbender	Peter Sellers
Michael James	Peter O'Toole
Carol Werner	Romy Schneider
Renee Lefebvre	Capucine
Liz	Paula Prentiss
Victor Shakapopolis	Woody Allen
Rita	Ursula Andress
Anna Fassbender	Edra Gale
Jacqueline	Catherine Schaake
Mr. Werner	Jess Hahn
Mrs. Werner	Eleanor Hirt
Tempest O'Brien	Nicole Karen
Marcel	Jean Paredes
Philippe	Michel Subor
Charlotte	Jacqueline Fogt
Car Renter	Robert Rollis
Gas Station Operator	Daniel Emilfork
Jean	Louis Falavigna
Etienne	Jacques Balutin
Emma	Annette Poivre

and Sabine Sun, Jean Yves Autrey, Pascal Wolf, Nadine Papin, Tanya Lopert, Colin Drake, Norbert Terry, Gordon Felio, Louise Lasser

Right: Peter O'Toole, Peter Sellers

Romy Schneider, Peter O'Toole

Peter O'Toole

Edra Gale, Ursula Andress, Peter Sellers. Top:
Paula Prentiss, (C) Woody Allen, Romy
Schneider, (R) Capucine

Romy Schneider, Peter O'Toole

(20th CENTURY-FOX) Director, Robert Parrish; Screenplay, Howard Clewes; Based on Novel by George Barr; Director of Photography, Walter Wottitz; In CinemaScope. June release.

CAST

Sgt. Edward Baxter	Cliff Robertson
Pfc. Harry Devine	Red Buttons
Lili Rolland	Irina Demick
Commandant, German Wehrmacht	Marius Goring
M. P. Major	Broderick Crawford
British Navy Beachmaster	James Robertson Justice
U.S. Army Colonel	Slim Pickens
Grandmother	Francoise Rosay

Left: Cliff Robertson, Francoise Rosay. Below: Cliff Robertson, Marius Goring, Red Buttons

HARVEY MIDDLEMAN, FIREMAN

(COLUMBIA) Produced by Robert L. Lawrence in association with Ernest Pintoff; Director, Ernest Pintoff; Screenplay, Ernest Pintoff; Music, Ernest Pintoff; Director of Photography, Karl Malkames; Associate Producer, Robert Gaffney; Costumes, Anna Hill Johnstone; Assistant Director, Roger Rothstein; In Eastman Color. July release.

CAST

Harvey Middleman	Gene Troobnick
Mrs. Koogleman	Hermione Gingold
Lois	Patricia Harty
Harriet	Arlene Golonka
Dinny	Will MacKenzie
The Mother	Ruth Jaroslow
Dooley	Charles Durning
Barratta	Peter Carew
Mookey	Stanley Myron Handelman
Cindy	Trudy Bordoff
Richie	Neil Rouda
Comet Receptionist	Gigi Chevalier
Librarian	Stacy Graham
Mr. Koogleman	Maurice Shrog

Gene Troobnick, Patricia Harty. Left: Hermione Gingold, Gene Troobnick

THE ART OF LOVE

(UNIVERSAL) Producer, Ross Hunter; Director, Norman Jewison; Screenplay, Carl Reiner; Story, Richard Alan Simmons, William Sackheim; Director of Photography, Russell Metty; Music, Cy Coleman; Costumes, Ray Aghayan; Choreographer, Hal Belfer; Assistant Directors, Douglas Green, Carl Beringer; In Technicolor. July release.

Ethel Merman, Astrid DeBrea, Miiko Taka, Sharon Shore, Dick Van Dyke, Dawn Villere, James Garner, Nancy Martin, Victoria Carroll

CAST

Casey	James Garner
Paul	Dick Van Dyke
Nikki	Elke Sommer
Laurie	Angie Dickinson
Madame Coco	Ethel Merman
Rodin	Carl Reiner
Carnot	Pierre Olaf
Chou Chou	Miiko Taka
Zorgus	Roger C. Carmel
Fromkis	Naomi Stevens
Janitor	Jay Novello
Mrs. Fromkis	Naomi Stevens
Pepe	Renzo Cesana
Prince	Leon Belasco
Judge	Louis Mercier
Prosecutor	Maurice Marsac
Fanny	Fifi D'Orsay
Executioner	Marcel Hillaire
Couchette	Dawn Villere
Margo	Nancy Martin
Yvette	Victoria Carroll
Betti	Sharon Shore
Cerise	Astrid DeBrea

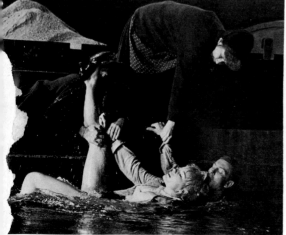

Emile Genest, Fifi D'Orsay, Elke Sommer, Dick Van Dyke. Top: Dick Van Dyke, James Garner

Elke Sommer, Dick Van Dyke. Above: James Garner, Elke Sommer, Paul Verdier

Frank Sinatra, Trevor Howard, Sergio Fantoni,
Edward Mulhare

John Leyton, Frank Sinatra, Trevor Howard,
Edward Mulhare

Wolfgang Preiss, Frank Sinatra, Edward Mulhare,
Trevor Howard, John Leyton. Above: Frank
Sinatra, Sergio Fantoni, Edward Mulhare, Trevor
Howard. Right: Trevor Howard, Raffaella Carra

VON RYAN'S EXPRESS

(20th CENTURY-FOX) Producer, Saul David;
Director, Mark Robson; Screenplay, Wendell
Mayes, Joseph Landon; Based on Novel by
David Westheimer; Music, Jerry Goldsmith; Di-
rector of Photography, William H. Daniels;
Assistant Director, Eli Dunn; A P-R Productions
Picture in DeLuxe Color. July release.

CAST

Col. Joseph L. Ryan	Frank Sinatra
Maj. Eric Fincham	Trevor Howard
Gabriella	Raffaella Carra
Sgt. Bostick	Brad Dexter
Capt. Oriani	Sergio Fantoni
Orde	John Leyton
Costanzo	Edward Mulhare
Maj. Von Klemment	Wolfgang Preiss
Pvt. Ames	James Brolin
Col. Gortz	John Van Dreelen
Battaglia	Adolfo Celi
Italian Train Engineer	Vito Scotti
Cpl. Giannini	Richard Bakalyan
Capt. Stein	Michael Goodliffe
Sgt. Dunbar	Michael St. Clair
Von Kleist	Ivan Triesault

Frank Sinatra, Vito Scotti, Sergio Fantoni,
Trevor Howard. Above: Frank Sinatra,
Trevor Howard

Trevor Howard, Edward Mulhare, Frank Sinatra
(also at top)

GENGHIS KHAN

(COLUMBIA) Producer, Irving Allen; Director, Henry Levin; Screenplay, Clarke Reynolds, Beverley Cross; Based on Story by Berkely Mather; Associate Producer, Euan Lloyd; Music, Dusan Radic; Director of Photography, Geoffrey Unsworth; Costumes, Cynthia Tingey; Assistant Directors, Buddy Coleman, Bluey Hill, Frank Winterstein; An Irving Allen/CCC/Avala Production in Panavision and Technicolor. July release.

CAST

Jamuga	Stephen Boyd
Temujin-Genghis Khan	Omar Sharif
Kam Ling	James Mason
Shah of Khwarezm	Eli Wallach
Bortei	Francoise Dorleac
Shan	Telly Savalas
Emperor of China	Robert Morley
Geen	Michael Hordern
Katke	Yvonne Mitchell
Sengal	Woody Strode
Subodai	Kenneth Cope
Kassar	Roger Croucher
Jebai	Don Borisenko
Kuchluk	Patrick Holt
Chin Yu	Suzanne Hsaio
Toktoa	George Savalas
Temujin as a child	Carlo Cura
Altan	Gustavo Rojo
Ho Mun Tim	Dusan Vujsic
Fut Su	Jovan Tesic
Chagedai	Andreja Marcic
Jochi	Thomas Margulies
Indian Girls	Yamata Pauli, Linda Loncar

Slave Dealers Branislav Radovic, Svonko Jovcic and Concubines: Dominique Don, Carmen Dene. Nora Forster, Jatta Falke, Hannalore Maeusel, Yvonne Shima, May Spils, Edwina Carroll, Sally Douglas, Chieko Huber, Elke Kroger, Ursel Mumoth, Lucille Soong, Ester Anderson

Left: James Mason, Omar Sharif. Top: Stephen Boyd, Omar Sharif, Woody Strode

Robert Morley   Eli Wallach   Omar Sharif   Stephen Boyd   Telly Savalas   James Mason

Omar Sharif, Woody Strode, Stephen Boyd, Telly Savalas

Francoise Dorleac, Omar Sharif

THE FOOL KILLER

(LANDAU) Producer, David Friedkin; Executive Producer, Worthington Miner; Director, Servando Gonzalez; Screenplay, Morton Fine, David Friedkin; Based on Novel by Helen Eustis; Director of Photography, Alex Phillips, Jr.; Music, Gustavo C. Carreon; Associate Producers, Harrison Starr, Alfred Markim; Costumes, Dorothy Jeakins. July release.

CAST

Milo Bogardus	Anthony Perkins
Mr. Dodd	Dana Elcar
George Mellish	Edward Albert
Dirty Jim Jelliman	Henry Hull
Mrs. Dodd	Salome Jens
Mrs. Ova Fanshawe	Charlotte Jones
Rev. Spotts	Arnold Moss
Blessing Angelina	Sindee Anne Richards
Old Crab	Frances Gaar
Old Man	Wendell Phillips

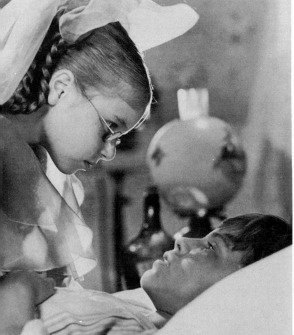

Sindee Anne Richards, Edward Albert. Top: Anthony Perkins. Right: Henry Hull, Edward Albert. Above: Dana Elcar, Salome Jens, Edward Albert. Top: Anthony Perkins, Edward Albert

McHALE'S NAVY JOINS THE AIR FORCE

(UNIVERSAL) Producer-Director, Edward J. Montagne; Associate Producer, Si Rose; Screenplay, John Fenton Murray; Story, William J. Lederer; Director of Photography, Lionel Lindon; Music, Jerry Fielding; Assistant Director, George Bisk; In Technicolor. July release.

CAST

Capt. Binghamton	Joe Flynn
Ensign Parker	Tim Conway
Lt. Carpenter	Bob Hastings
Christy	Gary Vinson
Tinker	Billy Sands
Virgil	Edson Stroll
Willy	John Wright
Fuji	Yoshio Yoda
Happy Haines	Gavin MacLeod
General Harkness	Tom Tully
Smitty	Susan Silo
Colonel Platt	Henry Beckman
Lt. Wilbur Harkness	Ted Bessell
Madge	Jean Hale
Major Grady	Cliff Norton
Dimitri	Jacques Aubuchon
Admiral Doyle	Willis Bouchey
Vogel	Berkeley Harris
Tresh	Tony Franke
Lt. Wilson	Clay Tanner
Russian Seamen	Jack Bernardi, Norman Leavitt, Joe Ploski, Andy Albin

Edson Stroll, Joe Flynn, Bob Hastings

HOW TO STUFF A WILD BIKINI

(AMERICAN INTERNATIONAL) Producers, James H. Nicholson, Samuel Z. Arkoff; Co-Producer, Anthony Carras; Screenplay, William Asher, Leo Townsend; Director, William Asher; Director of Photography, Floyd Crosby; Songs, Guy Hemric and Jerry Styner, Lynn Easton; Music, Les Baxter; Choreography, Jack Baker; Costumes, Richard Bruno; Assistant Director, Dale Hutchinson; In Panavision and Pathe-Color. July release.

CAST

Dee Dee	Annette Funicello
Ricky	Dwayne Hickman
B. D.	Brian Donlevy
Bwana	Buster Keaton
Peachy Keane	Mickey Rooney
Eric Von Zipper	Harvey Lembeck
Cassandra	Beverly Adams
Bonehead	Jody McCrea
Johnny	John Ashley
Animal	Marianne Gaba
North Dakota Pete	Len Lesser
Native Girl	Irene Tsu
Dr. Melamed	Arthur Julian
Khola Koku	Bobbi Shaw
Puss	Alberta Nelson
J. D.	Andy Romano

and John Macchia, Jerry Brutsche, Bob Harvey, Myrna Ross, Alan Fife, Sig Frohlich, Tom Quine, Hollis Morrison, Guy Hemric, George Boyce, Charlie Reed, Patti Chandler, Mike Nader, Ed Garner, John Fain, Mickey Dora, Brian Wilson, Bruce Baker, Ned Wynn, Kerry Berry, Rick Jones, Ray Atkinson, Ron Dayton, Marianne Gordon, Sheila Stephenson, Rosemary Williams, Sue Hamilton, Tonia Van Deter, Uta Stone, Toni Harper, Michele Barton, Victoria Carroll, Luree Holmes

Buster Keaton, Bobbi Shaw. Above: Brian Donlevy, Mickey Rooney. Right: Annette Funicello, Dwayne Hickman

John Wayne, Martha Hyer, Dean Martin,
Michael Anderson Jr., Earl Holliman

THE SONS OF KATIE ELDER

(PARAMOUNT) Producer, Hal Wallis; Associate Producer, Paul Nathan; Director, Henry Hathaway; Screenplay, William H. Wright, Allan Weiss, Harry Essex; Based on Story by Talbot Jennings; Director of Photography, Lucien Ballard; Music, Elmer Bernstein; Costumes, Edith Head; Assistant Director, D. Michael Moore; In Technicolor and Panavision. July release.

CAST

John Elder	John Wayne
Tom Elder	Dean Martin
Mary Gordon	Martha Hyer
Bud Elder	Michael Anderson, Jr.
Matt Elder	Earl Holliman
Deputy Sheriff Latta	Jeremy Slate
Curley	George Kennedy
Dave Hastings	Dennis Hopper
Judge Harry Evers	Sheldon Allman
Minister	John Litel
Undertaker Hyselman	John Doucette
Banker Vannar	James Westerfield
Charlie Bob Striker	Rhys Williams
Charlie Biller	John Qualen
Bondie Adams	Rodolfo Acosta
Jeb Ross	Strother Martin
Storekeeper Peevey	Percy Helton
Doc Isdell	Karl Swenson

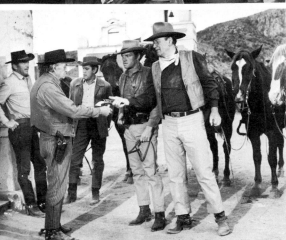

Dean Martin, Paul Fix, Earl Holliman,
Jeremy Slate, John Wayne. Above: Dean
Martin, Martha Hyer, John Wayne

John Wayne, Dean Martin. Above: Dean
Martin, Earl Holliman, Michael Anderson, Jr.,
John Litel

THE SANDPIPER

(M-G-M) Producer, Martin Ransohoff; Director, Vincente Minnelli; Screenplay, Dalton Trumbo, Michael Wilson; Adaptation, Irene Kamp, Louis Kamp; Story, Martin Ransohoff; Music, Johnny Mandel; Lyrics, Paul Francis Webster; Director of Photography, Milton Krasner; Costumes, Irene Sharaff; Associate Producer, John Calley; Assistant Director, William McGarry; A Filmways-Venice Picture in Panavision and Metrocolor. July release.

CAST

Laura Reynolds	Elizabeth Taylor
Dr. Edward Hewitt	Richard Burton
Claire Hewitt	Eva Marie Saint
Cos Erickson	Charles Bronson
Ward Hendricks	Robert Webber
Larry Brant	James Edwards
Judge Thompson	Torin Thatcher
Walter Robinson	Tom Drake
Phil Sutcliff	Doug Henderson
Danny Reynolds	Morgan Mason

Richard Burton, Elizabeth Taylor (also at top) James Edwards. Above: Eva Marie Saint, Richard Burton, Tom Drake

Richard Burton, Morgan Mason, Elizabeth Taylor Top: Charles Bronson, Richard Burton

Tom Drake, Richard Burton, Eva Marie Saint
Above: Richard Burton, Elizabeth Taylor
Top: Richard Burton, Eva Marie Saint

Richard Burton, Elizabeth Taylor (also above)

THE MONKEY'S UNCLE

(BUENA VISTA) Producer, Walt Disney; Co-Producer, Ron Miller; Director, Robert Stevenson; Screenplay, Tom and Helen August; Music, Buddy Baker; Title Song, Richard M. Sherman, Robert B. Sherman; Sung by The Beach Boys; Director of Photography, Edward Colman; Assistant Director, Joseph L. McEveety; Costumes, Chuck Keehne, Gertrude Casey; In Technicolor. July release.

CAST

Merlin Jones	Tommy Kirk
Jennifer	Annette
Judge Holmsby	Leon Ames
Mr. Dearborne	Frank Faylen
Darius Green III	Arthur O'Connell
Leon	Leon Tyler
Norman	Norman Grabowski
Prof. Shattuck	Alan Hewitt
Housekeeper	Connie Gilchrist
Lisa	Cheryl Miller
College President	Gage Clarke
Haywood	Mark Goddard
Board of Regents	Harry Holcombe, Alexander Lockwood, Harry Antrim

Right: Stanley, Tommy Kirk. Below: Stanley, Annette, Tommy Kirk, Leon Ames

Tom Tryon, Senta Berger, and above with Harve Presnell

THE GLORY GUYS

(UNITED ARTISTS) Producers, Arnold Laven, Arthur Gardner, Jules Levy; Director, Arnold Laven; Screenplay, Sam Peckinpah; Based on Novel "The Dice of God" by Hoffman Birney; Music, Riz Ortolani; Director of Photography, James Wong Howe; Assistant Director, Clarence Eurist; Costumes, Frank C. Beetson, Jr.; Filmed in Panavision and DeLuxe Color. July release.

CAST

Demas Harrod	Tom Tryon
Sol Rogers	Harve Presnell
Lou Woodward	Senta Berger
Dugan	James Caan
General McCabe	Andrew Duggan
Gregory	Slim Pickens
Hodges	Peter Breck
Mrs. McCabe	Jeanne Cooper
Beth	Laurel Goodwin
Crain	Adam Williams
Gentry	Erik Holland
Marcus	Robert McQueeney
Moyan	Wayne Rogers
Treadway	William Meigs
Mrs. Poole	Alice Backes
Lt. Cook	Walter Scott
Marshall Cushman	Michael Forest
Hanavan	George Ross
Gunsmith	Dal McKennon
Gen. Hoffman	Stephen Chase
Salesman	Henry Beckman
Martin Hale	Michael Anderson, Jr.

THE HALLELUJAH TRAIL

(UNITED ARTISTS) Producer-Director, John Sturges; Screenplay, John Gay; Based on Novel by Bill Gulick; Music, Elmer Bernstein; Associate Producer, Robert E. Relyea; Director of Photography, Robert Surtees; Costumes, Edith Head; Assistant Director, Jack N. Reddish; Lyrics, Ernie Sheldon; A Mirisch-Kappa Production in Ultra-Panavision and Technicolor. July release.

CAST

Narrator	John Dehner
Col. Thadeus Gearhart	Burt Lancaster
Cora Massingale	Lee Remick
Capt. Paul Slater	Jim Hutton
Louise Gearhart	Pamela Tiffin
Oracle Jones	Donald Pleasence
Frank Wallingham	Brian Keith
Chief Walks-Stooped-Over	Martin Landau
Sgt. Buell	John Anderson
Kevin O'Flaherty	Tom Stern
Five Barrels	Robert J. Wilke
Brother-in-Law #1	Jerry Gatlin
Brother-in-Law #2	Larry Duran
Elks-Runner	James Burk
Clayton Howell	Dub Taylor
Rafe Pike	John McKee
Henrietta	Helen Kleeb
Interpreter	Naom Pitlik
Phillips	Carl Pitti
Brady	Bill Williams
Carter	Marshall Reed
Simmons	Caroll Adams
Hobbs	Whit Bissell
Mrs. Hasselrad	Hope Summers

and Ted Markland, Buff Brady, Bing Russell, Billy Benedict, Karla Most, Elaina Martone, Carroll Henry, Val Avery

Right: Lee Remick, Burt Lancaster. Above:
Lee Remick (C)

Lee Remick, Burt Lancaster, and also above

Jim Hutton, Pamela Tiffin

Marvin Kaplan, Arthur O'Connell, Natalie Wood

Vivian Vance, Marvin Kaplan

Jack Lemmon, Natalie Wood, Tony Curtis
Above: Larry Storch, Tony Curtis. Right:
Natalie Wood, Dorothy Provine, Tony Curtis

THE GREAT RACE

(WARNER BROS.) Producer, Martin Jurow; Director, Blake Edwards; Screenplay, Arthur Ross; Story, Blake Edwards, Arthur Ross; Director of Photography, Russell Harlan; Choreography, Hermes Pan; Music, Henry Mancini; Assistant Directors, Mickey McCardle, Jack Cunningham, James Gordon; Associate Producer, Dick Crockett; Songs, Johnny Mercer, Henry Mancini; Clothes, Edith Head; Costumes, Donfeld; A Patricia-Jalem-Reynard Production in Panavision and Technicolor. July release.

CAST

Prof. Fate	Jack Lemmon
The Great Leslie	Tony Curtis
Maggie DuBois	Natalie Wood
Max	Peter Falk
Hezekiah	Keenan Wynn
Henry Goodbody	Arthur O'Connell
Hester Goodbody	Vivian Vance
Lily Olay	Dorothy Provine
Texas Jack	Larry Storch
Rolfe Von Stuppe	Ross Martin
General Kuhster	George Macready
Frisbee	Marvin Kaplan
Mayor of Boracho	Hal Smith
Sheriff	Denver Pyle
Baron's Guards	William Bryant, Ken Wales

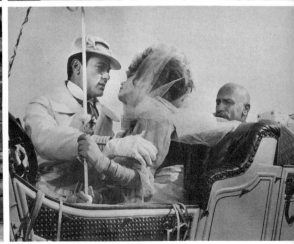

Tony Curtis, Ross Martin. Above: Jack Lemmon

Tony Curtis, Natalie Wood, Keenan Wynn
(also at top). Above: Tony Curtis, Jack Lemmon,
Natalie Wood

SHENANDOAH

(UNIVERSAL) Producer, Robert Arthur; Director, Andrew V. McLaglen; Screenplay, James Lee Barrett; Director of Photography, William H. Clothier; Music, Frank Skinner; Costumes, Rosemary Odell; Assistant Director, Terence Nelson; In Technicolor. August release.

CAST

Charlie	James Stewart
Sam	Doug McClure
Jacob	Glenn Corbett
James	Patrick Wayne
Jennie	Rosemary Forsyth
Boy	Phillip Alford
Ann	Katharine Ross
Nathan	Charles Robinson
John	James McMullan
Henry	Tim McIntire
Gabriel	Eugene Jackson, Jr.
Dr. Witherspoon	Paul Fix
Pastor Bjoerling	Denver Pyle
Col. Fairchild	George Kennedy
Carter	James Best
Lt. Johnson	Tom Simcox
Capt. Richards	Berkeley Harris
Jenkins	Harry Carey, Jr.
Mule	Kevin Hagen
Abernathy	Dabbs Greer
Carroll	Kelly Thordsen
Engineer	Strother Martin

Center: Eugene Jackson, James Stewart. Above: Glenn Corbett, James Stewart. Top: George Kennedy, James Stewart

Phillip Alford, James McMullan, Glenn Corbett, Tim McIntire, Patrick Wayne, Charles Robinson, Rosemary Forsyth, James Stewart, Katharine Ross. Above: Katharine Ross, Rosemary Forsyth Top: Douglas McClure, Rosemary Forsyth

MORITURI
(The Saboteur, Code Name—Morituri)

(20th CENTURY-FOX) Producer, Aaron Rosenberg; Director, Bernhard Wicki; Associate Producer, Barney Rosenzweig; Screenplay, Daniel Taradash; Based on Novel by Werner Joerg Luedecke; Music, Jerry Goldsmith; Director of Photography, Conrad Hill; Assistant Director, Joseph Silver; An Arcola-Colony Production. August release.

CAST

Robert Crain	Marlon Brando
Captain Mueller	Yul Brynner
Esther	Janet Margolin
Colonel Statter	Trevor Howard
Kruse	Martin Benrath
Donkeyman	Hans Christian Blech
Dr. Ambach	Wally Cox
Branner	Max Haufler
Milkereit	Rainer Penkert
Baldwin	William Redfield
Admiral	Oscar Beregi
Nissen	Martin Brandt
Kurz	Charles DeVries
Busch	Carl Esmond
Wilke	Martin Kosleck
Steward	Norbert Schiller
German Crew Member	Robert Sorrells
Crew Member	Rick Traeger
Lt. Brandt	Ivan Triesault

Yul Brynner, William Redfield. Above: Marlon Brando, Janet Margolin. Top: Yul Brynner, Janet Margolin

Marlon Brando, Trevor Howard. Above: Yul Brynner. Top: Janet Margolin, William Redfield

A VERY SPECIAL FAVOR

(UNIVERSAL) Executive Producer, Robert Arthur; Producer, Stanley Shapiro; Director, Michael Gordon; Screenplay, Stanley Shapiro, Nate Monaster; Director of Photography, Leo Tover; Music, Vic Mizzy; Wardrobe, Yves Saint Laurent; Choreography, David Robel; Assistant Director, Phil Bowles; In Technicolor. August release.

CAST

Paul	Rock Hudson
Lauren	Leslie Caron
Michel	Charles Boyer
Etienne	Walter Slezak
Arnold	Dick Shawn
Harry	Larry Storch
Mickey	Nita Talbot
Mother Plum	Norma Varden
Pete	George Furth
Claude	Marcel Hillaire
Rene	Jay Novello
Bartender	Stafford Repp
Jacqueline	Danica D'Hondt
Desk Clerk	Frank DeVol
Dr. Lambert	John Harding

Leslie Caron, Dick Shawn. Above: Rock Hudson, Leslie Caron, also left with Walter Slezak. Top: (L) Charles Boyer, Leslie Caron, (R) Leslie Caron, Rock Hudson

Oskar Werner, Simone Signoret
in
"SHIP OF FOOLS"

Vivien Leigh, Simone Signoret, Jose Ferrer, Lee Marvin, Oskar Werner, Elizabeth
Ashley, George Segal, Jose Greco, Michael Dunn, Charles Korvin, Heinz Ruehmann

Jose Ferrer, Christian Schmidtmer. Above:
George Segal, Elizabeth Ashley

Barbara Luna, Jose Greco. Above: Lee Marvin,
Vivien Leigh

SHIP OF FOOLS

(COLUMBIA) Producer-Director, Stanley Kramer; Screenplay, Abby Mann; Director of Photography, Ernest Laszlo; Music, Ernest Gold; Songs, Ernest Gold, Jack Lloyd; Costumes, Bill Thomas; Miss Leigh's Gowns, Jean Louis; Assistant Director, John Veitch; Based on Novel by Katherine Anne Porter. September release.

CAST

Mary Treadwell	Vivien Leigh
La Condesa	Simone Signoret
Rieber	Jose Ferrer
Tenny	Lee Marvin
Dr. Schumann	Oskar Werner
Jenny	Elizabeth Ashley
David	George Segal
Pepe	Jose Greco
Glocken	Michael Dunn
Capt. Thiele	Charles Korvin
Lowenthal	Heinz Ruehmann
Frau Hutten	Lilia Skala
Amparo	Barbara Luna
Lizzi	Christiane Schmidtmer
Freytag	Alf Kjellin
Lt. Heebner	Werner Klemperer
Graf	John Wengraf
Frau Schmitt	Olga Fabian
Elsa	Gila Golan
Lutz	Oscar Beregi
Hutten	Stanley Adams
Frau Lutz	Karen Verne
Johann	Charles de Vries
Pastora	Lydia Torea
Fat Man	Henry Calvin
Carlos	Paul Daniel
Woodcarver	David Renard
Ric	Rudy Carrella
Rac	Silvia Marino
Guitarist	Anthony Brand

Right: Werner Klemperer, Vivien Leigh
Above: Simone Signoret, Oskar Werner

Karen Verne, Gila Golan, Oskar Werner, Oscar Beregi. Above: Heinz Ruehmann, Michael Dunn, Alf Kjellin

Stanley Adams, Lilia Skala. Above: Oskar Werner, Charles Korvin

BILLIE

(UNITED ARTISTS) Producer-Director, Don Weis; Screenplay, Ronald Alexander; Based on his Play "Time Out For Ginger"; Executive Producer, Peter Lawford; Music, Dominic Frontiere; Choreography, David Winters; Director of Photography, John Russell; Assistant Directors, Dick Moder, Dale Coleman; A Chrislaw Production in Techniscope and Technicolor. September release.

CAST

Billie	Patty Duke
Howard Carol	Jim Backus
Agnes Carol	Jane Greer
Mike Benson	Warren Berlinger
Mayor Davis	Billy DeWolfe
Coach Jones	Charles Lane
Matt Bullitt	Dick Sargent
Jean Matthews	Susan Seaforth
Bob Matthews	Ted Bessell
Principal Wilson	Richard Deacon
Eddie Davis	Bobby Diamond
Ray Case	Michael Fox
Ted Chekas	Clive Clerk
Dr. Hall	Harlan Warde
Nurse Webb	Jean MacRae
Allan Grant	Himself
Mrs. Hosenwacker	Georgia Simmons
Mrs. Clifton	Arline Anderson
Miss Channing	Layte Bowden
Reporter	Mathew M. Jordan
Mrs. Harper	Shirley J. Shawn
Adele Colin	Maria Lennard
Mary Jensen	Breena Howard
Starter	Craig W. Chudy

Right: Patty Duke, Jim Backus, Dick Sargent, Jane Greer, Susan Seaforth. Above: Warren Berlinger, Patty Duke

THAT FUNNY FEELING

(UNIVERSAL) Producer, Harry Keller; Director, Richard Thorpe; Screenplay, David R. Schwartz; Based on Story by Norman Barasch, Carroll Moore; Director of Photography, Clifford Stine; Music, Bobby Darin; Gowns, Jean Louis; Assistant Director, Joseph Kenny; In Technicolor. September release.

CAST

Joan Howell	Sandra Dee
Tom Milford	Bobby Darin
Harvey Granson	Donald O'Connor
Audrey	Nita Talbot
Luther	Larry Storch
O'Shea	Leo G. Carroll
Officer Brokaw	James Westerfield
Bartenders	Robert Strauss, Ben Lessy
Taxi Driver	Benny Rubin

Leo G. Carroll, Bobby Darin, Sandra Dee. Above: Nita Talbot, Larry Storch, Sandra Dee. Left: Donald O'Connor, Bobby Darin

ONCE A THIEF

(M-G-M) Producer, Jacques Bar; Director, Ralph Nelson; Screenplay, Zekial Marko; From his Novel; Music, Lalo Schifrin; Director of Photography, Robert Burks; Assistant Director, Erich von Stroheim, Jr.; Produced by CIPRA in association with Ralph Nelson and Fred Engel in Panavision. September release.

CAST

Eddie Pedak	Alain Delon
Kristine Pedak	Ann-Margret
Mike Vido	Van Heflin
Walter Pedak	Jack Palance
James Sargatanas	John Davis Chandler
Lt. Kebner	Jeff Corey
Cleve Shoenstein	Tony Musante
Frank Kane	Steve Mitchell
Luke	Zekial Marko
Kathy Pedak	Tammy Locke
Drummer	Russell Lee
John Ling	Yuki Shimoda

Alain Delon, Van Heflin. Top: Alain Delon, Ann-Margret, and right with Tammy Locke

John Davis Chandler, Jack Palance, Tammy Locke, Alain Delon, Ann-Margret. Above: Alain Delon, Ann-Margret

Alain Delon, Ann-Margret
in
"ONCE A THIEF"

LAUREL AND HARDY'S LAUGHING '20'S

(M-G-M) Produced and Written by Robert Youngson; Music, Skeets Alquist; Associate Producers, Herbert Gelbspan, Hal Roach Studios, Alfred Dahlem. September release.

CAST

Oliver Hardy, Stan Laurel, Vivian Oakland, Glen Tryon, Edna Murphy, Anita Garvin, Tiny Sanford, Jimmy Finlayson, Charlie Chase, Viola Richard, Max Davidson, Del Henderson, Josephine Crowell, Anders Randolf, Edgar Kennedy, Dorothy Coburn, Lillian Elliott, "Spec" O'Donnell

A collection of classic bits from films in which Stan Laurel and Oliver Hardy appeared.

Below: Stan Laurel, Dorothy Coburn, Oliver Hardy. Left: Laurel and Hardy

I SAW WHAT YOU DID

(UNIVERSAL) Producer-Director, William Castle; Based on Novel "Out Of The Dark" by Ursula Curtiss; Director of Photography, Joe Biroc; Assistant Directors, Terry Morse, Jr., Charles Scott, Jr. September release.

CAST

Amy	Joan Crawford
Steve Marak	John Ireland
David Mannering	Leif Erickson
Ellie Mannering	Pat Breslin
Libby	Andi Garrett
Tess	Sharyl Locke
Kit Austin	Sarah Lane
John Austin	John Archer
Judith	Joyce Meadows
Tom Ward	Douglas Evans
Mary Ward	Barbara Wilkins

Andi Garrett, Sarah Lane, Sharyl Locke. Above: Joan Crawford, John Ireland. Left: John Ireland, Andi Garrett

MARRIAGE ON THE ROCKS

(WARNER BROS.) Producer and Director of Photography, William H. Daniels; Director, Jack Donohue; Screenplay, Cy Howard; Music, Nelson Riddle; Assistant Director, Richard Lang; Women's Costumes, Walter Plunkett; Choreography, Jonathan Lucas; A Sinatra Enterprise and A-C Production in Technicolor and Panavision. October release.

CAST

Dan Edwards	Frank Sinatra
Valerie Edwards	Deborah Kerr
Ernie Brewer	Dean Martin
Miguel Santos	Cesar Romero
Jeannie MacPherson	Hermione Baddeley
Jim Blake	Tony Bill
Shad Nathan	John McGiver
Tracy Edwards	Nancy Sinatra
Lisa Sterling	Davey Davison
David Edwards	Michel Petit
Trini Lopez	Trini Lopez
Lola	Joi Lansing
Bunny	Tara Ashton
Miss Blight	Kathleen Freeman
Rollo	Flip Mark
Mr. Turner	DeForest Kelley
Kitty	Sigrid Valdis

Nancy Sinatra, Tony Bill. Top: Frank Sinatra, Deborah Kerr, (R) Joi Lansing, Dean Martin

Frank Sinatra, Nancy Sinatra, Dean Martin, Joi Lansing, Hermione Baddeley, Tony Bill. Above: Frank Sinatra, Cesar Romero, Deborah Kerr

GIT!

(EMBASSY) Producer-Director, Ellis Kadison; Associate Producers, Bill Schwartz, Homer McCoy; Screenplay, Homer McCoy; Based on Story by Homer McCoy, Ellis Kadison; Director of Photography, Gordon Avil; Music, Philip Lambro; Assistant Director, Joe Wonder; A Joseph E. Levine Presentation in Technicolor; A World-Cine Associates Production. October release.

CAST

Deke	Jack Chaplain
Elaine	Heather North
Finney	Leslie Bradley
Andrew Garrett	Richard Webb
Mrs. Finney	Hannah Landy
T. C. Knox	Emory Parnell
Jed	Joseph Hamilton
District Attorney	Richard Valentine
Police Sergeant	Jeff Burton
Dr. Allen	Sherry Moreland
Sam Lewis	Shug Fisher
Rock	Seldom Seen Sioux

Right: Seldom Seen Sioux, Heather North, Jack Chaplain

THE REWARD

(20th CENTURY-FOX) Producer, Aaron Rosenberg; Director, Serge Bourguignon; Screenplay, Serge Bourguignon, Oscar Millard; Based on Novel by Michael Barrett; Music, Elmer Bernstein; Director of Photography, Joe MacDonald; Costumes, Moss Mabry; Assistant Director, Joseph E. Rickards; In Cinemascope and DeLuxe Color. October release.

CAST

Scott	Max von Sydow
Sylvia	Yvette Mimieux
Frank	Efrem Zimbalist, Jr.
Carbajal	Gilbert Roland
Lopez	Emilio Fernandez
Luis	Nino Castelnuovo
Joaquin	Henry Silva
Patron	Rodolfo Acosta
El Viejo	Julian Rivero

Gilbert Roland, Henry Silva, Yvette Mimieux, Efrem Zimbalist, Jr., Nino Castelnuovo. Above: (L) Yvette Mimieux, Max Von Sydow, (R) Max Von Sydow, Emilio Fernandez

A RAGE TO LIVE

(UNITED ARTISTS) Producer, Lewis J. Rachmil; Director, Walter Grauman; Screenplay, John T. Kelley; From the Novel by John O'Hara; Director of Photography, Charles Lawton; Music, Nelson Riddle; Theme Music, Ferrante and Teicher with Lyrics by Noel Sherman; Assistant Director, Emmett Emerson; Costumes, Howard Shoup; A Mirisch Corp. Presentation in Panavision. October release.

CAST
Grace Caldwell	Suzanne Pleshette
Sidney Tate	Bradford Dillman
Roger Bannon	Ben Gazzara
Jack Hollister	Peter Graves
Amy Hollister	Bethel Leslie
Dr. O'Brien	James Gregory
Emily Caldwell	Carmen Mathews
Mrs. Bannon	Ruth White
Connie Schoffstall	Sarah Marshall
Emma	Virginia Christine
Brock Caldwell	Linden Chiles
Charlie Jay	Mark Goddard
Paul Reichelderfer	George Furth
Jessie Jay	Brett Somers
George Jay	Frank Maxwell

Right: James Gregory, Suzanne Pleshette, Bradford Dillman

Suzanne Pleshette, Bradford Dillman. Above:
Suzanne Pleshette, Ben Gazzara

Bethel Leslie, Peter Graves, Suzanne Pleshette
Above: Carmen Mathews, James Gregory

MICKEY ONE

(COLUMBIA) Produced by Florin-Tatira; Director, Arthur Penn; Screenplay, Alan M. Surgal; Director of Photography, Ghislain Cloquet; Music, Jack Shaindlin, Eddie Sauter. October release.

CAST

Mickey One	Warren Beatty
Castle	Hurd Hatfield
Jenny	Alexandra Stewart
Berson	Teddy Hart
Fryer	Jeff Corey
The Artist	Kamatari Fujiwara
Ruby	Franchot Tone

Warren Beatty, Alexandra Stewart (also at top)
Above: Teddy Hart, Warren Beatty. Top right:
Alexandra Stewart, Warren Beatty, Hurd Hatfield

Pamela Curran, Jonathan Winters, Roxanne Arlen

John Gielgud, Asa Maynor, Roddy McDowall,
Jonathan Winters, Robert Easton

Robert Morse, Robert Morley, Jonathan Winters,
Anjanette Comer, Rod Steiger, Roddy McDowall,
John Gielgud. Above: Milton Berle, Margaret
Leighton. Right: Tab Hunter

THE LOVED ONE

(M-G-M) Producers, John Calley, Haskell
Wexler; Director, Tony Richardson; Screen-
play, Terry Southern, Christopher Isherwood;
Based on Novel by Evelyn Waugh; Director of
Photography, Haskell Wexler; Production and
Costume Design, Rouben Ter-Arutunian; Music,
John Addison; Assistant Director, Kurt Neu-
mann; Associate Producer, Neil Hartley; A
Filmways Picture; A Martin Ransohoff Pro-
duction. October release.

CAST

Dennis Barlow	Robert Morse
Wilbur and Harry Glenworthy	Jonathan Winters
Aimee Thanatogenos	Anjanette Comer
Mr. Joyboy	Rod Steiger
General Brinkman	Dana Andrews
Mr. Kenton	Milton Berle
Immigration Officer	James Coburn
Sir Francis Hinsley	John Gielgud
Guide	Tab Hunter
Mrs. Kenton	Margaret Leighton
Mr. Starker	Liberace
D. J., Jr.	Roddy McDowall
Sir Ambrose Abercrombie	Robert Morley
Sadie Blodgett	Barbara Nichols
The Guru Brahmin	Lionel Stander
Joyboy's Mother	Ayllene Gibbons
Assistant to Guru Brahmin	Bernie Kopell
Secretary to D. J., Jr.	Asa Maynor
English Club Official	Alan Napier

James Coburn, Robert Morse

Jonathan Winters, Dana Andrews

John Gielgud, Robert Morse, Roxanne Arlen,
Robert Morley. Above: Barbara Nichols,
Robert Morse

Liberace. Above: Robert Morse, Jonathan Winters

Carol Lynley, Keir Dullea, Anna Massey. Above:
Laurence Olivier, Martita Hunt, Keir Dullea

Noel Coward, Carol Lynley

BUNNY LAKE IS MISSING

(COLUMBIA) Producer-Director, Otto Preminger; Screenplay, John and Penelope Mortimer; From the Novel by Evelyn Piper; Director of Photography, Denys Coop; Music, Paul Glass; In Panavision. October release.

CAST

Steven	Keir Dullea
Ann	Carol Lynley
Cook	Lucie Mannheim
Wilson	Noel Coward
Elvira	Anna Massey
Ada Ford	Martita Hunt
Newhouse	Laurence Olivier
Andrews	Clive Revill
Doll Maker	Finlay Currie
Sister	Megs Jenkins

Clive Revill, Carol Lynley, Laurence Olivier,
Keir Dullea. Above: Carol Lynley, Keir Dullea
(L) Laurence Olivier, Keir Dullea

THE BEDFORD INCIDENT

(COLUMBIA) Producer-Director, James B. Harris; Co-Producer, Richard Widmark; Associate Producer, Dennis O'Dell; Screenplay, James Poe; Based on Novel by Mark Rascovich; Director of Photography, Gil Taylor; Assistant Director, Clive Reed. October release.

CAST

Capt. Eric Finlander	Richard Widmark
Ben Munceford	Sidney Poitier
Ensign Ralston	James MacArthur
Lt. Cmdr. Chester Potter	Martin Balsam
Sonarman Second Class	Wally Cox
Commodore Wolfgang Schrepke	Eric Portman
Cmdr. Allison	Michael Kane
Chief Pharmacist Mate McKinley	Phil Brown
Lt. Bascombe	Gary Cockrell
Lt. Beekman	Brian Davies
Pharmacist Mate Strauss	Warren Stanhope
Pharmacist Mate Nerney	Donald Sutherland
Seaman Jones	Colin Maitland
Lt. Hacker	Edward Bishop
Lt. Burger	George Roubicek

Right: Martin Balsam, Wally Cox. Top: Eric Portman, Sidney Poitier, Richard Widmark Below: Sidney Poitier, James MacArthur

Eleanor Roosevelt in 1905 in her wedding dress

THE ELEANOR ROOSEVELT STORY

(ALLIED ARTISTS) Created and Produced by Sidney Glazier; Written by Archibald MacLeish; Narrated by Eric Severeid, Archibald MacLeish, Mrs. Francis Cole; Directed by Richard Kaplan; Music, Ezra Laderman; A Landau-Unger Company Presentation. November release.

A full-length Documentary Film biography of Mrs. Roosevelt from her early years of unhappiness, to her later years as significant figure on the world scene as a trusted and respected stateswoman. Photos and motion picture footage were researched from private and government sources in 22 countries on all five continents and on both sides of the Iron Curtain.

Rose Andrews, Charlton Heston

PEER GYNT

(BRANDON) Producer-Director, David Bradley; Photography, David Bradley, Richard Roth; Music, Edward Grieg. November release.

CAST

Peer Gynt	Charlton Heston
Aase	Betty Hanisee
Old Woman	Mrs. Herbert Hyde
Kari	Lucielle Powell
Old Woman	Sue Straub
Aslak	Charles Paetow
Solveig	Kathryne Elfstrom
Haegstad	Morris Wilson
Drunk	George B. Moll
Ingrid	Betty Barton
Mads Moen	Alan Eckhart
Cowherd Girls	Katharine Bradley, Anty Ball, Alice Badgerow
Dovre-King	Roy Eggert, Jr.
The Boyg	Francis X. Bushman
Woman in Green	Audrey Wedlock
Woman in Green (now a Hag)	Sarah Merrill
Ugly Urchin	Alan Heston
Herr Trumpeterstraale	David Bradley
Anitra	Rose Andrews
Mr. MacPherson	Warren McKenzie
Monsieur Ballon	Roy Eggert, Jr.

and Robert Cooper, Rod Maynard, Jane Wilimovsky, Thomas A. Blair

Jack Kelly, Kristin Nelson, Madelyn Himes
Above and right: Kristin Nelson, Rick Nelson

LOVE AND KISSES

(UNIVERSAL) Producer-Director, Ozzie Nelson; Screenplay, Ozzie Nelson; Based on Play by Anita Rowe Block; Director of Photography, Robert Moreno; Music, William Loose, Jimmie Haskell; Assistant Director, Carl Beringer; Songs, Sonny Curtis, Clint Ballard, Jr. and Angela Riela; Sung by Rick Nelson; In Technicolor. November release.

CAST

Buzzy	Rick Nelson
Jeff Pringle	Jack Kelly
Rosemary	Kristin Nelson
Freddy	Jerry Van Dyke
Nanny	Pert Kelton
Carol	Madelyn Himes
Elizabeth	Sheilah Wells
Officer Jones	Alvy Moore
Stage Manager	Angelo Brovelli
Bobby	Barry Livingston
Assemblyman Potter	Ivan Bonar
Mr. Frisby	Howard McNear
Dancers	Betty Rowland, Nancy Lewis, Anita Mann

HARUM SCARUM

(M-G-M) Producer, Sam Katzman; Director, Gene Nelson; Screenplay, Gerald Drayson Adams; Director of Photography, Fred H. Jackman; Music, Fred Karger; Vocal Backgrounds, The Jordanaires; Choreography, Earl Barton; Assistant Director, Eddie Saeta; A Four Leaf Production in Metrocolor. November release.

CAST

Johnny Tyronne	Elvis Presley
Princess Shalimar	Mary Ann Mobley
Aishah	Fran Jeffries
Prince Dragna	Michael Ansara
Zacha	Jay Novello
King Toranshah	Philip Reed
Sinan	Theo Marcuse
Baba	Billy Barta
Mokar	Dirk Harvey
Julna	Jack Costanza
Capt. Herat	Larry Chance
Leilah	Barbara Werle
Emerald	Brenda Benet
Sapphire	Gail Gilmore
Amethyst	Wilda Taylor
Sari	Vicki Malkin
Mustapha	Ryck Rydon
Scarred Bedouin	Richard Reeves
Yussef	Joey Russo

Fran Jeffries, Elvis Presley. Left: MaryAnn Mobley, Elvis Presley

THE WAR LORD

(UNIVERSAL) Producer, Walter Seltzer; Director, Franklin Schaffner; Screenplay, John Collier, Millard Kaufman; Based on Play "The Lovers" by Leslie Stevens; Director of Photography, Russell Metty; Costumes, Vittorio Nino Novarese; Music, Jerome Moross; Choreography, Kenny Williams; Assistant Directors, Douglas Green, Carl Beringer; In Color and Panavision. November release.

CAST

Chrysagon	Charlton Heston
Bors	Richard Boone
Bronwyn	Rosemary Forsyth
Priest	Maurice Evans
Draco	Guy Stockwell
Odins	Niall MacGinnis
Frisian Prince	Henry Wilcoxon
Marc	James Farentino
Volc	Sammy Ross
Piet	Woodrow Parfrey
Holbracht	John Alderson
Tybald	Allen Jaffe
Rainault	Michael Conrad
Dirck	Dal Jenkins
Boy Prince	Johnny Jensen
Chrysagon Man	Forrest Wood
Old Woman	Belle Mitchell

Maurice Evans, Charlton Heston, Richard Boone Above: Rosemary Forsyth, Charlton Heston, Richard Boone

RETURN FROM THE ASHES

(UNITED ARTISTS) Producer-Director, J. Lee
Thompson; Screenplay, Julius J. Epstein; Based
on Novel by Hubert Monteilhet; Music, John
Dankworth; Associate Producer, Cecil Ford;
Director of Photography, Chris Challis; Cos-
tumes, Margaret Furse; Assistant Director, Kip
Gowans; A Mirisch Corp. Presentation in Pana-
vision. November release.

CAST
Stanislaus Pilgrin	Maximilian Schell
Fabienne	Samantha Eggar
Dr. Michele Wolf	Ingrid Thulin
Dr. Charles Bovard	Herbert Lom
Claudine	Talitha Pol
Chess Club Manager	Vladek Sheybal
Detectives	Jacques Brunius, Andre Maranne
Woman in Train	Yvonne Andre
Man in Train	John Serret
Mother in Train	Pamela Stirling

Maximilian Schell, Samantha Eggar. Top:
Herbert Lom, Ingrid Thulin

Samantha Eggar, Maximilian Schell, Ingrid Thulin
Above: Samantha Eggar, Maximilian Schell
Top: Maximilian Schell, Ingrid Thulin

A THOUSAND CLOWNS

(UNITED ARTISTS) Producer-Director, Fred Coe; Associate Producers, Ralph Rosenblum, Herb Gardner; Screenplay, Herb Gardner; Based on his Play; Costumes, Ruth Morley; Assistant Director, Dan Ericksen; Director of Photography, Arthur J. Ornitz; Presented by Harrell Productions, Inc. November release.

CAST

Murray	Jason Robards
Sandra	Barbara Harris
Arnold	Martin Balsam
Nick	Barry Gordon
Leo	Gene Saks
Albert	William Daniels

Barry Gordon, Jason Robards. Above: Barry Gordon, William Daniels, Barbara Harris. Top: Barbara Harris, Jason Robards

Jason Robards, Barbara Harris. Top: Jason Robards, Barry Gordon

99

THE CINCINNATI KID

(M-G-M) Producer, Martin Ransohoff; Director, Norman Jewison; Screenplay, Ring Lardner, Jr., Terry Southern; Based on Novel by Richard Jessup; Director of Photography, Philip H. Lathrop; Music, Lalo Schifrin; Title Song, Dorcas Cochran; Sung by Ray Charles; Associate Producer, John Calley; Costumes, Donfeld; Assistant Director, Kurt Neumann; A Filmways-Solar Picture in Metrocolor. November release.

CAST

The Cincinnati Kid	Steve McQueen
Lancey Howard	Edward G. Robinson
Melba	Ann-Margret
Shooter	Karl Malden
Christian	Tuesday Weld
Lady Fingers	Joan Blondell
Slade	Rip Torn
Pig	Jack Weston
Yeller	Cab Calloway
Hoban	Jeff Corey
Felix	Theo Marcuse
Sokal	Milton Selzer
Mr. Rudd	Karl Swenson
Cajun	Emile Genest
Danny	Ron Soble
Mrs. Rudd	Irene Tedrow
Mrs. Slade	Midge Ware
Dealer	Dub Taylor

Steve McQueen, Ann-Margret, Tuesday Weld
Above: Karl Malden, Joan Blondell, Cab Calloway, Edward G. Robinson

Ann-Margret, Steve McQueen. Above: Steve McQueen, Ann-Margret, Karl Malden, Joan Blondell, Edward G. Robinson. Top: Steve McQueen, Tuesday Weld

Jim Hutton, Connie Stevens, Paul Ford, Maureen
O'Sullivan (also above). Top: Paul Ford, Lloyd
Nolan, Jim Hutton, Maureen O'Sullivan
(R) Jim Hutton, Connie Stevens
Below: Paul Ford, Maureen O'Sullivan

NEVER TOO LATE

(WARNER BROS.) Producer, Norman Lear;
Director, Bud Yorkin; Screenplay, Sumner
Arthur Long from his Play; Director of Photog-
raphy, Phil Lathrop; Music, David Rose; Title
Song: Words, Jay Livingston, Ray Evans, Music,
David Rose; Sung by Vic Damone; Costumes,
Sheila O'Brien; Assistant Director, Bud Grace;
In Technicolor and Panavision. November
release.

CAST

Harry Lambert	Paul Ford
Kate Clinton	Connie Stevens
Edith Lambert	Maureen O'Sullivan
Charlie Clinton	Jim Hutton
Grace Kimbrough	Jane Wyatt
Dr. Kimbrough	Henry Jones
Mayor Crane	Lloyd Nolan

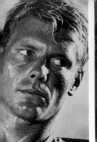
James Fox

Patrick O'Neal

Reg Lye

John Merivale

Tom Courtenay

Denholm Elliott

James Fox, Patrick O'Neal, Tom Courtenay, George Segal. Above: John Mills, Dale Ishimoto Right: George Segal, James Fox, William Fawcett, Sammy Reese, Joseph Turkel, Mike Stroka, Patrick O'Neal

KING RAT

(COLUMBIA) Producer, James Woolf; Directed and Written by Bryan Forbes; Based on Novel by James Clavell; Music, John Barry; Associate Producer, Marvin Miller; Director of Photography, Burnett Guffey; Assistant Director, Russell Saunders; A Coleytown Production. November release.

CAST

King	George Segal
Lt. Grey	Tom Courtenay
Flight Lt. Marlowe	James Fox
Max	Patrick O'Neal
Col. Larkin	Denholm Elliott
Dr. Kennedy	James Donald
Tex	Todd Armstrong
Col. Smedley Taylor	John Mills
Col. Brant	Alan Webb
Col. Jones	Gerald Sim
Maj. McCoy	Leonard Rossiter
Capt. Daven	John Standing
Capt. Hawkins	John Ronane
Chaplain Drinkwater	Hamilton Dyce
Dino	Joseph Turkel
Squadron Leader Vexley	Geoffrey Bayldon
Tinkerbell	Reg Lye
Maj. Barry	George Pelling
Yoshima	Dale Ishimoto
Pvt. Gurble	John Orchard
Torusumi	Louis Neervoort

and Sammy Reese, Michael Lees, Wright King, John Merivale, Arthur Malet, Hedley Mattingly, John Levington, Teru Shimada, Richard Dawson, Mike Stroka, William Fawcett, Roy Deane, Larry Conroy, John Warburton, David Haviland, Anthony Faramus, John Barclay, David Frankham

John Standing Gerald Sim Todd Armstrong Geoffrey Bayldon Joseph Turkel George Segal

James Fox, George Segal. Above: James Donald, Michael Lees, James Fox. Top: George Segal, Alan Webb, Tom Courtenay

Tom Courtenay, John Mills. Above: George Segal, Denholm Elliott, Todd Armstrong, Leonard Rossiter, James Fox. Top: James Fox, Denholm Elliott, Hamilton Dyce, Leonard Rossiter

103

Michael Romanoff, Doris Day, Reginald Gardiner

Maura McGiveney, Rod Taylor, Reginald Gardiner

Doris Day, Sergio Fantoni. Above: Doris Day, Hermione Baddeley

DO NOT DISTURB

(20th CENTURY-FOX) Producers, Aaron Rosenberg, Martin Melcher; Director, Ralph Levy; Screenplay, Milt Rosen, Richard Breen; Based on Play by William Fairchild; Music, Mort Garson; Songs, Ben Raleigh and Mark Barkan, Mort Garson and Bob Hillard; Director of Photography, Leon Shamroy; Costumes, Ray Aghayan; Assistant Director, Joseph E. Rickards; In CinemaScope and DeLuxe Color; An Arcola-Melcher Production. December release.

CAST

Janet Harper	Doris Day
Mike Harper	Rod Taylor
Vanessa Courtwright	Hermione Baddeley
Paul Bellasi	Sergio Fantoni
Simmons	Reginald Gardiner
Claire Hackett	Maura McGiveney
Culkos	Aram Katcher
Langsdorf	Leon Askin
Alicia	Lisa Pera
Man	Michael Romanoff
Reynard	Albert Carrier
Mrs. Ordley	Barbara Morrison
American Consul	Pierre Salinger

Doris Day, Rod Taylor. Above: Rod Taylo Sergio Fantoni

Frank Gorshin, Neville Brand, Grayson Hall

Dean Jones

Dorothy Provine, Hayley Mills

THAT DARN CAT

(BUENA VISTA) Producer, Walt Disney; Co-Producers, Bill Walsh, Ron Miller; Director, Robert Stevenson; Director of Photography, Edward Colman; Screenplay, The Gordons, Bill Walsh; Music, Bob Brunner; Title Song, Richard M. and Robert B. Sherman; Sung by Bobby Darin; Based on Book "Undercover Cat" by The Gordons; Costumes, Bill Thomas; Assistant Director, Joseph L. McEveety; In Technicolor. December release.

CAST

Patti Randall	Hayley Mills
Zeke Kelso	Dean Jones
Ingrid Randall	Dorothy Provine
Gregory Benson	Roddy McDowall
Dan	Neville Brand
Mr. Hofstedder	Ed Wynn
Mrs. MacDougall	Elsa Lanchester
Mr. MacDougall	William Demarest
Iggy	Frank Gorshin
Supervisor Newton	Richard Eastham
Margaret Miller	Grayson Hall
Canoe	Tom Lowell
Drive-In Manager	Richard Deacon
Landlady	Iris Adrian
Graham	Liam Sullivan
Spires	Don Dorrell
Cahill	Gene Blakely
Kelly	Karl Held

Hayley Mills, Dean Jones. Above: William Demarest, Elsa Lanchester

Roddy McDowall, Hayley Mills. Above: Hayley Mills, Dorothy Provine **105**

A PATCH OF BLUE

(M-G-M) Producer, Pandro S. Berman; Directed and Written by Guy Green; Based on "Be Ready With Bells and Drums" by Elizabeth Kata; Director of Photography, Robert Burks; Music, Jerry Goldsmith; Associate Producer, Kathryn Hereford; Assistant Director, Hank Moonjean; In Panavision.

CAST

Gordon Ralfe	Sidney Poitier
Rose-Ann D'Arcy	Shelley Winters
Selina D'Arcey	Elizabeth Hartman
Ole Pa	Wallace Ford
Mark Ralfe	Ivan Dixon
Sadie	Elizabeth Fraser
Mr. Faber	John Qualen
Yanek Faber	Kelly Flynn
Selina at 5	Debi Storm
Mrs. Favaloro	Renata Vanni
Mr. Favaloro	Saverio LoMedico

Elizabeth Hartman, Sidney Poitier (also above)

Elizabeth Hartman, Sidney Poitier, and above with Shelley Winters. Top: Wallace Ford, Shelley Winters, Elizabeth Hartman

BOEING BOEING

(PARAMOUNT) Producer, Hal Wallis; Associate Producer, Paul Nathan; Director, John Rich; Screenplay, Edward Anhalt; Based on Play by Marc Camoletti; Director of Photography, Lucien Ballard; Music, Neal Hefti; Assistant Director, Daniel J. McCauley; Costumes, Edith Head; In Technicolor. December release.

CAST

Bernard Lawrence	Tony Curtis
Robert Reed	Jerry Lewis
Jacqueline Grieux	Dany Saval
Lise Bruner	Christiane Schmidtmer
Vicky Hawkins	Suzanna Leigh
Bertha	Thelma Ritter
Pierre	Lomax Study

Left: Christiane Schmidtmer, Tony Curtis, Thelma Ritter

Jerry Lewis, Dany Saval, Tony Curtis, Suzanna Leigh, Christiane Schmidtmer. Above: Jerry Lewis, Suzanna Leigh, Tony Curtis

Jerry Lewis, Tony Curtis. Above: Jerry Lewis, Christiane Schmidtmer, Tony Curtis, Dany Saval

107

Telly Savalas, Pier Angeli   Barbara Werle, Robert Shaw   James MacArthur, Henry Fon

BATTLE OF THE BULGE

(WARNER BROS.) Producers, Milton Sperling, Philip Yordan; Director, Ken Annakin; Screenplay, Philip Yordan, Milton Sperling, John Melson; Director of Photography, Jack Hildyard; Costumes, Laure De Zarate; Music, Benjamin Frankel; Assistant Directors, Jose Lopez Rodero, Martin Sacristan, Luis Garcia; A Sidney Harmon, in association with United States Pictures Inc. Production; In Ultra-Panavision and Technicolor. December release.

CAST

Lt. Col. Kiley	Henry Fonda
Col. Hessler	Robert Shaw
Gen. Grey	Robert Ryan
Col. Pritchard	Dana Andrews
Sgt. Duquesne	George Montgomery
Schumacher	Ty Hardin
Louise	Pier Angeli
Elena	Barbara Werle
Wolenski	Charles Bronson
Gen. Kohler	Werner Peters
Conrad	Hans Christian Blech
Lt. Weaver	James MacArthur
Guffy	Telly Savalas

James MacArthur, Henry Fonda, Dana Andrews
Above: Henry Fonda, Robert Ryan, Dana
Andrews. Left: James MacArthur, George
Montgomery. Above: Robert Shaw,
Charles Bronson

Steven Hill, Anne Bancroft

Sidney Poitier, Indus Arthur, Jason Wingreen

Telly Savalas, Sidney Poitier. Above:
Anne Bancroft (also right)

THE SLENDER THREAD

(PARAMOUNT) Producer, Stephen Alexander; Director, Sydney Pollack; Screenplay, Stirling Silliphant; Suggested by Life Magazine article by Shana Alexander; Director of Photography, Loyal Griggs; Music, Quincy Jones; Assistant Director, Don Roberts; An Athene Production. December release.

CAST

Alan Newell	Sidney Poitier
Inga Dyson	Anne Bancroft
Doctor Coburn	Telly Savalas
Mark Dyson	Steven Hill
Detective Judd Ridley	Edward Asner
Marion	Indus Arthur
Sgt. Harry Ward	Paul Newlan
Charlie	Dabney Coleman
Doctor	H. M. Wynant
Patrolman Steve Peters	Robert Hoy
Chris Dyson	Greg Jarvis
Medical Technician	Jason Wingreen
Mrs. Thomas	Marjorie Nelson
Arthur Foss	Steven Marlo
Liquor Salesman	Thomas Hill
Al McCardle	Lane Bradford
Edna	Janet Dudley
Dr. Alden Van	John Napier

WHEN THE BOYS MEET THE GIRLS

(M-G-M) Producer, Sam Katzman; Director, Alvin Ganzer; Screenplay, Robert E. Kent; Based on Musical Play "Girl Crazy" with Music and Lyrics by George and Ira Gershwin; Choreography, Earl Barton; Other Songs by Graham Gouldman, Louis Armstrong and Billy Kyle, Johnny Farrow, Fred Karger, Ben Weisman and Sid Wayne, Jack Keller and Howard Greenfield, Liberace; Director of Photography, Paul C. Vogel; Assistant Director, Eddie Saeta; A Four Leaf Production in Panavision and Metrocolor. December release.

CAST

Ginger	Connie Francis
Danny	Harve Presnell
Herman's Hermits	Themselves
Louis Armstrong	Himself
Sam The Sham & The Pharaohs	Themselves
Liberace	Himself
Tess	Sue Ane Langdon
Bill	Fred Clark
Phin	Frank Faylen
Sam	Joby Baker
Tony Reese and Pepper Davis	Themselves
Kate	Hortense Petra
Lank	Stanley Adams
Pete	Romo Vincent
Delilah	Susan Holloway
Stokes	Russell Collins
Dean of Cody	William T. Quinn

Connie Francis, Harve Presnell. Top: Herman's Hermits. Right: Joby Baker, Harve Presnell, Connie Francis

THE FLIGHT OF THE PHOENIX

(20th CENTURY-FOX) Producer-Director, Robert Aldrich; Screenplay, Lukas Heller; From Novel by Elleston Trevor; Director of Photography, Joseph Biroc; Music, Frank DeVol; Assistant Directors, William F. Sheehan, Cliff Coleman, Alan Callow; In DeLuxe Color; An Associates & Aldrich Co. Production. December release.

CAST

Frank Towns	James Stewart
Lew Moran	Richard Attenborough
Captain Harris	Peter Finch
Heinrich Dorfmann	Hardy Kruger
Trucker Cobb	Ernest Borgnine
Crow	Ian Bannen
Sgt. Watson	Ronald Fraser
Dr. Renaud	Christian Marquand
Standish	Dan Duryea
Bellamy	George Kennedy
Gabriele	Gabriele Tinti
Carlos	Alex Montoya
Tasso	Peter Bravos
Bill	William Aldrich
Farida	Barrie Chase

Dan Duryea, Ronald Fraser, Ernest Borgnine, Alex Montoya, Ian Bannen, Peter Finch, Christian Marquand, Richard Attenborough, George Kennedy, James Stewart. Above: Richard Attenborough, James Stewart, Hardy Kruger

Ruth Gordon, Natalie Wood, Christopher Plummer

Betty Harford, Natalie Wood, Roddy McDowall

Paul Hartman, Natalie Wood
Above: Ottola Nesmith, Robert
Redford, Ruth Gordon,
Natalie Wood

Natalie Wood, Robert Redford
Right: Christopher Plummer,
Natalie Wood

INSIDE DAISY CLOVER

(WARNER BROS.) Producer, Alan J. Pakula; Director, Robert Mulligan; Screenplay, Gavin Lambert; Based on his Novel; Director of Photography, Charles Lang; Costumes, William Thomas; Miss Wood's Wardrobe, Edith Head; Music, Andre Previn; Songs, Dory and Andre Previn; Musical Numbers Staged by Herbert Ross; Assistant Director, Joseph E. Kenny; A Park Place Production in Technicolor and Panavision. December release.

CAST

Daisy	Natalie Wood
Raymond Swan	Christopher Plummer
Wade Lewis	Robert Redford
Baines	Roddy McDowall
The Dealer	Ruth Gordon
Melora Swan	Katharine Bard
Gloria Goslett	Betty Harford
Dancer	Paul Hartman
Harry Goslett	John Hale
Cop	Harold Gould
Old Lady in Hospital	Ottola Nesmith
Cynara	Edna Holland
Milton Hopwood	Peter Helm

111

Merry Anders, Ken Scott
in "Raiders From Beneath The Sea"

Annabelle Huggins, Conrad Maga, Jimmie
Rodgers in "Back Door To Hell"

MARA OF THE WILDERNESS (Allied Artists) Producer, Brice Mack; Executive Producer, Lindsley Parsons; Director, Frank McDonald; Screenplay, Tom Blackburn; Story, Rod Scott; Music, Harry Bluestone; Director of Photography, Robert Wyckoff; Assistant Director, Wilson Shyer; In De-Luxe Color; Unicorn Production. January release. CAST: Adam West, Linda Saunders, Theo Marcuse, Denver Pyle, Sean McClory, Eve Brent, Roberto Contreras, Ed Kemmer, Stuart Walsh, Lelia Walsh.

RAIDERS FROM BENEATH THE SEA (20th Century-Fox) Producer-Director, Maury Dexter; A Lippert Production. January release. CAST: Ken Scott, Merry Anders, Russ Bender, Booth Coleman, Garth Benton, Bruce Anson, Walter Maslow, Stacy Winters, Ray Dannis, Larry Barton, Roger Creed.

THE MAN FROM BUTTON WILLOW (United Screen Arts) Producer, Phyllis Bounds Detiege; Direction and Screenplay, David Detiege; Music, George Stoll, Robert Van Eps; Songs, Phil Bounds, Dale Robertson, George Bruns, Mel Henke; Director of Photography, Max Morgan; In Color. January release. Full length cartoon with the voices of Dale Robertson, Howard Keel, Edgar Buchanan, Barbara Jean Wong, Herschel Bernardi, Ross Martin, Verna Felton, Shep Menken, Pinto Colvig, Cliff Edwards, Thurl Ravenscroft, John Hiestand, Clarence Nash, Edward Platt, Buck Buchanan.

BACK DOOR TO HELL (20th Century-Fox) Producer, Fred Roos; Director, Monte Hellman; Screenplay, Richard A. Guttman, John Hackett; Music, Mike Velarde; Director of Photography, Mars Rasca; A Lippert-Medallion Production. January release. CAST: Jimmie Rodgers, Jack Nicholson, John Hackett, Anabelle Huggins, Conrad Maga, Johnny Monteiro, Joe Sison, Henry Duval.

THE GUIDE (Stratton) Producer-Director, Tad Danielewski; Screenplay, Pearl S. Buck; From Novel by R. K. Narayen. February release. CAST: Dev Anand, Waheeda Rehman, Kishore Sahu, Leela Chitnis, Anwar Hussein, K. N. Singh, Levy Aaron, Rashid Khan, Dilip Dutt, Iftikhar, John Voyantiz, Krishna Dhawan, Hazel, Satya Dev Duby, J. S. Kashyap, Sheila Burghart.

YOUNG FURY (20th Century-Fox) Producer, A. C. Lyles; Director, Chris Nyby; Director of Photography, Haskell Boggs; Screenplay, Steve Fisher; Assistant Directors, Hal Pereira, Arthur Lonergan; Music, Paul Dunlap; In Technicolor and Techniscope. February release. CAST: Rory Calhoun, Virginia Mayo, Lon Chaney, John Agar, Richard Arlen, Linda Foster, Merry Anders, Joan Huntington, Jody McCrea, Rex Bell, Jr., William Wellman, Jr., Reg Parton, William Bendix, Preston Pierce, Robert Biheller, Marc Cavell, Jay Ripley, Kevin O'Neal, Jerry Summers, Fred Alexander, Dal Jenkins.

Preston Pierce, Virginia Mayo, Rory Calhoun,
Linda Foster, John Agar in "Young Fury"

Linda Evans, Brandon DeWilde, Walter Brennan
in "Those Callaways"

SINDERELLA AND THE GOLDEN BRA (Manson) Producer, Paul Mart; Director, Loel Minnardi; Screenplay, Frank Squires; From Story by Loel Minnardi, Frank Squires, Les Szarvas; Assistant Director, Ronald Terry; Director of Photography, Fou; Music, Les Szarvas; In Eastman Color. January release. CAST: Suzanne Sybele, Bill Gaskin, David Duffield, Sid Lassick, Patricia Mayfield, June Faith, Joan Lemo, Gerald Strickland, John Bradley, Kay Hall, Althea Currier, Jackie DeWitt, Justine Scott, Lisa Carole, Beverly Frankell, Donna Anderson.

THOSE CALLOWAYS (Buena Vista) Producer, Walt Disney; Co-Producer, Winston Hibler; Director, Norman Tokar; Screenplay, Louis Pelletier; In Technicolor. January release. CAST: Brian Keith, Vera Miles, Brandon De Wilde, Linda Evans, Walter Brennan, Ed Wynn, Philip Abbott, John Larkin, Parley Baer, Renee Godfrey, Frank de Kova, Tom Skerritt, Russell Collins, Paul Hartman, John Davis Chandler, Chet Stratton, Roy Roberts, John Qualen.

The Three Stooges (R)
in "The Outlaws IS Coming!"

Davey Davison, Michael T. Mikler, Donald Barry
in "War Party"

THE OUTLAWS IS COMING! (Columbia) Producer-Director, Norman Maurer; Screenplay, Elwood Ullman; Story, Norman Maurer; A Normandy Production. February release. CAST: Larry Fine, Moe Howard, Joe DeRita (The Three Stooges), Adam West, Nancy Kovack, Mort Mills, Don Lammond, Rex Holman.

NIGHTMARE IN THE SUN (Zodiac-States Rights) Producers, Marc Lawrence, John Derek; Director, Marc Lawrence; Screenplay, Ted Thomas, Fanya Lawrence; Based on Story by Marc Lawrence, George Fass; In DeLuxe Color. February release. CAST: Ursula Andress, John Derek, Aldo Ray, Arthur O'Connell, Lurene Tuttle, George Tobias, Douglas Fowley, John Marley, Bill Challe, Michael Petit, James Waters, John Sebastian, and guest stars Sammy Davis, Jr., Allyn Joslyn, Keenan Wynn, Chick Chandler, Richard Jaeckel.

DEAD BIRDS A Documentary financed by Peabody Museum at Harvard and The Netherlands Government. Directed by Robert Gardner; Written by Peter Mathieson; Filmed by Eliot Elisofon in Color; Narrated by Robert Gardner. March release. It reveals the daily life in New Guinea of a personable tribesman and his family.

RACING FEVER (Allied Artists) Produced, Directed, and Written by William Grefe; Associate Producer, Joe A. Rodero; Songs and Music, Al Jacobs; Title Song sung by Gerry Granahan; In Eastman Color. March release. CAST: Joe Morrison, Dave Blanchard, Charles G. Martin, Barbara Biggart, Maxine Carroll, Ruth Nadel.

WAR PARTY (20th Century-Fox) Producer, Hal Klein; Director, Lesley Selander; Screenplay, George Williams, William Marks; Director of Photography, Gordon Avil; Music, Richard LaSalle; Assistant Director, Harold M. Klein; Costumes, Frank R. Budz; A Steve Production. March release. CAST: Michael T. Mikler, Davey Davison, Donald Barry, Laurie Mock, Dennis Robertson, Charles Horvath, Guy Wilkerson, Michael Carr, Fred Krone.

MORO WITCH DOCTOR (20th Century-Fox) Executive Producer, Kane Lynn; Producer-Director, Eddie Romero; Story and Screenplay, Eddie Romero; Director of Photography, Felipe Sacdalan; Music, Ariston Avelino; An Associated Producers-Hemisphere Pictures Production. March release. CAST: Jock Mahoney, Margia Dean, Pancho Magalona, Paraluman, Mike Parsons, Vic Diaz, Nemia Velasco, Bruno Punzalan, Jay Ilagan.

Cheryl MacDonald, Hanna Landy
in "Fort Courageous"

Pancho Magalona, Jock Mahoney, Margia Dean
in "Moro Witch Doctor"

FANNY HILL: MEMOIRS OF A WOMAN OF PLEASURE (Favorite Films) Producer, Albert Zugsmith; Director, Russ Meyer; Screenplay, Robert Hill; Based on Novel by John Cleland; Director of Photography, Heinz Hilscher; Music, Erwin Halletz; Assistant Director, Elfie Tillack. March release. CAST: Miriam Hopkins, Letitia Roman, Walter Giller, Alex D'Arcy, Helmut Weiss, Chris Howland, Ulli Lommel, Cara Garnett, Karin Evans, Syra Marty, Albert Zugsmith, Christiane Schmidtmer, Heide Hansen, Erica Ericson, Patricia Houstoun, Marshall Raynor, Hilda Sessack, Billy Frick, Jurgen Nesbach, Herbert Knippenberg, Susanne Hsiao, Renate Hutte, Ellen Velero.

A SWINGIN' SUMMER (United Screen Arts) Producer, Reno Carell; Executive Producers, Ken Raphael, Larry Goldblatt; Screenplay, Robert Sparr; Director of Photography, Ray Fernstrom; In Techniscope and Technicolor. April release. CAST: James Stacy, William Wellman, Jr., Quinn O'Hara, Martin West, Mary Mitchell, Robert Blair, Raquel Welch, Allan Jones, Lili Kardell, Diane Bond, Diane Swanson, Irene Sale, Kathy Francis, Laurie Williams, The Righteous Brothers, The Rip Chords, Donnie Brooks, Gary Lewis and The Playboys, Jody Miller.

Donna Michelle, Mike Nader, Annette Funicello,
Patti Chandler, Frankie Avalon, Jody McCrea
in "Beach Blanket Bingo"

Yvonne Craig, Deborah Walley, Aron Kincaid,
Robert Q. Lewis, Dwayne Hickman, Frankie
Avalon in "Ski Party"

BEACH BLANKET BINGO (American International) Producers, James H. Nicholson, Samuel Z. Arkoff; Director, William Asher; Co-Producer, Anthony Carras; Screenplay, William Asher, Leo Townsend; Director of Photography, Floyd Crosby; Music, Les Baxter; Songs, Jerry Styner, Guy Hemric; Choreography, Jack Baker; Costumes, Marjorie Corso; Assistant Director, Dale Hutchinson; In Panavision and Pathecolor. April release. CAST: Frankie Avalon, Annette Funicello, Deborah Walley, Harvey Lembeck, John Ashley, Jody McCrea, Donna Loren, Marta Kristen, Linda Evans, Timothy Carey, Donna Michelle, Mike Nadler, Patti Chandler, The Hondells, Andy Romano, Allen Fife, Jerry Brutsche, John Macchia, Bob Harvey, Alberta Nelson, Myrna Ross, Don Rickles, Paul Lynde, Buster Keaton, Earl Wilson, Bobbi Shaw.

YOUNG DILLINGER (Allied Artists) Producer, Alfred N. Zimbalist; Associate Executive Producer, Byron Roberts; Director, Terry O. Morse; Screenplay, Don Zimbalist, Arthur Hoerl. April release. CAST: Nick Adams, Robert Conrad, John Ashley, Mary Ann Mobley, Victor Buono, Dan Terranova, John Hoyt, Reed Hadley, Robert Osterloh, Anthony Caruso, Art Baker, Gene Roth, Ayleene Gibbons, Frank Gerstle, Emile Meyer, Beverly Hills, Harvey Gardner, Helen Stephens, Patty Joy Harmon, Sol Gorse, Wally Rose, Walter Sande, Ted Knight, Mike Masters.

MUTINY IN OUTER SPACE (Crest) Producers, Hugo Grimaldi, Arthur C. Pierce; Director, Hugo Grimaldi; Screenplay, Arthur C. Pierce; Director of Photography, Arch Dalzell; Assistant Director, Jack Voglin. May release. CAST: William Leslie, Dolores Faith, Pamela Curran, Richard Garland, Harold Lloyd, Jr., James Dobson, Glenn Langan.

STRANDED (Compton) Produced, Directed, and Written by Juleen Compton; Director of Photography, Demos Sakeyyariose; Music, John Sakellarides. May release. CAST: Juleen Compton, Gary Collins, Gian Pietro Calasso, Alkis Yanakis.

FORT COURAGEOUS (20th Century-Fox) Producer, Hal Klein; Director, Lesley Selander; Screenplay, Richard Landau; Director of Photography, Gordon Avil; Music, Richard LaSalle; Assistant Director, Joseph Wonder; Costumes, Patrick Cummings; A Steve Production. May release. CAST: Fred Bier, Donald Barry, Hanna Landy, Harry Lauter, Walter Reed, Joseph Patridge, Michael Carr, Fred Krone, George Sawaya, Cheryl MacDonald.

THE BUS (Harrison) Produced and Photographed by Haskell Wexler. A Documentary candid film taken by Wexler on a three-day trip from San Francisco to Washington, D.C. with a delegation of whites and Negroes to the historic March on Washington.

Rory Calhoun, Brud Talbot, Todd Martin
in "Finger On The Trigger"

Harry Lauter, Jodi Mitchell, Donald Barry
in "Convict Stage"

FINGER ON THE TRIGGER (Allied Artists) Producer-Director, Sidney Pink; Screenplay, Luis De Los Arcos, Sidney Pink; Music, Jose Sola; Assistant Director, Enrique Bergier; Director of Photography, M. Barquero. May release. CAST: Rory Calhoun, James Philbrook, Todd Martin, Silvia Solar, Brud Talbot, Leo Anchoriz, Jorge Rigaud, Eric Chapman, Beny Deus, Axol Anderson, Tito Garoia, John Clarke, Willy Ellie, Antonio Molino Rojo, Jose Antonio Reral, Gernan Grech, Fernando Bilbao, Sebastian Cavalier.

HARLOW (Magna) Producer, Lee Savin; Director, Alex Segal; Screenplay, Karl Tunberg; Music, Al Ham, Nelson Riddle; Executive Producer, Brandon Chase; An Electronovision Production; Presented by Marshall Naify. May release. CAST: Carol Lynley, Efrem Zimbalist, Jr., Barry Sullivan, Ginger Rogers, Hurd Hatfield, Lloyd Bochner, Hermione Baddeley, Audrey Totter, John Williams, Michael Dante, Jack Kruschen.

**Linda Marshall, Steve Rogers, Lana Wood,
Aron Kincaid, Gail Gilmore, Martin West
in "The Girls On The Beach"**

**Celia Kaye, Michael Parks
in "Wild Seed"**

THE GIRLS ON THE BEACH (Paramount) Producer, Harvey Jacobson; Director, William N. Witney; Associate Producer, Paul Rapp; Screenplay, David Malcolm; Music, Cary Usher; In Eastman Color. May release. CAST: Martin West, Noreen Corcoran, Peter Brooks, Michael Love, Alan Jardin, Carl Wilson, Dennis Wilson, Jerry Allison, Jerry Naylor, Sonny Curtis, Arnold Lessing, Linda Marshall, Steven Rogers, Anna Capri, Aron Kincaid, Sheila Bromley, Mary Mitchel, Gale Gerber, Linda Saunders, Mary Kate Denny, Nan Morris, Lana Wood, Pat Deming, Michele Corcoran, Larry Merrill, Dennis Jones, Bill Sampson, Carol Jean Lewis, Joan Conrath, Rick Newton, Lesley Gore, Nancy Spry, Ron Kennedy, Bruno Vesota, Lynn Cartwright, Richard Miller, Leo Gordon, Helen Kay Stephens.

CHINA (Janus) Produced and Written by Felix Greene; Photographed in Color by Felix Greene and Hsu Chih-Chang; Narrated by Alexander Scourby. A Documentary that provides a glimpse behind the bamboo curtain of Communist China.

GOLDSTEIN (Altura) Producer, Zev Braun; Direction and Screenplay, Philip Kaufman, Benjamin Manaster. May release. CAST: Lou Gilbert, Ellen Madison, Thomas Erhart, Benito Carruthers, Charles Fischer, Severn Darden, Anthony Holland, Nelson Algren.

THE HUMAN DUPLICATORS (Crest) Producers, Hugo Grimaldi, Arthur C. Pierce; Screenplay, Arthur C. Pierce; Director, Hugo Grimaldi; Director of Photography, Monroe Askins; Assistant Director, Juss Carrello; In Eastman Color. May release. CAST: George Nader, Barbara Nichols, George Macready, Dolores Faith, Richard Kiel, Hugh Beaumont, Richard Arlen.

SKI PARTY (American International) Executive Producers, James H. Nicholson, Samuel Z. Arkoff; Producer, Gene Corman; Director, Alan Rafkin; Screenplay, Robert Kaufman; Director of Photography, Arthur E. Arling; Assistant Director, Dale Hutchinson; Costumes, Richard Bruno; Music, Gary Usher; Songs, Gary Usher and Roger Christian, Bob Gaudio, Larry Kusic and Ritchie Adams, Guy Hemric and Jerry Styner, Marvin Hamlisch and Howard Liebling, Ted Wright; In Panavision and Pathecolor. June release. CAST: Frankie Avalon, Dwayne Hickman, Deborah Walley, Yvonne Craig, Robert Q. Lewis, Bobbi Shaw, Aron Kincaid, Steve Rogers, Mike Nader, John Boyer, Ronnie Dayton, Bill Sampson, Patti Chandler, Salli Sachse, Mikki Jamison, Mary Hughes, Luree Holmes, The Hondells, James Brown and The Famous Flames, Lesley Gore.

**George Baker (L)
in "The Curse Of The Fly"**

**Buster Crabbe, Dan Duryea
in "The Bounty Killer"**

THE CURSE OF THE FLY (20th Century-Fox) Producers, Robert L. Lippert, Jack Parsons; Director, Don Sharp; Director of Photography, Basil Emmott, Screenplay, Harry Spalding. May release. CAST: Brian Donlevy, Carole Gray, George Baker, Michael Graham, Jeremy Wilkins, Charles Carson, Bert Kwouk, Yvette Rees, Rachel Kempson, Mary Manson, Warren Stanhope, Arnold Bell, Stan Simmons.

CONVICT STAGE (20th Century-Fox) Producer, Hal Klein; Director, Lesley Selander; Screenplay, Daniel Mainwaring; Story, Donald Barry; Director of Photography, Gordon Avil; Music, Richard LaSalle; Assistant Director, Joseph Wonder; Costumes, Patrick Cummings; A Steve Production. June release. CAST: Harry Lauter, Donald Barry, Hanna Landy, Jodi Mitchell, Joseph Patridge, Eric Matthews, Walter Reed, Michael Carr, Fred Krone, George Sawaya, Karl MacDonald.

Frankie Avalon, Deborah Walley, Fred Clark
in "Sergeant Deadhead The Astronut!"

Mike Mazurki, Rod Cameron, Stephen McNally
in "Requiem For A Gunfighter"

THE INCREDIBLY STRANGE CREATURES WHO STOPPED LIVING AND BECAME MIXED-UP ZOMBIES (Hollywood Star) Executive Producer, George J. Morgan; Producer-Director, Ray Dennis Steckler; Screenplay, Gene Pollock, Robert Silliphant; Based on Story by E. M. Kevke; Director of Photography, Joseph V. Mascelli; Music, Henry Price; Songs, Libby Quinn; Assistant Director, Don Russell; In Color. June release. CAST: Cash Flagg, Brett O'Hara, Carolyn Brandt, Atlas King, Sharon Walsh, Madison Clarke, Erino Enyo, Jack Brady, Toni Camel, Neil Stillman, Joan Howard, James Bowie, Gene Pollock, Bill Ward, Son Hooker, Steve Clark, Don Snyder, Carol Kay, Teri Randal.

THE THRILL KILLERS (Hollywood Star) Producer, George J. Morgan; Director, Ray Dennis Steckler; Screenplay, Ray Dennis Steckler, Gene Pollock; Director of Photography, Joseph V. Mascelli; Music, Henry Price; Assistant Director, Don Russell. CAST: Cash Flagg, Liz Renay, Brick Bardo, Carolyn Brandt, Ron Burr, Gary Kent, Herb Robins, Keith O'Brien, Laura Benedict, Erina Enyo, Atlas King, Titus Moede, George J. Morgan.

THE BOUNTY KILLER (Embassy) Producer, Alex Gordon; Director, Spencer G. Bennet; Executive Producer, Pat B. Rooney; Director of Photography, Frederick E. West; Screenplay, R. Alexander, Leo Gordon; Music, Ronald Stein; A Premiere Productions Inc. Picture in Techniscope and Technicolor. July release. CAST: Dan Duryea, Rod Cameron, Audrey Dalton, Richard Arlen, Buster Crabbe, Fuzzy Knight, Johnny Mack Brown, Bob Steele, Bronco Billy Anderson.

WILD SEED (Universal) Executive Producers, Marlon Brando, Sr., Walter Seltzer; Producer, Albert S. Ruddy; Director, Brian G. Hutton; Screenplay, Les Pine; Story, Les Pine, Ike Jones; Director of Photography, Conrad Hall; Costumes, Ted Parvin; Music, Richard Markowitz; Assistant Director, Tom Shaw; A Pennebaker Production. July release. CAST: Michael Parks, Celia Kaye, Ross Elliott, Woodrow Chambliss, Rupert Crosse, Eva Novak, Norman Burton, Merritt Bohn, Anthony Lettieri.

WILLY McBEAN AND HIS MAGIC MACHINE (Magna) Produced, Directed, and Written by Arthur Rankin, Jr.; Associate Producers, Jules Bass, Larry Roemer; Music and Lyrics, Edward Thomas, Gene Forrell, James Polack; Presented by Marshall Naify; In Eastman Color and AniMagic. August release. CAST: Willie McBean and the Voices of Larry Mann, Billie Richards, Alfie Scopp, Paul Ligman, Bunny Cowan, Paul Soles, Pegi Loder.

George Peppard, Elizabeth Ashley
in "The Third Day"

The Astronauts with Sonny and Cher
in "Wild On The Beach"

THE THIRD DAY (Warner Bros.) Producer-Director, Jack Smight; Screenplay, Burton Wohl, Robert Presnell, Jr.; Based on Novel by Joseph Hayes; Director of Photography, Robert Surtees; Music, Percy Faith; Assistant Director, Victor Vallejo; Song, J. Livingston, R. Evans; Gowns, Donald Brooks; In Panavision and Technicolor. July release. CAST: George Peppard, Elizabeth Ashley, Roddy McDowall, Arthur O'Connell, Mona Washbourne, Herbert Marshall, Robert Webber, Charles Drake, Sally Kellerman, Arte Johnson, Bill Walker, Vincent Gardenia, Janine Gray.

WILD ON THE BEACH (20th Century-Fox) Producer-Director, Maury Dexter; Screenplay, Harry Spaulding; Story, Hank Tani; Director of Photography, Jack Marquette; Assistant Producer, Hank Tani; Assistant Director, Willard Kirkham; Associate Producer, "By" Dunham; Music, Jimmy Haskell; A Lippert Production. August release. CAST: Frankie Randall, Sherry Jackson, Jackie and Gayle, The Astronauts, Sonny and Cher, Cindy Malone, Sandy Nelson, Russ Bender, Booth Coleman, Justin Smith, Jerry Grayson, Marc Seaton, Robert Golden, Larry Gust.

Tommy Kirk, Charla Doherty, Toni Basil, Johnny Crawford in "Village Of The Giants"

Sal Mineo, Juliet Prowse in "Who Killed Teddy Bear?"

SERGEANT DEADHEAD THE ASTRONUT! (American International) Producers, James H. Nicholson, Samuel Z. Arkoff; Director, Norman Taurog; Screenplay, Louis M. Heyward; Co-Producer, Anthony Carras; Director of Photography, Floyd Crosby; Assistant Director, Claude Binyon, Jr.; Choreography, Jack Baker; Songs, Guy Hemric, Jerry Styner; In Panavision and Pathecolor. August release. CAST: Frankie Avalon, Deborah Walley, Cesar Romero, Fred Clark, Gale Gordon, Harvey Lembeck, John Ashley, Buster Keaton, Reginald Gardiner, Donna Loren, Romo Vincent. Tod Windsor, Norman Grabowski, Mike Nader, Ed Faulkner, Pat Buttram, Bobbi Shaw, Patti Chandler, Salli Sachse, Luree Holmes, Sue Hamilton, Jo Collins, Bob Harvey, Jerry Brutsche, Andy Romano, John Macchia, Mary Hughes, Astrid De Brea, Jean Ingram, Peggy Ward, Stephanie Nader, Lyzanne Ladue, Janice Levinson, Alberta Nelson, Sallie Dornan, Eve Arden.

REQUIEM FOR A GUNFIGHTER (Embassy) Producer, Alex Gordon; Director, Spencer G. Bennet; Executive Producer, Pat B. Rooney; Screenplay, R. Alexander; Story, Evans W. Cornell, Guy J. Tedesco; Director of Photography, Frederick E. West; Music, Ronald Stein; An Alex Gordon-Premiere Productions Inc. Picture in Techniscope and Technicolor. August release. CAST: Rod Cameron, Stephen McNally, Mike Mazurki, Olive Sturgess, Tim McCoy, Johnny Mack Brown, Bob Steele, Lane Chandler, Raymond Hatton.

ROPE OF FLESH (Eve) Producers, Russ Meyer, George Costello; Director, Russ Meyer; Screenplay, Raymond Friday Locke, William E. Sprague; Director of Photography, Walter Schenk; Music, Henri Price. August release. CAST: Hal Hopper, Lorna Maitland, Antoinette Cristiani, John Furlong, Stu Lancaster, Rena Horten, Princess Livingston, Sam Hanna, Nick Wolcuff, Frank Bolger, Lee Ballard, Mickey Foxx, F. Rufus Owens.

THE YOUNG SINNER (United Screen Arts) Produced, Directed, and Written by Tom Laughlin. August release. CAST: Tom Laughlin, Stephanie Powers, William Wellman, Jr., Robert Angelo, Linda March, Roxanne Heard, Jack Starrett, Ed Cook, Chris Robinson, Denni O'Flaherty, James Stacey, Bob Colonna, Jane Taylor, Julia Paul, Dorothy Downey, Harry Zumach, Clint Gunkel, Charles Stobert, Marlene Kelly, Terry Thompson.

LORNA (Eve) Produced, Directed, Photographed by Russ Meyer; Screenplay, James Griffith; Story, Russ Meyer; Song, Hal Hopper; Sung by Bob Grabeau. August release. CAST: Lorna Maitland, Mark Bradley, James Rucker, Hal Hopper, Doc Scortt, James Griffith.

BEACH GIRLS AND THE MONSTERS (U.S. Films) Producer, Edward Janis; Director, Jon Hall; Screenplay, Joan Gardner; Music, Frank Sinatra, Jr. September release. CAST: Jon Hall, Sue Casey, Walker Edmiston, Arnold Lessing.

Darren McGavin, Joseph Cotten in "The Great Sioux Massacre"

Boris Karloff, Nick Adams in "Die, Monster, Die!"

MOTOR PSYCHO (Eve) Produced, Directed, and Photographed by Russ Meyer; Screenplay, Russ Meyer, W. E. Sprague; Music, Igo Kanter; Theme, Paul Sawtell, Bert Shefter; Assistant Director, George Costello. August release. CAST: Stephen Oliver, Haji, Alex Rocco, Holle K. Winters, Joseph Cellini, Thomas Scott, Coleman Francis, Sharron Lee, Steve Masters, Arshalouis Alvasian, F. Rufus Owens, E. E. Meyer, George Costello, Richard Brummer.

DIE, MONSTER, DIE! (American International) Presented by James H. Nicholson, Samuel Z. Arkoff; Producer, Pat Green; Director, Daniel Haller; Screenplay, Jerry Sohl; From Story "Colour Out Of Space" by H. P. Lovecraft; Music, Don Banks; Director of Photography, Paul Beeson; Assistant Director, Dennis Hall; In Color. September release. CAST: Boris Karloff, Nick Adams, Freda Jackson, Suzan Farmer, Terence DeMarney, Patrick Magee, Paul Farrell, Leslie Dwyer, Sheila Raynor, Harold Goodwin, Sydney Bromley, Billy Milton.

117

Mark Richman, Werner Klemperer
in "Dark Intruder"

Dana Andrews, Terry Moore, Richard Jaeckel,
Richard Arlen in "Town Tamer"

THE GREAT SIOUX MASSACRE (Columbia) Producer, Leon Fromkess; Director, Sidney Salkow; Screenplay, Fred C. Dobbs; Story, Sidney Salkow, Marvin Gluck; Director of Photography, Irving Lippman; Music, Emil Newman, Edward B. Powell; Assistant Director, Abby Berlin; In Cinemascope and Color by Pathe. September release. CAST: Joseph Cotten, Darren McGavin, Philip Carey, Julie Sommars, Nancy Kovack, Michael Pate, John Matthews, Don Haggerty, Frank Ferguson, Stacy Harris, Iron Eyes Cody, House Peters, Jr., John Napier, William Tannen, Blair Davies, Louise Serpa.

ONE WAY WAHINI (United Screen Arts) Producer, Leon E. Whiteman; Co-Produced and Directed by William O. Brown; Screenplay, Rod Larson; Director of Photography, John Morrill; In Techniscope and Technicolor. September release. CAST: Joy Harmon, Anthony Eisley, Adele Claire, David Whorf, Edgar Bergen, Lee Kreiger, Ken Mayer, Harold Fong, Alvy Moore, Aime Luce, Ralph Nanalei.

THE GENTLE RAIN (Allied Artists) Executive Producer, Bert Caudle; Producer-Director, Burt Balaban; Screenplay, Robert Crean; Music, Luiz Bonfa; Director of Photography, Mario di Leo. October release. CAST: Christopher George, Lynda Day, Fay Spain, Maria Helena Dias, Lon Clark, Barbara Williams, Roberto Assumpcao, Herbert Moss, Lorena, Nadyr Fernandes.

VILLAGE OF THE GIANTS (Embassy) Producer-Director, Bert I. Gordon; Screenplay, Alan Caillou; Based on Novel "The Food of The Gods" by H. G. Wells; Music, Jack Nitzsche; Songs, Ron Elliott, Frank Slay and Frederick A. Picariello, Jack Nitzsche and Russ Titleman; Director of Photography, Paul C. Vogel; Choreography, Toni Basil; Assistant Director, Jim Rosenberger; Costumes, Leah Rhodes; In Perceptovision and Color. October release. CAST: Tommy Kirk, Johnny Crawford, Ronny Howard, The Beau Brummels, Freddy Cannon, Mike Clifford, Joy Harmon, Bob Random, Tisha Sterling, Charla Doherty, Tim Rooney, Kevin O'Neal, Gail Gilmore, Toni Basil, Hank Jones, Jim Begg, Vicki London, Joseph Turkel.

THE CRAZY QUILT (Farallon) Produced, Directed, and Written by John Korty; Based on Novel "Illusionless Man and The Visionary Maid" by Allen Wheelis; Director of Photography, John Korty; Music, Peter Schickele; Commentary, Burgess Meredith. October release. CAST: Tom Rosqui, Ina Mela, Ellen Frye, Harry Hunt, Calvin Kentfield, Robert Marquis, Doug Korty.

MURDER IN MISSISSIPPI (Tiger) Producer, Herbert S. Altman; Director, J. P. Mawra; Screenplay, Herbert S. Altman; Director of Photography, Warner Rose; Music, Joe Lesko. October release. CAST: Sheilla Britton, Sam Stewart, Derek Crane, Lou Stone, Martin St. John, John Steel, Wayne Foster, Dick Stone, Otis Young, Irv Seldin, Frank Philadelphia.

Gail Hire, James Ward
in "Red Line 7000"

Marla Landi, Ken Scott
in "The Murder Game"

WHO KILLED TEDDY BEAR? (Magna) Producer, Everett Rosenthal; Director, Joseph Cates; Screenplay, Leon Tokatyan, Arnold Drake; Story, Arnold Drake; Director of Photography, Joseph Brun; Music, Charles Calello; Title and Discotheque Songs, Al Kasha, Bob Gaudio; Presented by Marshall Naify. October release. CAST: Sal Mineo, Juliet Prowse, Jan Murray, Elaine Stritch, Margot Bennett, Dan Travanty, Diana Moore, Frank Campanella, Bruce Glover, Tom Aldredge, Rex Everhart, Alex Fisher, Stanley Beck, Casey Townsend.

THE PLAYGROUND (Jerand) Producer-Director, Richard Hilliard; Screenplay, George Garrett; Inspired by "My Brother Death" by Cyrus L. Sulzberger. October release. CAST: Rees Vaughn, Inger Stratton, Edmon Ryan, Andrea Blayne, Loretta Leversee, Richard Kilbride, Marian Blake, Carol White, Peter MacLean, Conrad Jameson, Roger Talbot, Stanley Greene, Philip Brown, Sol Schwade, Ethel Shutta, Paul Schmidt.

Judy Parker, Anthony Hayes, William Wellman, Jr.
Jill Donohue, James Stacy, Bucky Holland
in "Winter A-Go-Go"

Edd Byrnes, Chris Noel
in "Beach Ball"

WINTER A-GO-GO (Columbia) Producer, Reno Carell; Director, Richard Benedict; Screenplay, Bob Kanter; Story, Reno Carell; Director of Photography, Jacques Marquette; Choreography, Kay Carson; Costumer, Joe Simmitt; Music, Harry Betts; Songs, Howard Greenfield and Jack Keller, Steve Venet, Toni Wine, Tommy Boyce, Bob Hart and Harry Betts; Title Song Sung by The Astronauts; In Pathe Color. October release. CAST: James Stacy, William Wellman, Jr., Beverly Adams, Anthony Hayes, Jill Donohue, Tom Nardini, Duke Hobbie, Julie Parrish, Nancy Czar, Linda Rogers, Judy Parker, Bob Kanter, Walter Maslow, H. T. Tsiang, Buck Holland, The Nooney Rickett Four with Joni Lyman, The Reflections, Carey Foster, Cheryl Hurley, Arlene Charles, Cherie Foster.

DARK INTRUDER (Universal) Producer, Jack Laird; Director, Harvey Hart; Screenplay, Barre Lyndon; Director of Photography, John F. Warren; Assistant Director, Edward K. Dodds; Costumes, Vincent Dee. October release. CAST: Leslie Nielsen, Gilbert Green, Charles Bolender, Mark Richman, Judi Meredith, Werner Klemperer, Peter Brocco, Vaughn Taylor, Harriett Vine.

KNOCKOUT! (Trans-Lux) Producer-Director, William Cayton; Assistant Producer, Jim Jacobs; Narrator, Kevin Kennedy. November release. A feature length film showing highlights and actual knockout sequences from 19 historic boxing contests of the twentieth century.

SATURDAY NIGHT IN APPLE VALLEY (Emerson) Direction and Screenplay, John Myhers; Director of Photography, Alan Stensvold; Music, Foster Wakefield; An Empire Production. November release. CAST: Phil Ford, Mimi Hines, Cliff Arquette, Shanton Granger, Joan Benedict, Marvin Miller, Anthony Dexter.

TOWN TAMER (Paramount) Producer, A. C. Lyles; Director, Leslie Selander; Director of Photography, W. Wallace Kelley; Assistant Director, Howard Roessel; Screenplay, Frank Gruber; Based on his Novel; In Techniscope and Technicolor. November release. CAST: Dana Andrews, Terry Moore, Pat O'Brien, Lon Chaney, Bruce Cabot, Lyle Bettger, Coleen Gray, Barton MacLane, Richard Arlen, Richard Jaeckel, Philip Carey, DeForrest Kelley, Sonny Tufts, Roger Torres, James Brown, Richard Webb, Jeanne Cagney, Don Barry, Bob Steele.

DR. GOLDFOOT AND THE BIKINI MACHINE (American International) Producers, James H. Nicholson, Samuel Z. Arkoff; Director, Norman Taurog; Screenplay, Elwood Ullman, Robert Kaufman; Story, James Hartford; In Panavision and Color. November release. CAST: Vincent Price, Fred Clark, Frankie Avalon, Dwayne Hickman, Susan Hart, Jack Mullaney, Alberta Nelson, Milton Frome, Hal Riddle, Kay Elhardt, William Baskin, Vincent L. Barnett, Joe Ploski, Sam and The Ape Men with Diane DeMarco, Patti Chandler, Salli Sachse, Sue Hamilton, Marianne Gaba, Issa Arnal, Pam Rodgers, Sally Frei, Jan Watson, Mary Hughes, Luree Holmes, Laura Nicholson, China Lee, Deanna Lund, Leslie Summers, Kay Michaels, Arlene Charles.

PINOCCHIO IN OUTER SPACE (Universal) Producers, Norm Prescott, Fred Ladd; Director, Ray Goossens; Screenplay, Fred Laderman; From an original idea by Norm Prescott, and original tale by Collodi; A Swallow Ltd.-Belvision Production in Color; November release. Featuring VOICES of: Arnold Stang, Conrad Jameson, Cliff Owens, Peter Lazer, Mavis Mims, Kevin Kennedy, Minerva Pious, Jess Cain, Norman Rose.

RED LINE 7000 (Paramount) Producer-Director, Howard Hawks; Screenplay, George Kirgo; In Color. November release. CAST: James Caan, Laura Devon, Gail Hire, Charlene Holt, John Robert Crawford, Marianna Hill, James Ward, Norman Alden, George Takei, Diane Strom, Anthony Rogers, Carol Connors, Cissy Wellman.

SALT OF THE EARTH (Independent Productions Corp.) Producer, Paul Jarrico; Director, Herbert Biberman; Screenplay, Michael Wilson. November release. CAST: Rosuara Revueltas, Juan Chacon, Will Geer, Mervyn Williams, Herman Waldman, Frank Talevera, Mary Lou Castillo, Clinton Jeneks, Virginia Jencks.

ALL MEN ARE APES (Adelphia) Producers, Barnard L. Sackett, Charles E. Mazin; Director, J. P. Mawra; Screenplay, Charles E. Mazin, Barnard L. Sackett; Director of Photography, Richard E. Brooks; Music, Irv Dweir; Songs, Charles E. Mazin. November release. CAST: Mark Ryan, Grace Lynn, Steve Woods, Steve Vincent, Bonny Lee Noll, Mia Marlowe, Ted Teschner, Walter Teague, Tom O'Horgan, Wendy Winston, Jeanine Costa, Brigitta Batit, Bob Worms, Frank Geraci, Joe Boatner's Ink Spots, Sandi Brown.

THE MURDER GAME (20th Century-Fox) Producers, Robert L. Lippert, Jack Parsons; Director, Sidney Salkow; Screenplay, Harry Spalding; Story, Irving Yergin; Director of Photography, Geoffrey Faithful; Assistant Director, Gordon Gilbert; Music, Carlo Martelli. December release. CAST: Ken Scott, Marla Landi, Trader Faulkner, Conrad Phillips, Gerald Sim, Duncan Lamont, Rosamund Greenwood, Victor Brooks, Ballard Berkeley, Jimmy Gardner, Peter Bathurst, Jennifer White, Frank Thornton, Gretchen Franklyn, John Dunbar, Clement Freud, Derek Partridge.

BEACH BALL (Paramount) Producer, Bart Patton; Director, Lennie Weinrib; Screenplay, David Malcolm; Assistant Director, Gary Kurtz; Director of Photography, Alfred Taylor; Music, Frank Wilson; Songs, Chester Pipkin and Frank Wilson, Al Capps, Eddie Holland, Brian Holland and Lamonte Dozier; In Technicolor. December release. CAST: Edd Byrnes, Chris Noel, Robert Logan, Gail Gilmore, Aron Kincaid, Mikki Jamison, Don Edmonds, Brenda Benet, Anna Lavelle, James Wellman, The Supremes, The Four Seasons, The Righteous Brothers, The Hondells, The Walker Brothers.

PROMISING PERSONALITIES OF 1965

Julie Christie

David McCallum

Robert Redford

Barbara Harris

Michael Parks

Geraldine Chaplin

Samantha Eggar

Edward Mulhare

Virna Lisi

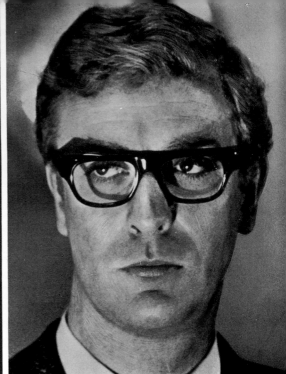

Michael Caine

Tom Nardini

Katharine Ross

Joi Lansing

Jaime Sanchez

Aron Kincaid

Catherine Deneuve

ACADEMY AWARD WINNERS

(1) Best Picture, (2) Actor, (3) Actress, (4) Supporting Actor, (5) Supporting Actress, (6) Director, (7) Special Award.

1927-28: (1) "Wings", (2) Emil Jannings in "The Way Of All Flesh", (3) Janet Gaynor in "Seventh Heaven", (6) Frank Borzage for "Seventh Heaven", (7) Charles Chaplin.

1928-29: (1) "Broadway Melody", (2) Warner Baxter in "Old Arizona", (3) Mary Pickford in "Coquette", (6) Frank Lloyd for "The Divine Lady".

1929-30: (1) "All Quiet On The Western Front", (2) George Arliss in "Disraeli", (3) Norma Shearer in "The Divorcee", (6) Lewis Milestone for "All Quiet On The Western Front".

1930-31: (1) "Cimarron", (2) Lionel Barrymore in "A Free Soul", (3) Marie Dressler in "Min and Bill", (6) Norman Taurog for "Skippy".

1931-32: (1) "Grand Hotel", (2) Fredric March in "Dr. Jekyll and Mr. Hyde", (3) Helen Hayes in "The Sin of Madelon Claudet", (6) Frank Borzage for "Bad Girl".

1932-33: (1) "Cavalcade", (2) Charles Laughton in "The Private Life of Henry VIII", (3) Katharine Hepburn in "Morning Glory", (6) Frank Lloyd for "Cavalcade".

1934: (1) "It Happened One Night", (2) Clark Gable in "It Happened One Night", (3) Claudette Colbert in "It Happened One Night", (6) Frank Capra for "It Happened One Night", (7) Shirley Temple.

1935: (1) "Mutiny On The Bounty", (2) Victor McLaglen in "The Informer", (3) Bette Davis in "Dangerous", (6) John Ford for "The Informer", (7) D. W. Griffith.

1936: (1) "The Great Ziegfeld", (2) Paul Muni in "The Story of Louis Pasteur", (3) Luise Rainer, in "The Great Ziegfeld", (4) Walter Brennan in "Come and Get It", (5) Gale Sondergaard in "Anthony Adverse", (6) Frank Capra for "Mr. Deeds Goes To Town".

1937: (1) "The Life of Emile Zola", (2) Spencer Tracy in "Captains Courageous", (3) Luise Rainer in "The Good Earth", (4) Joseph Schildkraut in "The Life of Emile Zola", (5) Alice Brady in "In Old Chicago", (6) Leo McCarey for "The Awful Truth", (7) Mack Sennett, Edgar Bergen.

1938: (1) "You Can't Take It With You", (2) Spencer Tracy in "Boys' Town", (3) Bette Davis in "Jezebel", (4) Walter Brennan in "Kentucky", (5) Fay Bainter in "Jezebel", (6) Frank Capra for "You Can't Take It With You", (7) Deanna Durbin, Mickey Rooney, Harry M. Warner, Walt Disney.

1939: (1) "Gone With The Wind", (2) Robert Donat in "Goodbye, Mr. Chips", (3) Vivien Leigh in "Gone With The Wind", (4) Thomas Mitchell in "Stagecoach", (5) Hattie McDaniel in "Gone With The Wind", (6) Victor Fleming for "Gone With The Wind", (7) Douglas Fairbanks, Judy Garland.

1940: (1) "Rebecca", (2) James Stewart in "The Philadelphia Story", (3) Ginger Rogers in "Kitty Foyle", (4) Walter Brennan in "The Westerner", (5) Jane Darwell in "The Grapes of Wrath", (6) John Ford for "The Grapes of Wrath", (7) Bob Hope.

1941: (1) "How Green Was My Valley", (2) Gary Cooper in "Sergeant York", (3) Joan Fontaine in "Suspicion", (4) Donald Crisp in "How Green Was My Valley", (5) Mary Astor in "The Great Lie", (6) John Ford for "How Green Was My Valley", (7) Leopold Stokowski, Walt Disney.

1942: (1) "Mrs. Miniver", (2) James Cagney in "Yankee Doodle Dandy", (3) Greer Garson in "Mrs. Miniver", (4) Van Heflin in "Johnny Eager", (5) Teresa Wright in "Mrs. Miniver", (6) William Wyler for "Mrs. Miniver", (7) Charles Boyer, Noel Coward.

1943: (1) "Casablanca", (2) Paul Lukas in "Watch On The Rhine", (3) Jennifer Jones in "The Song of Bernadette", (4) Charles Coburn in "The More The Merrier", (5) Katina Paxinou in "For Whom The Bell Tolls", (6) Michael Curtiz for "Casablanca".

1944: (1) "Going My Way", (2) Bing Crosby in "Going My Way", (3) Ingrid Bergman in "Gaslight", (4) Barry Fitzgerald in "Going My Way", (5) Ethel Barrymore in "None But The Lonely Heart", (6) Leo McCarey for "Going My Way", (7) Margaret O'Brien, Bob Hope.

1945: (1) "The Lost Weekend", (2) Ray Milland in "The Lost Weekend", (3) Joan Crawford in "Mildred Pierce", (4) James Dunn in "A Tree Grows In Brooklyn", (5) Anne Revere in "National Velvet", (6) Billy Wilder for "The Lost Weekend", (7) Walter Wanger, Peggy Ann Garner.

1946: (1) "The Best Years of Our Lives", (2) Fredric March in "The Best Years of Our Lives", (3) Olivia de Havilland in "To Each His Own", (4) Harold Russell in "The Best Years of Our Lives", (5) Anne Baxter in "The Razor's Edge", (6) William Wyler for "The Best Years of Our Lives", (7) Laurence Olivier, Harold Russell, Ernst Lubitsch, Claude Jarman, Jr.

1947: (1) "Gentleman's Agreement", (2) Ronald Colman in "A Double Life", (3) Loretta Young in "The Farmer's Daughter", (4) Edmund Gwenn in "Miracle On 34th Street", (5) Celeste Holm in "Gentleman's Agreement", (6) Elia Kazan for "Gentleman's Agreement", (7) James Baskette.

1948: (1) "Hamlet", (2) Laurence Olivier in "Hamlet", (3) Jane Wyman in "Johnny Belinda", (4) Walter Huston in "The Treasure of The Sierra Madre", (5) Claire Trevor in "Key Largo", (6) John Huston for "The Treasure of The Sierra Madre", (7) Ivan Jandl, Sid Grauman, Adolph Zukor, Walter Wanger.

Janet Gaynor

James Cagney

Luise Rainer

Paul Lukas

Claudette Colb

| Helen Hayes | Ray Milland | Katharine Hepburn | Paul Muni | Jane Wyman |

1949: (1) "All The King's Men", (2) Broderick Crawford in "All The King's Men", (3) Olivia de Havilland in "The Heiress", (4) Mercedes McCambridge in "All The King's Men", (6) Joseph L. Mankiewicz for "A Letter To Three Wives", (7) Bobby Driscoll, Fred Astaire, Cecil B. DeMille, Jean Hersholt.

1950: (1) "All About Eve", (2) Jose Ferrer in "Cyrano de Bergerac", (3) Judy Holliday in "Born Yesterday", (4) George Sanders in "All About Eve", (5) Josephine Hull in "Harvey", (6) Joseph L. Mankiewicz for "All About Eve", (7) George Murphy, Louis B. Mayer.

1951: (1) "An American in Paris", (2) Humphrey Bogart in "The African Queen", (3) Vivien Leigh in "A Streetcar Named Desire", (4) Karl Malden in "A Streetcar Named Desire", (5) Kim Hunter in "A Streetcar Named Desire", (6) George Stevens for "A Place In The Sun", (7) Gene Kelly.

1952: (1) "The Greatest Show On Earth", (2) Gary Cooper in "High Noon", (3) Shirley Booth in "Come Back, Little Sheba", (4) Anthony Quinn in "Viva Zapata", (5) Gloria Grahame in "The Bad and The Beautiful", (6) John Ford for "The Quiet Man", (7) Joseph M. Schenck, Merian C. Cooper, Harold Lloyd, Bob Hope, George Alfred Mitchell.

1953: (1) "From Here To Eternity", (2) William Holden in "Stalag 17", (3) Audrey Hepburn in "Roman Holiday", (4) Frank Sinatra in "From Here To Eternity", (5) Donna Reed in "From Here To Eternity", (6) Fred Zinnemann for "From Here To Eternity", (7) Pete Smith.

1954: (1) "On The Waterfront", (2) Marlon Brando in "On The Waterfront", (3) Grace Kelly in "The Country Girl", (4) Edmond O'Brien in "The Barefoot Contessa", (5) Eva Marie Saint in "On The Waterfront", (6) Elia Kazan for "On The Waterfront", (7) Greta Garbo, Danny Kaye, Jon Whitely, Vincent Winter.

1955: (1) "Marty", (2) Ernest Borgnine in "Marty", (3) Anna Magnani in "The Rose Tattoo", (4) Jack Lemmon in "Mister Roberts", (5) Jo Van Fleet in "East of Eden", (6) Delbert Mann for "Marty".

1956: (1) "Around The World in 80 Days", (2) Yul Brynner in "The King and I", (3) Ingrid Bergman in "Anastasia", (4) Anthony Quinn in "Lust For Life", (5) Dorothy Malone for "Written On The Wind", (6) George Stevens for "Giant", (7) Eddie Cantor.

1957: (1) "The Bridge On The River Kwai", (2) Alec Guinness in "The Bridge On The River Kwai", (3) Joanne Woodward in "The Three Faces of Eve", (4) Red Buttons in "Sayonara", (5) Miyoshi Umeki in "Sayonara", (6) David Lean for "The Bridge On The River Kwai", (7) Charles Brackett, B. B. Kahane, Gilbert M. (Broncho Billy) Anderson.

1958: (1) "Gigi", (2) David Niven in "Separate Tables", (3) Susan Hayward in "I Want To Live", (4) Burl Ives in "The Big Country", (5) Wendy Hiller in "Separate Tables", (6) Vincente Minnelli for "Gigi", (7) Maurice Chevalier.

1959: (1) "Ben-Hur", (2) Charlton Heston in "Ben-Hur", (3) Simone Signoret in "Room At The Top", (4) Hugh Griffith in "Ben-Hur", (5) Shelley Winters in "The Diary of Anne Frank", (6) William Wyler for "Ben-Hur", (7) Lee de Forest, Buster Keaton.

1960: (1) "The Apartment", (2) Burt Lancaster in "Elmer Gantry", (3) Elizabeth Taylor in "Butterfield 8", (4) Peter Ustinov in "Spartacus", (5) Shirley Jones in "Elmer Gantry", (6) Billy Wilder for "The Apartment", (7) Gary Cooper, Stan Laurel, Hayley Mills.

1961: (1) "West Side Story", (2) Maximilian Schell in "Judgment At Nuremberg", (3) Sophia Loren in "Two Women", (4) George Chakiris in "West Side Story", (5) Rita Moreno in "West Side Story", (6) Robert Wise for "West Side Story", (7) Jerome Robbins, Fred L. Metzler.

1962: (1) "Lawrence of Arabia", (2) Gregory Peck in "To Kill A Mockingbird", (3) Anne Bancroft in "The Miracle Worker", (4) Ed Begley in "Sweet Bird of Youth", (5) Patty Duke in "The Miracle Worker", (6) David Lean for "Lawrence of Arabia".

1963: (1) "Tom Jones", (2) Sidney Poitier in "Lilies of The Field", (3) Patricia Neal in "Hud", (4) Melvyn Douglas in "Hud", (5) Margaret Rutherford in "The V.I.P.'s", (6) Tony Richardson for "Tom Jones".

1964: (1) "My Fair Lady", (2) Rex Harrison in "My Fair Lady", (3) Julie Andrews in "Mary Poppins", (4) Peter Ustinov in "Topkapi", (5) Lila Kedrova in "Zorba The Greek", (6) George Cukor for "My Fair Lady", (7) William Tuttle.

| Burl Ives | Greer Garson | Fredric March | Ginger Rogers | Melvyn Douglas |

FOREIGN FILMS

Sandra Milo. Above: Giulietta Masina

Jose de Vilallonga. Above: Sandra Milo

JULIET OF THE SPIRITS

(RIZZOLI) Created and Directed by Federico Fellini; Executive Producer, Clemente Fracassi; Screenplay, Federico Fellini, Tullio Pinelli, Ennio Flaiano, Brunello Rondi; Original Story, Federico Fellini, Tullio Pinelli; Director of Photography, Gianni Di Venanzo; Music, Nino Rota; A Federiz Production in Technicolor.

CAST

Juliet's World:

Juliet	Giulietta Masina
Juliet as a child	Alba Cancellieri
Giorgio	Mario Pisu
The Mother	Caterina Boratto
Adele	Luisa della Noce
Sylva	Sylva Koscina
Granddaughters	Sabrina Gigli, Rosella di Sepio
Grandfather	Lou Gilbert
Valentina	Valentina Cortese
Dolores	Silvana Jachino
Elena	Elena Fondra
Friends of Giorgio	Jose de Vilallonga, Cesarino Miceli Picardi
Maids	Milena Vucotich, Elisabetta Gray
Susy, Iris, Fanny	Sandra Milo

Susy's Coterie:

Grandmother	Irina Alexeieva
Mother	Alessandra Mannoukine
Chauffeur	Gilberto Galvan
Massageuse	Seyna Seyn
Maids	Yvonne Casadei, Hildegarde Golez, Dina de Santis
Russian Teacher	Edoardo Torricella
Desperate Friend	Dany Paris
Oriental Lover	Raffaele Guida
Arabian Prince	Fred Williams
Lynx-Eyes	Alberto Plebani
Bhishma	Waleska Gert

Advisers and Adversaries:

Don Raffaele	Felice Fulchignoni
Psychoanalyst	Anne Francine
Family Lawyer	Mario Conocchia
Headmaster	Fredrich Ledebur
Medium	Genius
Valentina's Lover	Massimo Sarchielli
Models	Giorgio Ardisson, Bob Edwards, Nadir Moretti

Sandra Milo

Giulietta Masina

Giulietta Masina
in
"JULIET OF THE SPIRITS"

Andre Bourvil, also above, and right with
Francis Blanche, top with Jean Poiret

THANK HEAVEN FOR
SMALL FAVORS
(Deo Gratias)

(INTERNATIONAL CLASSICS) Producers,
Henri Diamant-Berger, Jerome Goulven; Di-
rector, Jean-Pierre Mocky; Screenplay, Jean-
Pierre Mocky, Michel Servin, Alain Moury;
From Novel by Michel Servin; Music, Joseph
Kosma; Director of Photography, L. H. Burel;
A Film D'Art-Atica-Corflor Production.

CAST

George..Andre Bourvil
Inspector Cucherat....................Francis Blanche
Raoul...Jean Poiret
and Jean Yonnel, Jean Tissier, Veronique Nor-
den, Bernard Lavalette

THE TRUTH ABOUT SPRING

(UNIVERSAL) Producer, Alan Brown; Director, Richard Thorpe; Director, James Lee Barrett; Based on Story by Henry de Vere Stacpoole; Director of Photography, Edward Schaife; Music, Robert Farnon; Assistant Directors, Ted Sturgis, Pedro Vidal; A Quota Rentals Ltd. Presentation in Technicolor.

CAST

Spring Tyler	Hayley Mills
Tommy Tyler	John Mills
William Ashton	James MacArthur
Cark	Lionel Jeffries
Sellers	Harry Andrews
Cleary	Niall MacGinnis
Simmons	Lionel Murton
Skelton	David Tomlinson

Right: James MacArthur, John Mills,
Harry Andrews

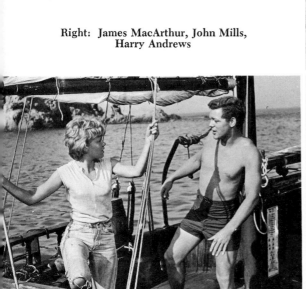

John Mills, Hayley Mills. Above:
Hayley Mills, James MacArthur

Hayley Mills, David Tomlinson. Above:
James MacArthur, Niall MacGinnis,
John Mills, Hayley Mills

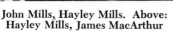

THE LITTLE NUNS

(EMBASSY) Producer, Ferruccio Brusarosco; Director, Luciano Salce; Screenplay, Franco Castellano, Giuseppe Moccia; Associate Producers, G. Carlo Marchetti, Mario Tugnoli; Director of Photography, Erico Menczer; Assistant Director, Emilio Miraglia; Music, Ennio Morricone; Costumes, Giuliano Papi; Presented by Joseph E. Levine.

CAST

Sister Celeste	Catherine Spaak
Elena	Sylva Koscina
Livio Bertana	Amedeo Nazzari
Mother Rachele	Didi Perego
Spugna	Umberto D'Orsi
Damiano	Sandro Bruni
Bertana's Secretary	Annie Gorassini
Mr. Batistucchi	Alberto Bonucci

Left: Sylva Koscina, Catherine Spaak,
Didi Perego, Sandro Bruni

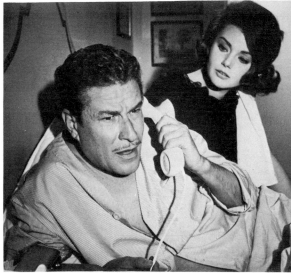

Catherine Spaak, Sandro Bruni, Umberto d'Orsi,
Didi Perego. Above: Catherine Spaak,
Sylva Koscina, Didi Perego

Didi Perego, Amedeo Nazzari, Catherine Spaak
Above: Amedeo Nazzari, Sylva Koscina

131

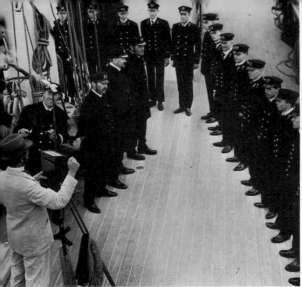

Center: Jack Hawkins, Peter O'Toole

Peter O'Toole, Andrew Keir

Eli Wallach, Daliah Lavi, Peter O'Toole. Above:
Peter O'Toole, Paul Lukas, Akim Tamiroff

Daliah Lavi, Peter O'Toole. Above:
Curt Jurgens, Eli Wallach

Tatsuo Saito, Paul Lukas, Daliah Lavi,
Peter O'Toole, Ruon

LORD JIM

(COLUMBIA) Directed and Written by Richard
Brooks; Based on Novel by Joseph Conrad;
Director of Photography, Frederick A. Young;
Music, Bronislau Kaper; Costumes, Phyllis
Dalton; Assistant Director, Roy Stevens; A
Columbia-Keep Films Co-Production in Super
Panavision and Technicolor.

CAST

Lord Jim	Peter O'Toole
Gentleman Brown	James Mason
Cornelius	Curt Jurgens
The General	Eli Wallach
Marlow	Jack Hawkins
Stein	Paul Lukas
The Girl	Daliah Lavi
Schomberg	Akim Tamiroff
Waris	Ichizo Itami
Du-Ramin	Tatsuo Saito
Brierly	Andrew Keir
Robinson	Jack MacGowran
Malay	Eric Young
Capt. Chester	Noel Purcell
Capt. of Patna	Walter Gotell
Moslem Leader	Rafik Anwar
Elder	Marne Maitland
Doctor	Newton Blick
Magistrate	A. J. Brown
French Officer	Christian Marquand

James Mason, Akim Tamiroff. Above: Peter
O'Toole. Left: Daliah Lavi, Ichizo Itami,
Paul Lukas, Tatsuo Saito

Daliah Lavi, Peter O'Toole
in
"LORD JIM"

BAMBOLE
(The Dolls)

(COLUMBIA) Producer, Gianni Hecht Lucari for Documento Film-Orsay Films; Based on "Tales of The Decameron" by Giovanni Boccaccio; A Royal Films International Release.

CAST

"The Telephone Call":
Director, Dino Risi; Screenplay, Gianni Polidori; Photography, Ennio Guarnieri; Music, Armando Trovaioli

Luisa......................................Virna Lisi
Giorgio..................................Nino Manfredi
Armenia..................................Alicia Bradet

"Treatise On Eugenics":
Director, Luigi Comencini; Music, Armando Trovaioli; Photography, Carlo Montuori

Ulla......................................Elke Sommer
Massimo..................................Maurizio Arena
Valerio..................................Piero Focaccia

"The Soup":
Director, Franco Rossi; Screenplay, Rodolfo Sonego; Photography, Roberto Gerardy; Music, Armando Trovaioli

Giovanna..................................Monica Vitti
with Orazio Orlando, John Karlsen, Roberto De Simone

"Monsignor Cupid":
Director, Mauro Bolognini; Screenplay, Leo Benvenuti, Piero De Bernardi; Photography, Leonida Barboni; Music, Armando Trovaioli

Beatrice..................................Gina Lollobrigida
Vincenzo..................................Jean Sorel
Monsignor Arcudi..................................Akim Tamiroff

Nino Manfredi, Virna Lisi

Monica Vitti

Jean Sorel, Akim Tamiroff, Gina Lollobrigida
Above: Elke Sommer

135

YOUNG CASSIDY

(M-G-M) Producers, Robert D. Graff, Robert Emmett Ginna; Director, Jack Cardiff; Screenplay, John Whiting; Based on "Mirror In My House" by Sean O'Casey; Director of Photography, Ted Scaife; Music, Sean O'Riada; Associate Producer, Michael Killanin; Costumes, Margaret Furse; Assistant Director, John Quested; A Sextant Films Lt. Picture in Technicolor; A John Ford Film. April release.

CAST

John Cassidy	Rod Taylor
Mrs. Cassidy	Flora Robson
Archie	Jack MacGowran
Ella	Sian Phillips
Tom	T. P. McKenna
Sara	Julie Ross
Michael	Robin Sumner
Mick Mullen	Philip O'Flynn
Nora	Maggie Smith
Daisy Battles	Julie Christie
Bessie Ballynoy	Pauline Delaney
Lady Gregory	Edith Evans
W. B. Yeats	Michael Redgrave
Foreman	Arthur O'Sullivan
Constable	Tom Irwin
Barman	John Cowley
Publisher's Clerk	William Foley
Bank Teller	John Franklyn
Murphy	Harry Brogan
Charlie Ballynoy	James Fitzgerald

and Joe Lynch, Vincent Dowling, Anne Dalton, Donal Donnelly, Martin Crosbie, Fred Johnson, Edward Golden, Christopher Curran, Shivaun O'Casey, Harold Goldblatt, Ronald Ibbs, May Craig, May Cluskey, and members of The Abbey Theatre Company

Rod Taylor, Julie Christie. Above: Edith Evans, Rod Taylor (Left with Maggie Smith). Top: Rod Taylor with Flora Robson, Michael Redgrave

LA BOHEME

(WARNER BROS.) An Opera in 4 Acts by Giuseppe Giacosa and Lugi Illica; Based on Novel by Henri Murger; Music, Giacomo Puccini; Directed and Designed by Franco Zeffirelli; Artistic Director and Conductor, Herbert von Karajan; Costumes, Marcel Escoffier; Associate Director, Wilhelm Semmelroth; Director of Photography, Werner Krein; A Cosmotel Production in Technicolor and New High Fidelity Sound; Filmed at La Scala, Milan, Italy.

CAST

Rodolfo	Gianni Raimondi
Marcello	Rolando Panerai
Schaunard	Gianni Maffeo
Colline	Ivo Vinco
Benoit	Carlo Badioli
Alcindoro	Birgilio Carbonari
Mimi	Mirella Freni
Musetta	Adriana Martino
Parpignol	Franco Ricciardi
Sergeant	Giuseppe Morresi
Customs Official	Carlo Forti
Salesman	Angelo Mercuriali

and the Orchestra and Chorus of La Scala

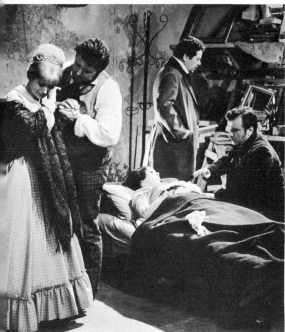

Adriana Martino, Gianni Raimondi, Mirella Freni, Rolando Panerai, Gianni Maffeo. Top: Ivo Vinco, Gianni Raimondi, Gianni Maffeo, Rolando Panerai

Gianni Raimondi, Mirella Freni. Above: Adriana Martino

137

TRIAL OF JOAN OF ARC

(PATHE CONTEMPORARY) Producer, Agnes Delahaie; Direction and Screenplay, Robert Bresson; Adapted from the original records; Director of Photography, Leonce-Henri Burel.

CAST

Joan	Florence Carrez
Bishop Cauchon	Jean-Claude Fourneau
Interrogator Beaupere	Roger Honorat
Inquisitor LeMaitre	Marc Jacquier
Joan's Confessor	Philippe Martin
Jean de Chatillon	Jean Gillibert
Brother Isambart	Michel Herubel

Left and below: Florence Carrez

NOBODY WAVED GOODBYE

(CINEMA V) Producers, Roman Kroitor, Don Owen; Executive Producer, Tom Daly; Direction and Screenplay, Don Owen; Music, Eldon Rathburn; Director of Photography, John Spotton; A National Film Board of Canada Production.

CAST

Peter	Peter Kastner
Julie	Julie Biggs
Father	Claude Rae
Sister	Toby Tarnow
Mother	Charmion King
Boy Friend	Ron Taylor
Patrolman	Robert Hill
Sergeant	Jack Beer
Probation Officer	John Sullivan
Julie's Mother	Lynne Gorman
Interviewer	Ivor Barry
Waitress	Sharon Bonin
Landlord	Norman Ettlinger
Lot Supervisor	John Vernon

Peter Kastner, Julie Biggs, also above

BANANA PEEL

(PATHE CONTEMPORARY) Producer, Paul-Edmonde DeCharme; Director, Marcel Ophuls; Screenplay, Marcel Ophuls, Claude Sautet; Director of Photography, Jean Rabier.

CAST
Cathy	Jeanne Moreau
Michel	Jean-Paul Belmondo
Charlie	Claude Brasseur
Lachard	Gert Frobe
Reynaldo	Jean-Pierre Marielle
Bontemps	Alain Cuny

Right: Jean-Paul Belmondo, Jeanne Moreau

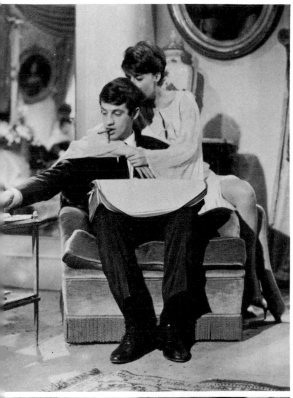

Jean-Paul Belmondo, Gert Frobe. Above: Jean-Paul Belmondo with Jeanne Moreau

Jeanne Moreau, Gert Frobe, Jean-Paul Belmondo
Above: Jean-Paul Belmondo, Jean-Pierre Marielle

CRACK IN THE WORLD

(**PARAMOUNT**) Producers, Bernard Glasser, Lester A. Sansom; Director, Andrew Marton; Screenplay, Jon Manchip White, Julian Halevy; Story, Jon Manchip White; Assistant Director, Jose-Maria Ochoa; Costumes, Laure DeZarate; Director of Photography, Manuel Berenguer; Music, John Douglas; A Philip Yordan Production in Technicolor.

CAST

Dr. Stephen Sorensen	Dana Andrews
Mrs. Maggie Sorensen	Janette Scott
Ted Rampion	Kieron Moore
Sir Charles Eggerston	Alexander Knox
Masefield	Peter Damon
Markov	Gary Lasdun
Steele	Mike Steen
Simpson	Todd Martin
Rand	Jim Gillen

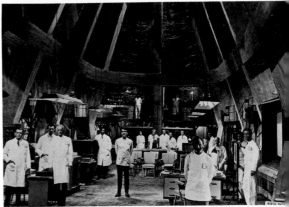

Janette Scott, Kieron Moore. Top: Dana Andrews, Gary Lasdun, Kieron Moore

Dana Andrews, Kieron Moore, Janette Scott Top: Alexander Knox, Janette Scott

RAPTURE

(INTERNATIONAL CLASSICS) Producer, Christian Ferry; Director, John Guillermin; Screenplay, Stanley Mann; Based on Novel by Phyllis Hastings; Director of Photography, Marcel Grignon; Costumes, Jacques Fonteray; Assistant Directors, Louis Pitzele, Rik Wise; In CinemaScope.

CAST

Larbaud	Melvyn Douglas
Joseph	Dean Stockwell
Agnes	Patricia Gozzi
Karen	Gunnel Lindblom
Elder Policeman	Leslie Sands
Younger Policeman	Murray Evans
Genevieve	Sylvia Kay
Armand	Peter Sallis

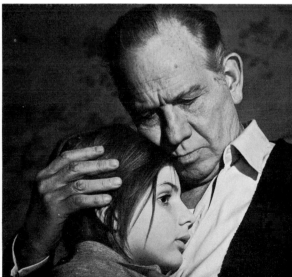

Gunnel Lindblom, Dean Stockwell, and above with Patricia Gozzi. Top: Patricia Gozzi, Dean Stockwell

Patricia Gozzi, Melvyn Douglas, also at top

141

THE TRAIN

(UNITED ARTISTS) Producer, Jules Bricken; Director, John Frankenheimer; Screen Story and Screenplay, Franklin Coen, Frank Davis; Based on "Le Front de L'Art" by Rose Valland; Directors of Photography, Jean Tournier, Walter Wottitz; Associate Producer, Bernard Farrel; Music, Maurice Jarre; A Co-Production of Productions Artistes Associés Films Ariane, Dear Films.

CAST

Labiche	Burt Lancaster
Col. Von Waldheim	Paul Scofield
Christine	Jeanne Moreau
Papa Boule	Michel Simon
Miss Villard	Suzanne Flon
Herren	Wolfgang Preiss
Von Lubitz	Richard Munch
Didont	Albert Remy
Pesquet	Charles Millot
Jacques	Jacques Marin
Spinet	Paul Bonifas
Schmidt	Jean Bouchaud
Schwartz	Donal O'Brien
Octave	Jean-Pierre Zola
Pilzer	Art Brauss
Major	Jean-Claude Bercq
Dietrich	Howard Vernon
Bernard	Bernard La Jarrige
Priest	Daniel Lecourtois
Grote	Richard Bailey
Robert	Christian Fuin
Gestapo Chief	Max From
Tauber	Christian Remy

Paul Scofield, Suzanne Flon. Above: Jeanne Moreau, Burt Lancaster (also at top, and right with Paul Scofield, below with Michel Simon)

THE AMOROUS ADVENTURES OF MOLL FLANDERS

(PARAMOUNT) Producer, Marcel Hellman; Associate Producer, Richard Hellman; Director, Terence Young; Director of Photography, Ted Moore; Assistant Director, David Anderson; Screenplay, Denis Cannan, Roland Kibbee; Based on works of Daniel DeFoe; Costumes, Elizabeth Haffenden, Joan Bridge; Music, John Addison; Choreography, Pauline Grant; Song sung by Lionel Long; A Winchester Film in Panavision and Technicolor.

CAST

Moll Flanders	Kim Novak
Young Moll	Claire Ufland
Jemmy	Richard Johnson
Lady Blystone	Angela Lansbury
The Count	Vittorio DeSica
Squint	Leo McKern
The Banker	George Sanders
Dutchy	Lilli Palmer
Grunt	Peter Butterworth
Orphanage Superintendent	Dandy Nichols
Bishop	Noel Howlett
The Mayor	Cecil Parker
Mayor's Wife	Barbara Couper
Elder Brother	Daniel Massey
Younger Brother	Derren Nesbitt
Elder Sister	Ingrid Hafner
Younger Sister	June Watts
Miss Glowber	Judith Furse
Officer of Dragoons	Anthony Dawson
Drunken Parson	Roger Livesey
Prison Governor	Hugh Griffith

and Jess Conrad, Noel Harrison, Alex Scott, Alexis Kahner, Mary Merrall, Richard Wattis, Terence Lodge, Reginald Beckwith, Lionel Long, David Lodge, David Hutcheson, Michael Trubshawe, Richard Goolden, Leonard Sachs, Basil Dignam, Michael Brennan, Liam Redmond, Neville Jason

Angela Lansbury, Hugh Griffith, Kim Novak Above: Kim Novak with Vittorio DeSica (L) and Daniel Massey (R), and top with Richard Johnson (L), and George Sanders (R)

Donal Donnelly, Michael Crawford, Ray Brooks,
Rita Tushingham. Above: Ray Brooks,
Rita Tushingham

Donal Donnelly, Michael Crawford
Above: Ray Brooks

144

THE KNACK . . .
and how to get it

(LOPERT) Producer, Oscar Lewenstein; Director, Richard Lester; Screenplay, Charles Wood; Based on Play by Ann Jellicoe; Music, John Barry; Director of Photography, David Watkins; Associate Producers, Leigh Aman, Michael Deeley; Costumes, Jocelyn Rickards; Solo Jazz Organ, Alan Haven; A Woodfall Film.

CAST

Nancy	Rita Tushingham
Tolen	Ray Brooks
Colin	Michael Crawford
Tom	Donal Donnelly
Dress Shop Owner	William Dexter
Man in Photo Booth	Charles Dyer
Female Teacher	Margot Thomas
Angry Father	John Bluthal
Blonde in Photo Booth	Helen Lennox
Teacher	Wensley Pithey
Man in Phone Both	Edgar Wreford
Surveyor	Frank Sieman
His Assistant	Bruce Lacey
Left Luggage Porter	George Chisholm
Third Guardsman	Kenneth Farrington
Picture Owner	Peter Copley
Junk Yard Owner	Timothy Batesom
Tom's Landlady	Dandy Nichols

Rita Tushingham, Donal Donnelly, Michael Crawford, also above

145

SWINGERS' PARADISE

(AMERICAN INTERNATIONAL) Producer, Kenneth Harper; Director, Sidney J. Furie; Story and Screenplay, Peter Myers, Ronald Cass; An Ivy Production.

CAST

Johnnie	Cliff Richard
Lloyd Davis	Walter Slezak
Jenny	Susan Hampshire
Mood Musicians	Hank B. Marvin,
Bruce Welch, Brian Bennett, John Rostill	
Jerry	Melvyn Hayes
Edward	Richard O'Sullivan
Barbara	Una Stubbs
Miguel	Joseph Cuby
Douglas Leslie	Derek Bond
Senior Sheik, Scotsman,	
Harold	Gerald Harper

Right: Una Stubbs, Joseph Cuby, Cliff Richard

Stanley Baker, Juliet Prowse, and above with Ken Gampu. Right: Fuzi Zazayokwe (C)

148

DINGAKA

(EMBASSY) Producer-Director, Jamie Uys; Screenplay, Jamie Uys; Directors of Photography, Manie Botha, Judex C. Viljoen; Music, Bertha Egnos, Eddie Domingo, Basil Gray; Costumes, Ruth St. Moritz, Anna Richter-Visser; Choreography, Sheila Wartski; Presented by Joseph E. Levine; In Wide-Screen and Color.

CAST

Tom Davis	Stanley Baker
Marion Davis	Juliet Prowse
Ntuku Makwena	Ken Gampu
The Judge	Siegfried Mynhardt
Prison Chaplain	Bob Courtney
Prosecutor	Gordon Hood
Legal Aid Society Secretary	George Moore
Bantu Commissioner	Hugh Rouse
The Doctor	Simon Swindell
Court Clerk	Willem Botha
Witch Doctor	John Sithebe
Masaba	Paul Makgoba
Choir Soloist	Sophie MqCina
Lead Singer	Jimmy Sabe
Priest	Daniel Marolen
Dancer	Clement Mehlomakulu
Priest	Cocky Tlhotlhalemji
Rurari	Flora Motaung
Stick Fighter	Fuzi Zazayokwe

MALE HUNT
(La Chasse à l'Homme)

(PATHE CONTEMPORARY) Producers, Robert Amon, Claude Jaeger; Director, Edouard Molinaro; Screenplay, France Roche; From an Idea by Yvon Guezel, and Stories by Albert Simonin and Michel Duran; A Co-Production of Procinex-Mondex Films & Filmsonor, and Euro International Films.

CAST

Fernand	Jean-Paul Belmondo
Tony	Jean-Claude Brialy
Denise	Catherine Deneuve
Sandra	Francoise Dorleac
Isabelle	Micheline Presle
Julien	Claude Rich
Gisele	Marie Laforet
Sophie	Marie Dubois
M. Heurtin	Bernard Blier
Mme. Armande	Helene Duc
Papatakes	Francis Blanche
Prof. Lartois	Michel Serrault
Flora	Bernadette Lafont
Georgina	Mireille Darc

Jean-Paul Belmondo, Jean-Claude Brialy, Claude Rich (also at top). Above: Jean-Paul Belmondo, Francoise Dorleac, Jean-Claude Brialy

Marie Dubois, Jean-Paul Belmondo. Above: Micheline Presle, Catherine Deneuve, Claude Rich

Edmund Purdom, Jeanne Moreau, Rex Harrison

Shirley MacLaine, George C. Scott, Art Carney,
Riccardo Garrone

Moira Lister, Rex Harrison, and above
with Jeanne Moreau

Art Carney, George C. Scott, Shirley MacLaine,
Alain Delon. Above: Shirley MacLaine,
Art Carney

Omar Sharif, Ingrid Bergman

THE YELLOW ROLLS-ROYCE

(M-G-M) Producer, Anatole De Grunwald; Director, Anthony Asquith; Screenplay, Terence Rattigan; Director of Photography, Jack Hildyard; Music, Riz Ortolani; Assistant Director, Kip Gowans; Associate Producer, Roy Parkinson; Clothes, Castillo of Paris, Edith Head, Pierre Cardin; In Panavision and Metrocolor.

CAST

Marquess of Frinton	Rex Harrison
Marchioness of Frinton	Jeanne Moreau
John Fane	Edmund Purdom
Lady St. Simeon	Moira Lister
Duchesse d'Angouleme	Isa Miranda
Norwood	Roland Culver
Harmsworth	Michael Hordern
His Assistant	Lance Percival
Taylor	Harold Scott
Mae Jenkins	Shirley MacLaine
Paolo Maltese	George C. Scott
Stefano	Alain Delon
Joey	Art Carney
Bomba	Riccardo Garrone
Mrs. Gerda Millett	Ingrid Bergman
Davich	Omar Sharif
Miss Hortense Astor	Joyce Grenfell
Ferguson	Wally Cox
Mayor	Guy Deghy
Mrs. Millett's Chauffeur	Carlo Groccolo

Omar Sharif, Wally Cox, Ingrid Bergman, Joyce Grenfell. Above: Omar Sharif, Ingrid Bergman Left: Alain Delon, Shirley MacLaine

149

A BOY TEN FEET TALL

(PARAMOUNT) Producer, Hal Mason; Director, Alexander Mackendrick; Screenplay, Denis Cannan; Based on Novel "Sammy Going South" by W. H. Canaway; Director of Photography, Erwin Hillier; Music, Tristram Cary; Assistant Director, Peter Price; A Seven Arts-Bryston Presentation.

CAST

Cocky Wainwright	Edward G. Robinson
Sammy	Fergus McClelland
Gloria van Imhoff	Constance Cummings
Lem	Harry H. Corbett
Spyros Dracondopolous	Paul Stassino
The Syrian	Zia Mohyeddin
Abu Lubaba	Orlando Martins
Heneker	John Turner
Aunt Jane	Zena Walker
District Commissioner	Jack Gwillim
Cathie	Patricia Donahue
Bob	Jared Allen
Doctor	Guy Deghy
Hassan	Marnie Maitland
Egyptian Policeman	Steven Scott
Head Porter	Frederick Schiller
Members of Cocky's Camp	Swaleh, Tajiri, Faith Brown

150   Fergus McClelland, Edward G. Robinson, and above with Harry H. Corbett

Zena Walker, Fergus McClelland and Above: Paul Stassino, Orlando Martins, Fergus McClelland (also at top)

HIGH INFIDELITY

(MAGNA) Produced by Gianni Hecht Lucari for Documento Film; Story and Screenplay, Age and Scarpelli, Scola and Maccari; Presented by Marshall Naify.

CAST

The Scandal: (Directed by Franco Rossi)
Francesco.....................................Nino Manfredi
Raffaella..Fulvia Franco
Ronald...John Philip Law

Sin In The Afternoon: (Directed by Elio Petri)
Giulio...Charles Aznavour
Laura..Claire Bloom

The Victim: (Directed by Luciano Salce)
Gloria...Monica Vitti
Tonino.....................................Jean-Pierre Cassel
Paolo..Sergio Fantoni

Modern People: (Directed by Mario Monicelli)
Cesare..Ugo Tognazzi
Tebaide.......................................Michele Mercier
Reguzzoni...Bernard Blier

Left: Claire Bloom, Charles Aznavour

Monica Vitti, Jean-Pierre Cassel. Above:
Michele Mercier, Ugo Tognazzi

Fulvia Franco, John Philip Law. Above:
Sergio Fantoni, Monica Vitti

151

ROTTEN TO THE CORE

(**CINEMA V**) Producer, Roy Boulting; Director, John Boulting; Associate Producer, Philip Shipway; Director of Photography, Freddie Young; Story and Screenplay, Jeffrey Dell, John Warren, Roy Boulting; A British Lion Film.

CAST

Duke	Anton Rodgers
Hunt	Eric Sykes
Sara	Charlotte Rampling
Vine	Ian Bannen
Countess	Avis Bunnage
Jelly	Dudley Sutton
Lenny	Kenneth Griffith
Scapa	James Beckett
Preston	Thorley Walters
Anxious	Victor Maddern
Prison Governor	Raymond Huntley

Anton Rodgers, Kenneth Griffith, Dudley Sutton, Kenneth Griffith. Above: Ian Bannen, Dudley Sutton, Anton Rodgers. Left: Charlotte Rampling, Anton Rodgers. Top: (L) Kenneth Griffith, Anton Rodgers, (R) Avis Bunnage, Victor Maddern

George Peppard, Sophia Loren
in
"OPERATION CROSSBOW"

OPERATION CROSSBOW

(M-G-M) Producer, Carlo Ponti; Director, Michael Anderson; Screenplay, Richard Imrie, Derry Quinn, Ray Rigby; Music, Ron Goodwin; Director of Photography, Erwin Hillier; Assistant Director, Basil Rayburn; In Panavision and Metrocolor.

CAST

Nora	Sophia Loren
John Curtis	George Peppard
Prof. Lindemann	Trevor Howard
Boyd of M.I.6	John Mills
Duncan Sandys	Richard Johnson
Robert Henshaw	Tom Courtenay
Phil Bradley	Jeremy Kemp
Bamford	Anthony Quayle
Frieda	Lilli Palmer
Ziemann	Paul Henreid
Linz	Helmut Dantine
Hanna Reitsch	Barbara Rueting
Wing Cmdr. Kendall	Richard Todd
Constance Babington Smith	Sylvia Syms
Flight Lt. Kenny	John Fraser
R.A.F. Officer	Maurice Denham
Winston Churchill	Patrick Wymark
Prof. Hoffer	Karl Stepanek
Col. Kenneth Post	Moray Watson
Sir Charles Sims	Richard Wattis
German Technical Examiner	Allan Cuthbertson
Air Commodore	Robert Brown

Left: John Fraser, Trevor Howard, Richard Todd, John Mills

Paul Henreid, Helmut Dantine. Above: George Peppard, John Mills, Tom Courtenay (R)

Sylvia Syms, Richard Wattis. Above: Basil Dignam, Richard Johnson, Moray Watson, John Mills

Milo Sperber, Lilli Palmer. Above: Jeremy Kemp,
George Peppard. Top: Tom Courtenay,
Anthony Quayle

Sophia Loren. Above: George Peppard, Jeremy
Kemp. Top: Barbara Rueting

CASANOVA '70

(EMBASSY) Producer, Carlo Ponti; Director, Mario Monicelli; Screenplay, Furio Scarpelli, Agenore Incrocci, Mario Monicelli; Story, Tonino Guerra; Director of Photography, Aldo Tonti; Assistant Director, Renzo Marignano; Music, Armando Trovaioli; Costumes, Giulio Coltellacci; Presented by Joseph E. Levine in Wide-Screen and Color.

CAST

Maj. Andrea Rossi-Colombetti	Marcello Mastroianni
Gigliola	Virna Lisi
Noelle	Michele Mercier
Thelma	Marisa Mell
Count Ferreri	Marco Ferreri
Psychoanalyst	Enrico Maria Salerno
The Monsignor	Guido Alberti
Dolly Greenwater	Margaret Lee
Chambermaid	Rosemarie Dexter
Addolarata	Yolanda Modio
Indonesian Airline Hostess	Seyna Seyn
Santina	Moira Orfei
Lion Tamer	Liana Orfei
Girl in Museum	Beba Loncar
General Greenwater	Frank Gregory
Grocer's Wife	Luciana Paoli
Gigliola's Mother	Augusta Checcotti
Gigliola's Father	Mario Banchelli

Virna Lisi. Top: Marcello Mastroianni

Marcello Mastroianni, Virna Lisi (also at top)
Above: Marcello Mastroianni, Marisa Mell

MASQUERADE

(UNITED ARTISTS) Producer, Michael Relph; Director, Basil Dearden; Screenplay, Michael Relph, William Goldman; From the Novel "Castle Minerva" by Victor Canning; Music, Philip Green; Title Song sung by Danny Williams; Lyrics, Norman Newell; Director of Photography, Otto Heller; Costumes, Beatrice Dawson; In Eastman Color.

CAST

David Frazer	Cliff Robertson
Colonel Drexel	Jack Hawkins
Sophie	Marisa Mell
Sarrassin	Michel Piccoli
Dunwoody	Bill Fraser
Prince Jamil	Christopher Witty
Paviot	Tutte Lemkow
Gustave	Keith Pyott
El Mono	Jose Burgos
Benson	Charles Gray
Sir Robert	John LeMesurier
Ahmed Ben Fa'id	Roger Delgado
Brindle	Jerold Wells
Henrickson	Felix Aylmer
King Ahmed	Denis Bernard
Minister	Ernest Clark
Photographer	David Nettheim
His Assistant	Anthony Singleton
Bishop	Norman Fisher
General	Eric Blyth
James Mossman	Himself

Cliff Robertson, Marisa Mell. Above: Michel Piccoli, Tutte Lemkow, Jose Burgos, Jack Hawkins Top: Jack Hawkins, Christopher Witty

Marisa Mell. Top: Cliff Robertson

REPULSION

(ROYAL FILMS INTERNATIONAL) Producer, Eugene Gutowski; Director, Roman Polanski; Associate Producers, Robert Sterne, Sam Waynberg; Screenplay, Roman Polanski, Gerard Brach; Assistant Director, Ted Sturgis; Music, Chico Hamilton.

CAST

Carol	Catherine Deneuve
Michael	Ian Hendry
Colin	John Fraser
Landlord	Patrick Wymark
Helen	Yvonne Furneaux
Miss Balch	Renee Houston
Bridget	Helen Fraser
Madame Denise	Valerie Taylor
John	James Villiers
Reggie	Hugh Futcher
Workman	Mike Pratt
Mrs. Rendlesham	Monica Merlin
Manicurist	Imogen Graham

Top Left: Yvonne Furneaux, Ian Hendry

Catherine Deneuve (also above)

Yvonne Furneaux, Catherine Deneuve
Above: John Fraser, Catherine Deneuve

BACKFIRE

(ROYAL FILMS INTERNATIONAL) Executive Producer, Paul-Edmond Decharme; Director, Jean Becker; Screenplay, Didier Goulard, Maurice Fabre, Jean Becker; From the Novel by Clet Coroner; Director of Photography, Edmond Sechan; Music, Martial Solal; In French with English subtitles.

CAST

David .... Jean-Paul Belmondo
Olga .... Jean Seberg
Mario .... Enrico Maria Salerno
Fehrman .... Gert Frobe
and Renate Ewert, Jean-Pierre Marielle, Wolfgang Preiss, Diana Lorys, Fernando Rey, Michel Beaune, Roberto Camardiel, Xan Das Bolas, Petar Martinovitch, Carmen De Lirio, Fernando Sancho, Margarita Gil

Jean Seberg, Jean-Paul Belmondo (also left and top). Above: Jean-Paul Belmondo, Gert Frobe 159

Gert Frobe. Above: Sarah Miles, Stuart Whitman
Top: Red Skelton

Terry-Thomas, Eric Sykes. Above: Irina Demick,
Jean-Pierre Cassel

THOSE MAGNIFICENT MEN IN THEIR FLYING MACHINES
or: How I Flew From London To Paris In 25 Hours and 11 Minutes

(20th CENTURY-FOX) Producer, Stan Margulies; Associate Producer, Jack Davies; Director, Ken Annakin; Screenplay, Jack Davies, Ken Annakin; Music, Ron Goodwin; Director of Photography, Christopher Challis; Costumes, Osbert Lancaster; Assistant Director, Clive Reed; In Todd-AO(R) and DeLuxe Color.

CAST

Orvil Newton	Stuart Whitman
Patricia Rawnsley	Sarah Miles
Richard Mays	James Fox
Count Emilio Ponticelli	Alberto Sordi
Lord Rawnsley	Robert Morley
Col. Manfred Von Holstein	Gert Frobe
Pierre Dubois	Jean-Pierre Cassel
Courtney	Eric Sykes
Sir Perby Ware-Armitage	Terry-Thomas
Brigitte, Ingrid, Marlene, Francois, Yvette, Betty	Irina Demick
Fire Chief Perkins	Benny Hill
Yamamoto	Yujiro Ishihara
Mother Superior	Flora Robson
Capt. Rumpelstrosse	Karl Michael Vogler
George Gruber	Sam Wanamaker
Neanderthal Man	Red Skelton
French Postman	Eric Barker
Elderly Colonel	Fred Emney
McDougal	Gordon Jackson
Jean	Davy Kaye
French Painter	John LeMesurier
Lt. Parsons	Jeremy Lloyd
Sophia Ponticelli	Zena Marshall
Airline Hostess	Millicent Martin
Italian Mayor	Eric Pohlman
Waitress in Old Mill	Marjorie Rhodes
Tremayne Gascoyne	William Rushton
Niven	Michael Trubshawe
Popperwell	Tony Hancock

Right: Robert Morley, Sarah Miles, James Fox
Top: Sarah Miles, Stuart Whitman, James Fox

Jean-Pierre Cassel

Stuart Whitman, Sam Wanamaker

THE BATTLE OF THE VILLA FIORITA

(WARNER BROS.) Directed and Written by Delmer Daves; Based on Novel by Rumer Godden; Director of Photography, Oswald Morris; Music, M. Spoliansky; Special Wardrobe, Biki of Milano, Emilio Pucci; In Panavision and Technicolor.

CAST

Moira	Maureen O'Hara
Lorenzo	Rossano Brazzi
Darrell	Richard Todd
Margot	Phyllis Calvert
Michael	Martin Stephens
Debby	Elizabeth Dear
Donna	Olivia Hussey
Charmian	Maxine Audley
Lady Anthea	Ursula Jeans
Father Rossi	Ettore Manni
Travel Agent	Richard Wattis
M. C.	Finlay Currie
Celestina	Clelia Matania
Giuletta	Rosi Di Pietro

Rossano Brazzi, Maureen O'Hara. Above: Martin Stephens, Richard Todd, Elizabeth Dear

162

Rossano Brazzi, Maureen O'Hara and above with Martin Stephens, Elizabeth Dear, Olivia Hussey. Top: Maureen O'Hara, Richard Todd

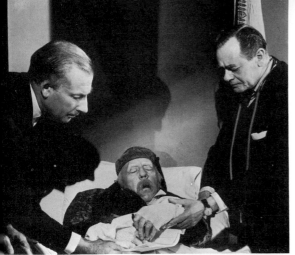

THE SECRET OF MY SUCCESS

(M-G-M) A Virginia and Andrew Stone Production; Direction and Screenplay, Andrew L. Stone; Director of Photography, David Boulton; Wardrobe, John B. Cavanagh; In Panavision and Color.

CAST

Marigold Marado	Shirley Jones
Violet Lawson	Stella Stevens
Baroness Von Lukenburg	Honor Blackman
Arthur Tate	James Booth
Inspector Hobart, Baron Von Lukenburg, President Esteda, Earl of Aldershot	Lionel Jeffries
Mrs. Tate	Amy Dolby
Mrs. Pringle	Joan Hickson
Colonel Armandez	Robert Barnete
Pallazio	Nicolau Breyner

Left: Ernest Clark, Lionel Jeffries, Duncan Lewis

Lionel Jeffries, Shirley Jones, James Booth
Above: Joan Hickson, Amy Dolby, James Booth

Lionel Jeffries, Honor Blackman. Above: James Booth, Lionel Jeffries, Stella Stevens

Ringo Starr

Eleanor Bron. Above and Top:
The Beatles

HELP!

(UNITED ARTISTS) Producer, Walter Shenson; Director, Richard Lester; Original Screenplay, Marc Behm, Charles Wood; Story, Marc Behm; Director of Photography, David Watkins; Assistant Director, Clive Reed; Dress Designers, Julie Harris, Dinah Greet; A Walter Shenson-Subafilms Production in Eastman Color.

CAST

John	John Lennon
Paul	Paul McCartney
Ringo	Ringo Starr
George	George Harrison
Clang	Leo McKern
Ahme	Eleanor Bron
Foot	Victor Spinetti
Algernon	Roy Kinnear
Bhuta	John Bluthal
Superintendent	Patrick Cargill
Priests/Thugs	Ronnie Brody, Bob Godfrey, Louis Mansi, Rupert Evans
Austrian Waiter	Andreas Malandrinos
Cleaner in Temple	Golda Casimir
High Priestesses	Deborah du'Lacey, Gai Wright, Zorenah Osborne, Eve Eden, Zienia Merton, Marie-Lise
Lawn Mower	Bruce Lacey
Abdul	Warren Mitchell
Belly Dancer	Durra

and Alfie Bass, Danny Almond, Edith Savile, Vera Cook, Joe Gibbons, Sue Reid, Stewart Guidotti, Wally Shufflebottom, Blake Butler, Ian Wilson, Jenny Till, Mary Ford, Jenny Landry, Glenda Warrington, Alex Macintosh, Pat Roberts, Thomas Baptiste, Dandy Nichols, Jeremy Lloyd, Gretchen Franklin

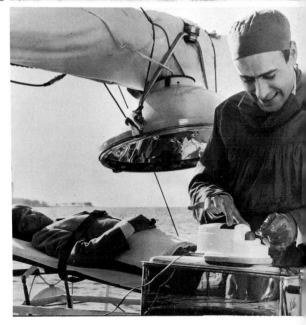

Ringo Starr, Victor Spinetti
Left: Ringo Starr. Above: The Beatles 165

HIGH WIND IN JAMAICA

(20th CENTURY-FOX) Producer, John Croydon; Director, Alexander Mackendrick; Director of Photography, Douglas Slocombe; Assistant Director, Tom Pevsner; Screenplay, Stanley Mann, Ronald Harwood, Denis Cannan; From the Novel by Richard Hughes; In CinemaScope and DeLuxe Color.

CAST

Juan Chavez	Anthony Quinn
Zac	James Coburn
Rosa	Lila Kedrova
Dutch Captain	Gert Frobe
Alberto	Benito Carruthers
Margaret	Viviane Ventura
Mr. Thornton	Nigel Davenport
Mrs. Thornton	Isabel Dean
Emily	Deborah Baxter
Captain Marpole	Kenneth J. Warren
Curtis	Brian Phelan

Lila Kedrova, James Coburn, Anthony Quinn
(also above)

Anthony Quinn, James Coburn. Above: Kenneth J. Warren, Deborah Baxter. Top: Nigel Davenport, Isabel Dean, Deborah Baxter

IL SUCCESSO

(EMBASSY) Producer, Mario Cecchi Gori; Director, Mauro Morassi; Story and Screenplay, Ettore Scola, Ruggero Maccari; Director of Photography, Alessandro D'Eva; Assistant Director, Vana Caruso; Music, Ennio Morriconi; Costumes, Ugo Pericoli; Presented by Joseph E. Levine.

CAST

Giulio Ceriani	Vittorio Gassman
Laura	Anouk Aimee
Sergio	Jean-Louis Trintignant
Grassi	Leopoldo Trieste
The Maid	Cristina Gaioni
Fascist-Capitalist	Umberto D'Orsi
Laura's Ex-fiance	Riccardo Garrone
Giulio's Father	Filippo Scelzo
Giulio's Brother-in-law	Gastone Moschin
Sergio's Girl Friend	Maria Grazia Spina
Laura's Boss	Daniele Vargas
Call Girls	Annie Gorassini, Franca Polesello

Vittorio Gassman, Anouk Aimee. Above: Gastone Moschin, Vittorio Gassman. Top: Vittorio Gassman, Filippo Scelzo

Vittorio Gassman, Cristina Gaioni. Above: Vittorio Gassman, Jean-Louis Trintignant

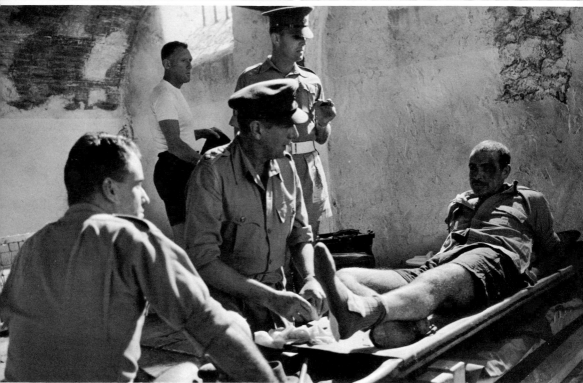

Ian Hendry, Roy Kinnear, Harry Andrews

Harry Andrews, Sean Connery. Above: Ian Bannen, Jack Watson, Ian Hendry, Michael Redgrave, Sean Connery

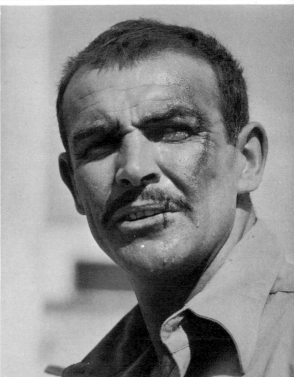

THE HILL

(M-G-M–7 ARTS) Producer, Kenneth Hyman; Director, Sidney Lumet; Screenplay, Ray Rigby; Based on Play by Ray Rigby, R. S. Allen; Director of Photography, Oswald Morris; Associate Producer, Raymond Anzarut; Assistant Directors, Frank Ernst, Pedro Vidal.

CAST

Joe Roberts	Sean Connery
Sgt/Major Wilson	Harry Andrews
Sgt. Harris	Ian Bannen
George Stevens	Alfred Lynch
Jacko King	Ossie Davis
Monty Bartlett	Roy Kinnear
Jock McGrath	Jack Watson
Medical Officer	Sir Michael Redgrave
Sgt. Williams	Ian Hendry
Commandant	Norman Bird

Sean Connery, above, and top with Harry Andrews (R), Ian Hendry (L). Left Center: Ian Hendry, Ossie Davis, Sean Connery, Jack Watson 169

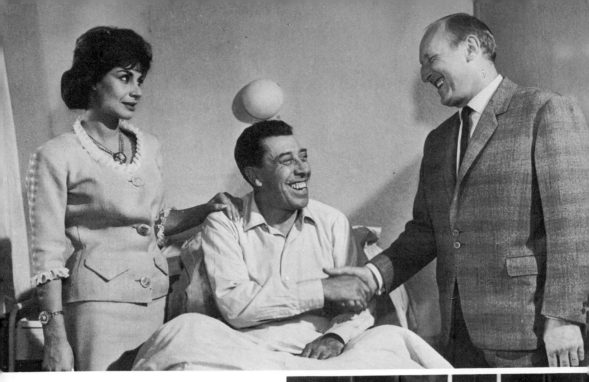

MY WIFE'S HUSBAND

(LOPERT) Producer, Robert Dorfmann; Director, Gilles Grangier; Associate Producer, Claude Haymann; Screenplay, Jean Levitt, Pierre Levy-Corti; Director of Photography, Roger Hubert; Assistant Director, Serge Piollet.

CAST

Fernand	Fernandel
Andre	Bourvil
Christiane	Claire Maurier
Me Sarrazin	Henri Vilbert
Maximin	Michel Galabru
Pellatan	Andrex
Mme. Rose	Mag Avril
Louise	Evelyne Selena
Marinette	Laurence Ligueres
The Mayor	Henri Arius
Espinasse	Gaston Rey
Carlotti	Ardisson
Gervasoni	Andre Tomasi
Gerda	Anne Marie Carriere

Fernandel, Anne Marie Carriere

Bourvil (L), (C) Claire Maurier, Fernandel, and also at top. Above: Claire Maurier, Fernandel

THE IPCRESS FILE

(UNIVERSAL) Producer, Harry Saltzman; Director, Sidney J. Furie; Executive Producer, Charles Kasher; Assistant Director, Fred Slark; Associate Producer, Ronald Kinnoch; Screenplay, Bill Canaway, James Doran; From Novel by Len Deighton; Music, John Barry; Director of Photography, Otto Heller; In Techniscope and Technicolor.

CAST

Harry Palmer	Michael Caine
Dalby	Nigel Green
Ross	Guy Doleman
Jean	Sue Lloyd
Carswell	Gordon Jackson
Radcliffe	Aubrey Richards
Bluejay	Frank Gatliff
Barney	Thomas Baptiste
Housemartin	Oliver MacGreevy
Alice	Freda Bamford
Charlady	Pauline Winter
Edwards	Anthony Blackshaw
Gray	Barry Raymond
Chilcott-Oakes	David Glover
Inspector Keightley	Stanley Meadows
Sir Robert	Peter Ashmore
Raid Inspector	Michael Murray
Raid Sergeant	Anthony Baird
O.N.I. Man	Tony Caunter
Taylor	Charles Rea
Records Officer	Ric Hutton
Murray	Douglas Blackwell
Operator	Richard Burrell
Police Station Sergeant	Glynn Edwards
Prison Doctor	Zsolt Vadaszffy
Prison Guards	Joseph Behrmann, Max Faulkner, Paul S. Chapman

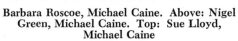

Barbara Roscoe, Michael Caine. Above: Nigel Green, Michael Caine. Top: Sue Lloyd, Michael Caine

Michael Caine

172　　　Charlton Heston (also top). Above:
　　　　 Harry Andrews, Rex Harrison

Charlton Heston, Diane Cilento. Above:
Charlton Heston, and top with Rex Harrison

THE AGONY AND THE ECSTASY

(20th CENTURY-FOX) Director, Carol Reed; Screen Story and Screenplay, Philip Dunne; Based on Novel by Irving Stone; Music, Alex North; Director of Photography, Leon Shamroy; Assistant Director, Gus Agosti; Costumes, Vittorio Nino Novarese; In Todd-AO(R) and DeLuxe Color.

CAST

Michelangelo	Charlton Heston
Pope Julius II	Rex Harrison
Contessina de'Medici	Diane Cilento
Bramante	Harry Andrews
Duke of Urbino	Alberto Lupo
Giovanni de'Medici	Adolfo Celi
Paris DeGrassis	Venantino Venantini
Sangallo	John Stacy
Foreman	Fausto Tozzi
Woman	Maxine Audley
Raphael	Tomas Milian

Charlton Heston, Rex Harrison (also left). Above: Charlton Heston, Diane Cilento. Top: (L) Sistine Chapel, (R) Rex Harrison

Charlton Heston, Rex Harrison (also above)
in
"THE AGONY AND THE ECSTASY"

WEEKEND AT DUNKIRK

(20th CENTURY-FOX) Producers, Robert and Raymond Hakim; Director, Henri Verneuil; Based on Novel by Robert Merle; Adapted by Francois Boyer; Music, Maurice Jarre; Director of Photography, Henri Decae; Assistant Director, Claude Pinoteau; Costumes, Jean and Leon Zay; In DeLuxe Color.

CAST
Maillat	Jean-Paul Belmondo
Jeanne	Catherine Spaak
Pinot	Georges Geret
Pierson	Jean-Pierre Marielle
Dhery	Pierre Mondy
Helene	Marie Dubois
Alexandre	Francois Perier
Atkins	Kenneth Haigh
Robinson	Ronald Howard
Burnt Man	Nigel Stock
Virrel	Albert Remy
Lieutenant	Francois Guerin
Blackguard	J. P. Roussillon
Cirilli	Michel Barbey
Giant	Christian Barbier
Happy Undertaker	Pierre Vernier
Infantryman	Raoul Delfosse
Antoinette	Marie-France Mignal

and Rolf Spath, Gerard Darrieu, Robert Deslandes, Julien Verdier, Dominique Zardi, Alan Adair, Donald O'Brien, Anthony Stuart, Robert Napier, Rene Panetra, Paul Preboist, Robert Rollins, Charles Bouillaud

Left and above: Jean-Paul Belmondo

Jean-Paul Belmondo

Catherine Spaak, Jean-Paul Belmondo. Above: Francois Perier, Jean-Paul Belmondo

175

CHRONICLE OF A SUMMER

(PATHE CONTEMPORARY) Producers, Anatole Dauman, Philippe Lipchitz; Directors, Jean Rouch, Edgar Morin; Photographers, Roger Marillere, Raoul Coutard, Jean-Jacques Torbes, Michel Brault; Assistant Directors, Claude Beausoleil, Louis Boucher; An Argos Film.

CAST

Main Participants⸺ Jean Rouch, Edgar Morin,
  Marceline, Angelo, Marilou, Jean-Pierre
Factory Workers⸺⸺⸺⸺⸺⸺⸺ Jean, Jacques
Students⸺⸺⸺⸺⸺⸺⸺ Regis, Celine, Jean-Marc,
  Nadine, Landry, Raymond
Office Workers⸺⸺⸺⸺⸺⸺⸺ Jacques, Simone
Artists⸺⸺⸺⸺⸺⸺⸺ Henri, Madi, Catherine
Model ⸺⸺⸺⸺⸺⸺⸺⸺⸺⸺⸺ Sophie

Sophie. Above: Angelo, Landry. Top: (L) Jean-Pierre, Marceline. (R) Two Parisian Students

Julie Christie, Dirk Bogarde
in
"DARLING"

DARLING

(EMBASSY) Producer, Joseph Janni; Associate Producer, Victor Lyndon; Director, John Schlesinger; Screenplay, Frederic Raphael; Music, John Dankworth; Director of Photography, Kenneth Higgins; Costumes, Julie Harris; Presented by Joseph E. Levine.

CAST

Miles Brand	Laurence Harvey
Robert Gold	Dirk Bogarde
Diana Scott	Julie Christie
Malcom	Roland Curram
Cesare	Jose Luis De Vilallonga
Sean Martin	Alex Scott
Alec Prosser-Jones	Basil Henson
Felicity Prosser-Jones	Helen Lindsay
Estette Gold	Pauline Yates
William Prosser-Jones	Tyler Butterworth
Lord Grant	Peter Bayliss
Kurt	Ernst Walder
Allie	Lucille Soong
Gillian	Sidonie Bond
Gerhard	John G. Heller
Basildon	James Cossins
Lady Brentwood	Lydia Sherwood
Carlotta Hale	Georgina Cookson
Willett	Brian Wilde
Charles Glass	David Harrison
Mrs. Glass	Irene Richmond
Sybil	Ann Firbank
Rupert Crabtree	Richard Bidlake

and Angus MacKay, Margaret Gordon, Trevor Bowen, Jane Downes, Carlo Palmucci, Dante Posani, Umberto Raho, Helen Stirling

Julie Christie, Tyler Butterworth
Above: Julie Christie

Julie Christie, Laurence Harvey

Julie Christie, Ann Firbank, Alex Scott. Above: Julie Christie, Roland Curram

Laurence Harvey, Julie Christie. Above: Julie Christie, Jose Luis De Vilallonga. Top: Julie Christie, Dirk Bogarde

NOT ON YOUR LIFE
(El Verdugo)

(PATHE CONTEMPORARY) Director, Luis Berlanga; Screenplay, Luis Berlanga, Rafael Azcona, Ennio Flaiano; Story, Luis Berlanga; Music, Miguel Asins Arbo; Director of Photography, Tonino Delli Colli; A Naga Films S.A.-Zebra Films Co-Production.

CAST

Jose Luis	Nino Manfredi
Carmen	Emma Penella
Amedeo	Jose Isbert
Antonio	Jose Luis Lopez Vazquez
Alvarez	Angel Alvarez
Prison Warden	Guido Alberti
Estefania	Maria Luisa Ponte
Ignacia	Maruja Isbert

Emma Penella, Nino Manfredi, Jose Isbert, and top. Above: Nino Manfredi with Angel Alvarez (R) and Emma Penella (L)

Robert Redford, Michael Connors, Alec Guinness
(also at top). Above: Alec Guinness. Right:
Michael Connors, Robert Redford

SITUATION HOPELESS—
BUT NOT SERIOUS

(PARAMOUNT) Producer-Director, Gottfried
Reinhardt; Screenplay, Silvia Reinhardt; Adap-
tation, Jan Lustig; Based on Novel "The Hiding
Place" by Robert Shaw; Director of Photog-
raphy, Kurt Hasse; Costumes, Ilse Dubois;
Assistant Producer, Jose de Villaverde; Assist-
ant Director, Henry Sokal; Music, Harold
Byrns.

CAST

Herr Frick	Alec Guinness
Lucky	Michael Connors
Hank	Robert Redford
Edeitraud	Anita Hoefer
Lissie	Mady Rahl
Herr Neusel	Paul Dahlke
QM Master Sergeant	Frank Wolff
Sergeant	John Briley
Wanda	Elisabeth Von Molo
Senta	Carola Regnier

CIRCLE OF LOVE

(WALTER READE-STERLING) Director, Roger Vadim; Screenplay by Jean Anouilh from Arthur Schnitzler's Play "Reigen"; Music, Michel Magne; Costumes, Marc Doelnitz; A Robert and Raymond Hakim Production in Eastman Color.

CAST

The Wife	Jane Fonda
The Husband	Maurice Ronet
The Count	Jean Sorel
The Young Girl	Catherine Spaak
The Chambermaid	Anna Karina
The Young Gentleman	Jean-Claude Brialy
The Actress	Francine Berg
The Author	Bernard Noel
The Prostitute	Marie Dubois
The Soldier	Claude Giraud

Jane Fonda, Jean-Claude Brialy (also above),
Top: Jean-Claude Brialy, Anna Karina

Jean Sorel, Marie Dubois. Above: Jean Sorel,
Francine Berg. Top: Marie Dubois, Claude Giraud
Below: Maurice Ronet, Catherine Spaak

Richard Burton
in
"THE SPY WHO CAME IN FROM THE COLD"

Sam Wanamaker

George Voskovec

Oskar Werner

Claire Bloom

Robert Hardy

Cyril Cusack

Sam Wanamaker, Richard Burton. Above: Robert
Hardy, Michael Hordern, Richard Burton
Right: Claire Bloom, Richard Burton

THE SPY WHO CAME IN FROM THE COLD

(PARAMOUNT) Producer-Director, Martin Ritt;
Director of Photography, Oswald Morris; Screen-
play, Paul Dehn, Guy Trosper; Based on Novel
by John LeCarré; Assistant Director, Colin
Brewer; Costumes, Motley; Music, Sol Kaplan;
A Salem Films Production.

CAST

Alec Leamas	Richard Burton
Nan Perry	Claire Bloom
Fiedler	Oskar Werner
Hans-Dieter Mundt	Peter Van Eyck
Peters	Sam Wanamaker
East German Defense Attorney	George Voskovec
Smiley	Rupert Davies
Control	Cyril Cusack
Ashe	Michael Hordern
Carlton	Robert Hardy
Patmore	Bernard Lee
President of Tribunal	Beatrix Lehmann
Old Judge	Esmond Knight
Holten	Walter Gotel
C.I.A. Agent	Tom Stern
German Guards	Niall MacGinnis, George Mikell
German Guide	Scott Finch
Stripper	Kathy Keeton
Mr. Pitt	Richard Caldicot
Frau Floerdke	Marianne Deeming
Lofthouse	Michael Ripper
Passport Officer	Henk Mobenberg
Vopo Captain	Richard Marner
Young Judge	David Bauer
Security Officer	Michael Ritterman
Man in Shop	Edward Harvey
Mrs. Zanfrello	Nancy Nevinson
Mr. Zanfrello	Warren Mitchell
Miss Crail	Anne Blake

Michael Hordern, Richard Burton. Above: Richard
Burton, Oskar Werner. Top: Oskar Werner,
Michael Ritterman, Richard Burton,
Peter Van Eyck

Richard Burton, Claire Bloom (also above). Top:
Richard Burton (C), Peter Van Eyck (R)

VARIETY LIGHTS
(Luci del Varieta)

(PATHE CONTEMPORARY) Produced and Directed by Alberto Lattuada and Federico Fellini; Screenplay, Federico Fellini, Ennio Flaiano, Alberto Lattuada, Tullio Pinelli; Story, Federico Fellini; Music, Felice Lattuada; Director of Photography, Otello Martelli; A Capitolium Production.

CAST

Checco Dal Monte	Peppino De Filippo
Liliana	Carla Del Poggio
Melina Amour	Giulietta Masina
Adelmo Conti	Folco Lulli
Johnny	John Kitzmiller
Remo	Dante Maggio
La Rosa	Carlo Romano
Valeria del Sole	Gina Mascetti
Theatre Owner	Checco Durante
Bill	Joe Falletta
Melina's Father	Enrico Piergentili
Maestro	Mario De Angelis
Soubrette	Fanny Marchio
Duke	Giacomo Furia
Journalist	Silvio Bagolini
Gypsy Singer	Vanja Orico

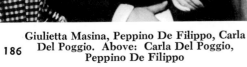

186 Giulietta Masina, Peppino De Filippo, Carla Del Poggio. Above: Carla Del Poggio, Peppino De Filippo

Giulio Cali, Giulietta Masina, Peppino De Filippo Gina Mascetti, Dante Maggio. Above: Peppino De Filippo, Giulietta Masina

THE OVERCOAT

(CINEMASTERS INTERNATIONAL) Director, Alexi Batalov; Screenplay, L. Solovyov; Based on Story by Nicolai Gogol; Director of Photography, G. Marandjyan; Music, N. Sidelnikov; A Lenfilm Studios Production.

CAST

Akaky Akakyevich	Roland Bykov
Petrovich	Y. Tolubeyev
Petrovich's Wife	A. Yezhkina
Landlady	Y. Ponsova

A. Yezhkina, Y. Ponsova, Y. Tolubeyev, Roland Bykov. Above, Left, and Top: Roland Bykov

Rudolf Nureyev, Margot Fonteyn
in
"LE CORSAIRE"

AN EVENING WITH THE ROYAL BALLET

(SIGMA III) Producer, Anthony Havelock-Allan;
Directors, Anthony Asquith, Anthony Havelock-Allan; An A.B.H.E. Production in Technicolor.

CAST
Margot Fonteyn   Rudolf Nureyev
and The Royal Ballet Company

PROGRAM
"La Valse," "Les Sylphides," "Le Corsaire,"
"The Sleeping Beauty" (Act III).

Rudolf Nureyev in "Les Sylphides"
Above: "La Valse"

Margot Fonteyn in "Les Sylphides"
Above: "The Sleeping Beauty." Top:
"Le Corsaire"

DIE! DIE! MY DARLING!

(COLUMBIA) Producer, Anthony Hinds; Director, Silvio Narizzano; Screenplay, Richard Matheson; Based on Novel "Nightmare" by Anne Blaisdell; Director of Photography, Arthur Ibbetson; Music, Wilfred Josephs; Assistant Director, Claude Watson; A Hammer Film Production.

CAST

Mrs. Trefoile	Tallulah Bankhead
Pat Carroll	Stefanie Powers
Harry	Peter Vaughan
Alan Glentower	Maurice Kaufmann
Anna	Yootha Joyce
Joseph	Donald Sutherland
Gloria	Gwendolyn Watts
Ormsby	Robert Dorning
Oscar	Philip Gilbert
Shopkeeper	Winifred Dennis
Woman Shopper	Diana King

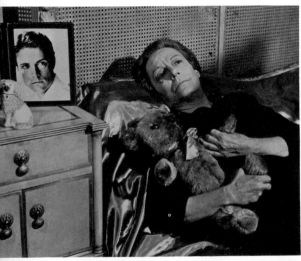

Yootha Joyce, Stefanie Powers, Tallulah Bankhead (also above)

Donald Sutherland, Maurice Kaufmann, Yootha Joyce. Above: Tallulah Bankhead, Stefanie Powers. Top: Stefanie Powers, Donald Sutherland, Tallulah Bankhead, Yootha Joyce, Peter Vaughan

Tom Adams, Karel Stepanek, and also top with
Veronica Hurst. Above: Carol Blake, Tom Adams
Right: Tom Adams

THE SECOND BEST SECRET AGENT IN THE WHOLE WIDE WORLD

(EMBASSY) Executive Producer, S. J. H. Ward; Director, Lindsay Shonteff; Screenplay, Howard Griffiths, Lindsay Shonteff; Music, Bertram Chappell; Director of Photography, Terry Maher; Assistant Director, Ernie Lewis; Presented by Joseph E. Levine; In Pathe Color.

CAST

Charles Vine	Tom Adams
Henrik Jacobsen	Karel Stepanek
Julia Lindberg	Veronica Hurst
Masterman	Peter Bull
Rockwell	John Arnatt
Walter Pickering	Francis DeWolff
Tetchinov	Felix Felton
Russian Commissar	George Pastell
Computer Center Girl	Judy Huxtable
Army Officer	Gary Hope
Maltby	Denis Holmes
Wilson	Billy Milton
"Crossword Puzzle" Girl	Carole Blake
Sadistikov	Tony Wall
Russian Commissar	Oliver MacGreevy
Police Inspector	Stuart Saunders
Vladimir Sheehee	Paul Tann
Governess	Shelagh Booth
"Killer"	John Evitts
August Jacobsen	Robert Marsden

and Mona Chong, Michael Godfrey, Julian Strange, Claire Gordon, J. B. Dubin-Behrmann, Sarah Maddern

James Villiers, Bette Davis, William Dix. Above:
Wendy Craig, Bette Davis. Top: Bette Davis

192

Jill Bennett, Bette Davis, William Dix. Above:
Bette Davis, William Dix, Jack Watling. Top:
William Dix, Wendy Craig, Bette Davis

THE NANNY

(20th CENTURY-FOX) Producer, Jimmy Sangster; Director, Seth Holt; Screenplay, Jimmy Sangster; Based on Novel by Evelyn Piper; Director of Photography, Harry Waxman; Assistant Director, Christopher Dryhurst; Music, Richard Rodney Bennett; A Seven Arts-Hammer Film Production.

CAST

Nanny	Bette Davis
Virgie	Wendy Craig
Pen	Jill Bennett
Bill	James Villiers
Joey	William Dix
Bobby	Pamela Franklin
Dr. Medman	Jack Watling
Dr. Beamaster	Maurice Denham
Dr. Wills	Alfred Burke
Mrs. Griggs	Nora Gordon
Sarah	Sandra Power
Milkman	Harry Fowler
Susay	Angharad Aubrey

Bette Davis, Wendy Craig, and above with William Dix

Bette Davis, Jill Bennett. Top: Bette Davis, William Dix

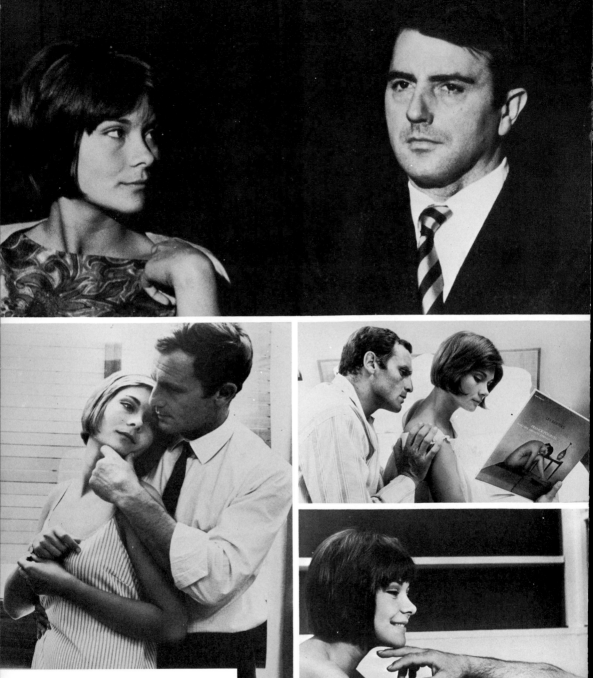

THE MARRIED WOMAN

(ROYAL FILMS INTERNATIONAL) Produced,
Directed and Written by Jean-Luc Godard;
Director of Photography, Paoul Coutard; In
French with English subtitles.

CAST
Charlotte	Macha Meril
The Lover	Bernard Noel
The Husband	Philippe Leroy

Macha Meril, above and left with Philippe
Leroy, and top with Bernard Noel

THE LEATHER BOYS

(ALLIED ARTISTS) Producer, Raymond Stross; Director, Sidney J. Furie; Screenplay, Gillian Freeman; Based on Novel by Eliot George; Assistant Director, Roy Baird; Music, Bill McGuffie; Director of Photography, Gerald Gibbs; In CinemaScope; Presented by R. Lee Platt Associates.

CAST

Dot	Rita Tushingham
Reggie	Colin Campbell
Pete	Dudley Sutton
Gran	Gladys Henson
Reggie's Mother	Avice Landon
Reggie's Father	Lockwood West
Dot's Mother	Betty Marsden
Uncle Arthur	Martin Mathews
Boy Friend	Johnny Briggs
Les	James Chase
Mr. Lunnis	Geoffrey Dunn
Mrs. Stanley	Dandy Nicholls
Brenda	Valerie Varnam
June	Jill Meredith
Receptionist	Elizabeth Begley
Man-in-jeans	Brian Phelan
Merchant Seaman	Oliver MacGreevy
School Teacher	Sylvia Kaye

and Sandra Caron, Tracey Rogers, Carmel McSharry, Joyce Henson

Rita Tushingham, Dudley Sutton, Colin Campbell
Above: Rita Tushingham, Colin Campbell,
Avice Landon. Top: (L & R) Rita Tushingham,
Colin Campbell

Laurence Olivier
in
"OTHELLO"

OTHELLO

(WARNER BROS.) Producers, Anthony Have-lock-Allan, John Brabourne; Directed for Screen by Stuart Burge, based on National Theatre Production Staging by John Dexter; Based on Play by William Shakespeare; Director of Photography, Geoffrey Unsworth; Music, Richard Hampton; A B.H.E. Production in Panavision and Technicolor.

CAST

Othello	Laurence Olivier
Iago	Frank Finlay
Desdemona	Maggie Smith
Emilia	Joyce Redman
Cassio	Derek Jacobi
Roderigo	Robert Lang
Brabantio	Anthony Nicholls
Duke of Venice	Harry Lomax
Bianca	Sheila Reid
Gratiano	Michael Turner
Lodovico	Kenneth Mackintosh
Montano	Edward Hardwicke
Clown	Roy Holder
Senate Officers	David Hargreaves, Malcolm Terris
Duke's Officer	Terence Knapp
Senator	Keith Marsh
Sailor	Tom Kempinski
Messenger	Nicholas Edmett
Cypriot Officers	William Hobbs, Trevor Martin

Right: Laurence Olivier, Maggie Smith

Laurence Olivier, Maggie Smith, Joyce Redman
Above: Joyce Redman, Maggie Smith, Frank Finlay

Frank Finlay, Laurence Olivier. Above: Laurence Olivier, Anthony Nicholls, Maggie Smith

VIVA MARIA

(UNITED ARTISTS) Producers, Louis Malle, Oscar Dancigers; Director, Louis Malle; Screenplay, Louis Malle, Jean-Claude Carriere; Director of Photography, Henri Decae; Assistant Directors, Volker Schloendorf, Jean Luis Bunuel; Costumes, Ghislain Uhry; Music, Georges Delerue; A Franco-Italian Co-Production in Panavision and EastmanColor.

CAST

Maria II	Brigitte Bardot
Maria I	Jeanne Moreau
Flores	George Hamilton
Diogene	Gregor Von Rezzori
Madam Diogene	Paulette Dubost
Rodolfo	Claudio Brook
Rodriguez	Carlos Lopez Moctezuma
Werther	Poldo Bendandi
Father Superior	Francisco Reiguera
Juanito	Jonathan Eden
Janine	Adriana Roel
Don Alvaro	Jose Baviera
El Presidente	Jose Angel Espinoza (Ferresquilla)
Father of Maria II	Fernando Wagner
The "Turcos"	Jose Luis Campa, Roberto Campa, Eduardo Murillo, Jose Esqueda

Paulette Dubost, Jeanne Moreau, Brigitte Bardot, Claudio Brook, Poldo Bendandi. Above: Jeanne Moreau, Brigitte Bardot, Poldo Bendandi. Left and Top: Brigitte Bardot, Jeanne Moreau

Jeanne Moreau, Claudio Brook, Brigitte Bardot
Above: George Hamilton, Jeanne Moreau
(also at top)

Jeanne Moreau, Brigitte Bardot. Above: Brigitte
Bardot, Claudio Brook. Top: Brigitte Bardot

Laurence Harvey, Jean Simmons, And top with
Paul A. Martin, Ambrosine Phillpotts,
Donald Wolfit

200

Jean Simmons (L), Michael Craig (R). Above: Jean
Simmons, Paul A. Martin, Laurence Harvey. Top:
Robert Morley, Laurence Harvey. Below: Donald
Wolfit, Jean Simmons, Ambrosine Phillpotts

LIFE AT THE TOP

(COLUMBIA) Producer, James Woolf; Director, Ted Kotcheff; Screenplay, Mordecai Richler; Based on Novel by John Barine; Director of Photography, Oswald Morris; Assistant Director, Kip Gowans; Music, Richard Addinsell; A Romulus Production.

CAST

Joe Lampton	Laurence Harvey
Norah Hausley	Honor Blackman
Susan Lampton	Jean Simmons
Mark	Michael Craig
Abe Brown	Donald Wolfit
Tiffield	Robert Morley
Sybil	Margaret Johnston
Mrs. Brown	Ambrosine Phillpotts
George Aisgill	Allan Cuthbertson
Harry	Paul A. Martin
Barbara	Frances Cosslet
Hethersett	Ian Shand
Graffham	George A. Cooper
Mottram	Nigel Davenport
McLelland	Andrew Laurence
Psychologist	Geoffrey Bayldon
Ben	Dennis Quilley
Tim	David Oxley
Oscar	David McKail
Keatley	Paul Whitsun Jones
Wincastle	Charles Lamb
Newspaper Boy	Michael Newport
Doctor	Richard Leech
Stripper	Ingrid Anthofer

Laurence Harvey, Honor Blackman. Above: Donald Wolfit, Laurence Harvey

Honor Blackman, Laurence Harvey. Top: Jean Simmons, Laurence Harvey

201

SANDS OF THE KALAHARI

(PARAMOUNT) Co-Producers, Cy Endfield,
Stanley Baker; Associate Producer, Bob Porter;
Director, Cy Endfield; Screenplay, Cy Endfield;
Based on Novel by William Mulvihill; Director
of Photography, Erwin Hillier; Assistant Direc-
tor, Jack Causey; Costumes, James Smith; Music,
John Dankworth; In Panavision and Techni-
color.

CAST

O'Brien	Stuart Whitman
Bain	Stanley Baker
Grace	Susannah York
Grimmelman	Harry Andrews
Bondarahkai	Theodore Bikel
Sturdevant	Nigel Davenport

Top: Stanley Baker, Susannah York, Harry
Andrews, Theodore Bikel. Below: Theodore Bikel,
Susannah York, Nigel Davenport

Susannah York, Stuart Whitman (both above),
Stanley Baker, and left with Nigel Davenport

HEROES OF TELEMARK

(COLUMBIA) Producer, S. Benjamin Fisz; Director, Anthony Mann; Screenplay, Ivan Moffat; Based on "Skis Against The Atom" by Knut Hauklid, and "But For These Men" by John Drummond; Director of Photography, Robert Krasker; Assistant Director, Derek Cracknell; A Benton Film Production in Panavision and ColumbiaColor.

CAST

Dr. Rolf Pedersen	Kirk Douglas
Knut Straud	Richard Harris
Uncle	Michael Redgrave
Anna	Ulla Jacobsson
Jensen	Roy Dotrice
Terboven	Eric Porter
Major Frick	Anton Diffring
Col. Wilkinson	Mervyn Johns
Prof. Logan	Barry Jones
Gen. Bolts	Geoffrey Keen
Sigrid	Jennifer Hilary
Nilssen	Ralph Michael
Arne	David Weston
Claus	William Marlowe
Oli	Alan Howard
Freddy	John Golightly
Gunnar	Sebastian Breaks
Henrik	Patrick Jordan
Einar	Brook Williams
Hartmuller	Karel Stepanek

and Gerard Heinz, George Murcell, Victor Beaumont, Wolf Frees, Russell Waters, Elvi Hale, Maurice Denham, Jan Conrad, Faith Brook, Alf Joint, Robert Ayres, Robert Bruce, David Davies, Brian Jackson, Paul Hansard, Annette Andre, Pamela Conway, Grace Arnold, Howard Douglas, Philo Hauser, Jemma Hyde, Terry Plummer, Joe Powell

Kirk Douglas, Ulla Jacobsson, Richard Harris, also Top and above with Michael Redgrave

Ulla Jacobsson, Kirk Douglas, Richard Harris
Above: Jennifer Hilary, Richard Harris

Alec Guinness   Maria Martin   Rod Steiger   Ralph Richardson Siobhan McKenna   Tom Courtenay

Rod Steiger, Julie Christie, Omar Sharif (also above). Top: Julie Christie, Omar Sharif Below: Virgilio Texeira

Rita Tushingham, Alec Guinness. Above: Adrienne Corri, Rod Steiger, Maria Martin. Top: Ralph Richardson, Mercedes Ruiz, Siobhan McKenna, Tarek Sharif

DOCTOR ZHIVAGO

(M-G-M) Producer, Carlo Ponti; Director, David Lean; Screenplay, Robert Bolt; From Novel by Boris Pasternak; Director of Photography, Fred A. Young; Music, Maurice Jarre; Executive Producer, Arvid L. Griffen; Assistant Directors, Roy Stevens, Pedro Vidal, Jose Maria Ochoa; Costumes, Phyllis Dalton; In Panavision and Color.

CAST

Tonya	Geraldine Chaplin
Lara	Julie Christie
Pasha	Tom Courtenay
Yevgraf	Alec Guinness
Anna	Siobhan McKenna
Alexander	Ralph Richardson
Yuri	Omar Sharif
Komarovsky	Rod Steiger
The Girl	Rita Tushingham
Amelia	Adrienne Corri
Prof. Kurt	Geoffrey Keen
Sasha	Jeffrey Rockland
Katya	Lucy Westmore
Razin	Noel Willman
Liberius	Gerard Tichy
Kostoyed	Klaus Kinski
Petya	Jack MacGowran
Gentlewoman	Maria Martin
Yuri (at 8)	Tarek Sharif
Tonya (at 7)	Mercedes Ruiz
Colonel	Roger Maxwell
Major	Inigo Jackson
Captain	Virgilio Texeira
Bolshevik	Bernard Kay
Old Soldier	Eric Chitty
Priest	Jose Nieto
Young Engineer	Mark Eden
Mr. Sventytski	Emilio Carrer
David	Gerhard Jersch
Comrade Yelkin	Wolf Frees
Comrade Kaprugina	Gwen Nelson
Militiaman	Jose Caffarel
Streetwalker	Brigitte Trace
Mrs. Sventytski	Luana Alcaniz
Raddled Woman	Lili Murati
Raped Woman	Catherine Ellison
Demented Woman	Maria Vico
Dragoon Colonel	Dodo Assad Bahador

Geraldine Chaplin   Omar Sharif   Julie Christie

Geraldine Chaplin, Jeffrey Rockland, Omar Sharif, Jack MacGowran, Ralph Richardson. Above: Julie Christie, Tom Courtenay, Rod Steiger, Omar Sharif

Omar Sharif, Julie Christie, Rod Steiger
Top: Geraldine Chaplin, Omar Sharif

Geraldine Chaplin, Omar Sharif, also at top,
and above with Geoffrey Keen

Julie Christie, Omar Sharif, and at top
Above: Omar Sharif, Siobhan McKenna

in "DOCTOR ZHIVAGO"

THE TENTH VICTIM

(EMBASSY) Producer, Carlo Ponti; Director, Elio Petri; Executive Producer, Joseph E. Levine; Screenplay, Elio Petri, Ennio Flaiano, Tonino Guerra, Giorgio Salvione; Based on Novel by Robert Sheckley; Director of Photography, Gianni Di Venanzo; Assistant Director, Berto Pelosso; Costumes, Giulio Coltellacci; Music, Piero Piccioni; Choreographer, Gino Landi; In Wide-Screen and Color.

CAST

Marcello Polletti	Marcello Mastroianni
Caroline Meredith	Ursula Andress
Olga	Elsa Martinelli
Professor	Salvo Randone
Lawyer	Massimo Serato
The Victim	Evi Rigano
Rudi	Milo Quesada
Lidia	Luce Bonifassy
Relaxatorium Girl	Anita Sanders
Chet	Mickey Knox
Cole	Richard Armstrong
Martin	Walter Williams
Chinese Assailant	George Wang

Marcello Mastroianni, Elsa Martinelli. Above and Top: Marcello Mastroianni, Ursula Andress

Ursula Andress, George Wang. Above: Marcello Mastroianni, Ursula Andress

HOW <u>NOT</u> TO ROB A DEPARTMENT STORE

(ARTIXO) Producer-Director, Pierre Grimblat; Based on Novel by Clarence Weff; Adaptation and Dialogue, Clarence Weff, Pierre Grimblat; Music, Georges Garvarentz; Director of Photography, Michel Kelber; Assistant Directors, Michel Pezin, Francis Girod; Production Director, Julien Riviere; Associate Producer, Mario Chabert; Presented by Artie Shaw; A French-Italian Co-Production with English subtitles.

CAST

Marcel	Jean-Claude Brialy
Ida	Marie Laforet
Moune	Sophie Daumier
Justin	Jean-Pierre Marielle
Meloune	Michel Serrault
Leon	Daniel Ceccaldi
Etienne	Albert Remy
Raf	Pierre Clementi
Curly	Roland Blanche
Charles	Renaud Verlay
Limonade	Madeleine Barbulee
Palmoni	Robert Manuel
Shopkeeper	Rene Genin
His Wife	Gabrielle Doulcet
The Cousin	Paul Preboist
Poulaine	Dominique Davray
Zecca	Philippe Brizard
Store Manager	J. P. Rambal
Brigadier	Roger Trapp
Cop	Bernard Fresson

Roland Blanche, Renaud Verlay, Pierre Clementi
Above: Jean-Pierre Marielle, Michel Serrault
Top: (L) Gabrielle Doulcet, Sophie Daumier, Pierre Clementi, (R) Marie Laforet, Jean-Claude Brialy, Michel Serrault, Jean-Pierre Marielle
Left: Jean-Pierre Marielle, Marie Laforet

Sean Connery
in
"THUNDERBALL"

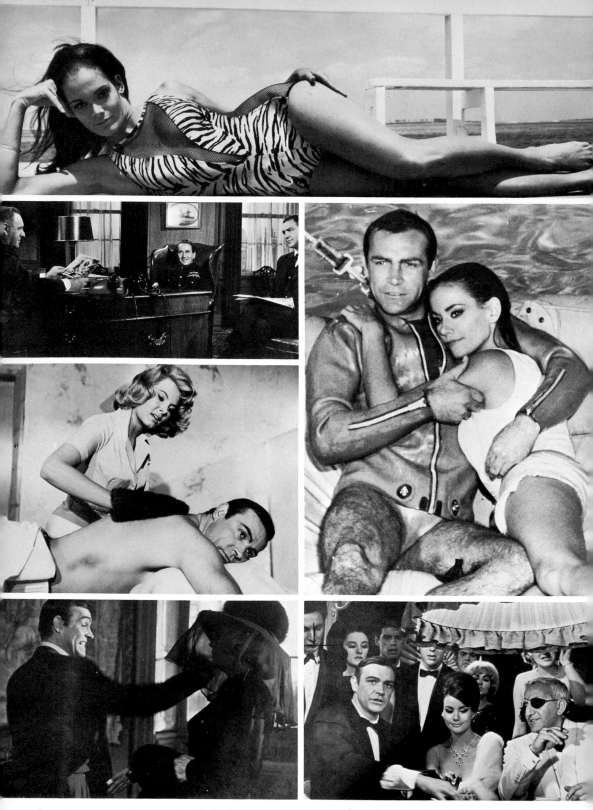

Sean Connery, and above with Molly Peters

Sean Connery, Claudine Auger (both above),
Adolfo Celi. Top: Martine Beswick. Below Left:
Bernard Lee, Roland Culver, Sean Connery

THUNDERBALL

(UNITED ARTISTS) Producer, Kevin McClory; Director, Terence Young; Director of Photography, Ted Moore; Screenplay, Richard Maibaum, John Hopkins; Based on Story by Kevin McClory, Jack Whittingham, Ian Fleming; Assistant Director, Gus Agosti; Costumes, Anthony Mendleson; Music, John Barry; Title Song lyrics by Don Black; Sung by Tom Jones; Presented by Albert R. Broccoli, Harry Saltzman; In Panavision and Technicolor.

CAST

James Bond	Sean Connery
Domino	Claudine Auger
Emilio Largo	Adolfo Celi
Fiona	Luciana Paluzzi
Felix Leiter	Rik Van Nutter
"M"	Bernard Lee
Paula	Martine Beswick
Count Lippe	Guy Doleman
Patricia	Molly Peters
"Q"	Desmond Llewelyn
Moneypenny	Lois Maxwell
Foreign Secretary	Roland Culver
Pinder	Earl Cameron
Major Derval	Paul Stassino
Madame Boitier	Rose Alba
Vargas	Philip Locke
Kutze	George Pravda
Janni	Michael Brennan
Group Captain	Leonard Sachs
Air Vice Marshal	Edward Underdown
Kenniston	Reginald Beckwith
Quist	Bill Cummings
Mlle. La Porte	Maryse Guy Mitsouko
Jacques Boiter	Bob Simmons

Sean Connery, Luciana Paluzzi
Above: Claudine Auger

Sean Connery, Adolfo Celi. Top:
Rik Van Nutter, Sean Connery

Simone Signoret, Marcello Mastroianni (L)
in "Love A La Carte"

Topol (L) in "Sallah"

LOVE A LA CARTE (Promenade) Producer, Moris Ergas; Director, Antonio Pietrangeli; A Zebra Films Production. CAST: Simone Signoret, Marcello Mastroianni, Sandra Milo, Emmanuelle Riva, Gina Rovere, Claudio Gora, Gianrico Tedeschi, Ivo Garrani, Domenico Modugno.

THE MAGNIFICENT CUCKOLD (Walter Reade-Sterling) Director, Antonio Pietrangeli; Screenplay, Diego Fabbri, Ruggero Maccari, Ettore Scola, Stefano Strucchi; Adapted from Play by Fernand Crommelynck; Director of Photography, Armando Nannuzzi; Costumes, Maurizio Chiari; Music, Armando Travajoli; Produced by Alfonso Sansone and Henryk Chroscicki for Sancro Film and Les Films Copernic. CAST: Claudia Cardinale, Ugo Tognazzi, Bernard Blier, Michele Girardon, Salvo Randone, Jose Luis de Villalonga, Gian Maria Volonte, Paul Guers, Philippe Nicaud, Suzy Andersen.

MALAMONDO (Magna) Producer, Goffredo Lombardo; Director, Paolo Cavara; Music, Ennio Morricone; "Funny World" sung by Catherine Spaak and Jane Morgan; English Version Adapted and Directed by Jack Lewis; "Sad Saturday Night" sung by Adriano Celentano; Director of Photography, Ennio Guarnieri, Marvin Miller; Narrator, Marvin Miller; In Eastman Color; Presented by Marshall Naify. A cinematic probe into the lives of today's youth.

THE BLACK DUKE (Eldorado) Producer, Tullio Bruschi; Director, Pino Mercanti; In Wide Screen and Eastman Color; Presented in Association with East/West Films. CAST: Cameron Mitchell, Gloria Milland, Conrado Sanmartin, Franco Fantasia, Robert Dean, Dina de Santis, Grazia Maria Spina.

THE EYE OF THE NEEDLE (Eldorado) Director, Marcello Andrei; Screenplay, G. Mangione, A. Vevilacqua, T. Dembi, M. Andrei; Story, G. Berto, D. Troisi; Music, Carlo Rustichelli; Director of Photography, Riccardo Pallottini; A Co-Production of MEC Cinematografica and Les Films Agiman. CAST: Vittorio Gassman, Annette Stroyberg, Gerard Blain, Nino Castelnuovo, Gino Cervi, Mariangela Giordano, Ernesto Calindri, Leopoldo Trieste, Umberto Spadaro, Ignazio Balsamo, Alfredo Varelli.

GO-GO BIGBEAT! (Eldorado) Producer-Director, Kenneth Hume; Music by The Beatles; In Eastman Color. CAST: Millie Small, The Animals, Lulu and The Luvvers, The Four Pennies, The Applejacks, The Merseybeats, The Hollies, The Wackers, The Cockneys, Brian Poole and The Tremeloes, The Magil 5, The Swinging Blue Jeans, The Tornadoes, Mods and The Rockers, The Western Theatre Ballet Company, The Cheynes.

SALLAH (Palisades International) Producer, Menachem Golan; Director, Ephraim Kishon; Story and Screenplay, Ephraim Kishon; Director of Photography, Floyd Crosby; Music, Yohanan Zarai; Costumes, Gina Rosenbach; Assistant Director, Joseph Gross. CAST: Topol, Geula Noni, Gila Almogor, Arik Einstein, Shraga Friedman, Zaharira Harifai, Nathan Meisler, Shaika Levi, Esther Greenberg, Mordecai Arnon.

CARRY ON CLEO (Governor) Producer, Peter Rogers; Director, Gerald Thomas; Screenplay, Talbot Rothwell; From an original idea by William Shakespeare; Associate Producer, Frank Bevis; Assistant Director, Peter Bolton; Music, Eric Rogers; In Exoticolor. CAST: Sidney James, Amanda Barrie, Kenneth Williams, Joan Sims, Kenneth Connor, Charles Hawtrey, Jim Dale, Julie Stevens, Victor Maddern, Sheila Hancock, David Davenport, Michael Ward, Tanya Dinning, Francis De Wolff, Tom Clegg, Jon Pertwee, Brian Oulton, Warren Mitchell.

THE BLACK TORMENT (Governor) Producer-Director, Robert Harford-Davis; Associate Producer, Robert Sterne; Screenplay, Donald and Derek Ford; Director of Photography, Peter Newbrook; Music, Robert Richards; In Diabolicolor. CAST: Heather Sears, John Turner, AnnLynn, Peter Arne, Norman Bird, Raymond Huntley, Annette Whiteley, Francis De Wolff, Joseph Tomelty, Patrick Troughton, Roger Croucher, Charles Houston, Derek Newark, Kathy MacDonald, Jack Taylor, Bill Cummings, Frank Hayden, Edina Ronay.

CARRY ON SPYING (Governor) Producer, Peter Rogers; Director, Gerald Thomas; Screenplay, Talbot Rothwell, Sid Colin; Associate Producer, Frank Bevis; Director of Photography, Alan Hume; Music, Eric Rogers. CAST: Kenneth Williams, Barbara Windsor, Bernard Cribbins, Charles Hawtrey, Eric Barker, Dilys Laye, Jim Dale, Richard Wattis, Eric Pohlmann, Victor Maddern, Judith Furse, John Bluthal, Frank Forsyth, Gerton Glauber, Jill Mai Meredith, Nora Gordon, Angela Ellison, Norman Mitchell, Hugh Futcher, Tom Clegg, Renee Houston, Derek Sydney, Jack Taylor, Bill Cummings, Anthony Baird, Patrick Durkin.

HERCULES AGAINST THE MOON MEN (Governor) In Cosmicolor and Lunarscope. Starring Alan Steel.

THE BRAIN (Governor) Producer, Raymond Stross; Director, Freddie Francis; Screenplay, Robert Stewart, Phillip Mackie; Based on Novel "Donovan's Brain" by Curt Siodmak; Music, Ken Jones; Director of Photography, Bob Huke. CAST: Anne Heywood, Peter Van Eyck, Cecil Parker, Bernard Lee, Ellen Schwiers, Maxine Audley, Jeremy Spenser, Siegfried Lowitz, Hans Nielsen, Miles Malleson, Jack MacGowran, George A. Cooper, Irene Richmond, Ann Sears, Victor Brooks, Alistair Williams, Kenneth Kendall, John Junkin, Frank Forsythe, Bandana Das Gupta, Allan Cuthbertson, Richard McNeff, John Watson, Patsy Rowlands, Brian Pringle.

THE HOURS OF LOVE (Cinema V) Producers, Isidoro Broggi, Renato Libassi; Director, Luciano Salce; Story and Screenplay, Castellano, Pipolo, Salce; Revision and Dialogue, Diego Fabbri; Music, Luiz Bonfa; Director of Photography, Erico Menczer; Assistant Director, Emilio Miraglia; Costumes, Giuliano Papi.

THE RESTLESS NIGHT (Casino) Producers, Carlton Film, Filmaufbau, Realfilm; Director, Falk Harnack; Screenplay, Horst Budjuhn; Music, Hans-Martin Majewski; Based on Story by Albrecht Goes. CAST: Bernard Wicki, Ulla Jacobson, Hansjorg Felmy, Ann Savo, Erik Schuman, Werner Hinz, Werner Peters.

Emmanuele Riva, Ugo Tognazzi
in "The Hours Of Love"

David DeKeyser, Barbara Ferris, Dave Clark
in "Having A Wild Weekend"

CITY OF FEAR (Allied Artists) Producers, Sandy Howard, Arthur Steloff; Director, Peter Bezencenet; Screenplay, Peter Welbeck. CAST: Paul Maxwell, Terry Moore, Marisa Mell, Albert Lieven, Pinkas Braun, Zsu Zaa Banki, Birgit Heiberg, Marie Rohm.

GUNMEN OF THE RIO GRANDE (Allied Artists) Producer, Ike Zingermann; Director, Tulio Demicheli; Screenplay, Gene Luotto; Based on Story by Chen Morrison; Director of Photography, M. A. Capriotti; Music, A. F. Lavagnino; A West Film-Flora Film-Llama Films-S.N. Pathe Cinema Co-Production. CAST: Guy Madison, Madeline Lebeau, Carolyn Davys, Massimo Serato, Gerard Tichy, Fernando Sancho, Olivier Hussenot, D. Michaelis, E. Maran, B. Deus, H. Morrow, X. Das Bolas, A. DeLuna, J. Majan.

PROSTITUTION (Stratford) Produced and Written by Maurice Boutel; Director of Photography, Q. Albicocco. CAST: Etchika Choreau, Evelyn Dassas, Alain Lionel, Jean Werner, Alicia Buttierez, Ann Darden, Rita Cadillac, Gabrille Robinne, Victor Guyay, Robert Dalban, Carl Eich, Raoul Dantes.

BLOOD AND BLACK LACE (Allied Artists) Story and Screenplay, Marcel Fondat, Joe Borilla, Mario Bava; Director of Photography, Mario Bava; Music, Carlo Rustichelli; A Woolner Brothers Picture in Technicolor. CAST: Cameron Mitchell, Eva Bartok, Mary Arden, and the 30 most glamorous models in the world.

VICE AND VIRTUE (M-G-M) Direction and Screenplay, Roger Vadim; Based on Novel "Justine" by Marquis de Sade; A Gaumont Production. CAST: Annie Girardot, Catherine Deneuve, Robert Hossein, Otto Hasse, Philippe Lemaire, Serge Marquand, Luciana Paluzzi.

KIMBERLEY JIM (Embassy) Producer-Director, Emil Nofal; Story and Screenplay, Emil Nofal; Director of Photography, Judex C. Viljoen; Assistant Director, Jans Rautenbach; Choreography, Sheila Wartski; Music, Bill Walker; Costumes, Anna Richter-Visser; A Jamie Uys Films Production. CAST: Jim Reeves, Madeleine Usher, Clive Parnell, Arthur Swemmer, Tromp Terre Blanche, Vonk DeRidder, Mike Holt, Dawid Van Der Walt, June Neethling, George Moore, Freddie Prozesky, Don Leonard, Morrie Blake.

SEASIDE SWINGERS (Embassy) Producers, Maurice J. Wilson, Ronald J. Kahn; Director, James Hill; Screenplay, Anthony Marriot, Jeri Matos, James Hill; Story, Anthony Marriot; Director of Photography, Nicholas Roeg; Music, Tony Osborne; Choreography, Gillian Lynne; Assistant Director, Patrick Marsden; A Fitzroy-Maycroft Production in Cinemascope and Technicolor. CAST: John Leyton, Mike Sarne, Freddie and The Dreamers, Ron Moody, Liz Fraser, Grazina Frame, Susan Baker, Jennifer Baker, The Mojos, Nicholas Parsons, Richard O'Sullivan, Michael Ripper, Hazel Hughes, Tony Daines, Peter Gilmore, Charles Lloyd Pack, Patrick Newell, Gaby Vargas, Coral Morphew, Nicola Riley, Marion Grimaldi, The Leroys.

THE FASCIST (Embassy) Producers, Isidoro Broggi, Renato Libassi; Director, Luciano Salce; Screenplay, Castellano-Pipolo, Luciano Salce. CAST: Ugo Tognazzi, Georges Wilson, Mireille Granelli, Stefania Sandrelli, Gianrico Tedeschi, Elsa Vazzoler, Franco Giacobini.

THE SECRET OF MAGIC ISLAND (Embassy) Director, Jean Tourane; Screenplay, Louis de Vilmorin; Narrated by Robert Lamoureux; In Color. A fantasy with live animals as actors.

HAVING A WILD WEEKEND (Warner Bros.) Producer, David Deutsch; Director, John Boorman; Screenplay, Peter Nichols; Associate Producer, Basil Keys; Assistant Director, David Tringham; Director of Photography, Manny Wynn; Costumes, Sally Jacobs. CAST: Dave Clark, Barbara Ferris, Lenny Davidson, Rick Huxley, Mike Smith, Denis Payton, David Lodge, Robin Bailey, Yootha Joyce, David DeKeyser, Robert Lang, Clive Swift, Ronald Lacey, Hugh Walters, Michael Gwynn, Marianne Stone, Donald Morley, Michael Blakemore, Julian Holloway, Edgar Harrison, John Jones, Peter Nichols, Susan Hanson, Sheila Fearn, Andrew Tyrrell, Roland Arblaster, Alan Lake, Ronald Cunliffe, Anthony Gardner, Peter Eyre.

I WAS ALL HIS (Casino) Produced by Carlton-Eichberg; Director, Wolfgang Becker; Screenplay, Kurt Heuser; Music, Klaus Ogermann. CAST: Barbara Ruetting, Carlos Thompson, Wolfgang Preiss, Kai Fischer, Siegfried Lowitz, Maria Stadler, Michl Lang, Lina Carstons, Korny Collins, Lukas Ammann.

A DAY IN COURT (Ultra) Director, Steno; Screenplay, Lucio Fulci, Alberto Sordi, Alessanoro Continenza; Based on Idea by Lucio Fulci; Music, Armando Trovaioli; A Bellotti Film. CAST: Sophia Loren, Alberto Sordi, Silvana Pampanini, Walter Chiari, Peppino De Filippo, Tania Weber.

ECCO (Cresa-Roma) Producer, Francesco Mazzei; Director, Gianni Proia; Executive Producer, Mario Russo; Photography, Baldi Schwarze, Emanuele DiCola; Music, Riz Ortolani; A Julia Film Production; Presented by Dick Randall and Howard Smith; In Technicolor and Wide Screen; Narrated by George Sanders.

THE SWORD OF EL CID (Eldorado) Director, M. Iglesias; In Supercinescope and Eastman Color; Presented in Association with East/West Films. CAST: Chantel Deberg, Roland Carey, Sandro Moretti, Iliana Grimandi, Ray Myles, Jeff Russel.

LOVE IN 4 DIMENSIONS (Eldorado) Executive Producer, Luciano Cattania; Directors, Massimo Mida, Jacques Romain, Gianni Puccini, Mino Guerrini; Screenplays, Bruno Baratti, Mino Guerrini, Massimo Mida, Gianni Puccini; Music, Franco Mannino; Photography, Tonino Delli Colli, Dario Di Palma, Carlo Di Palma; English Subtitles, Noelle Gillmor; An Italian-French Co-Production. CAST: Carlo Giuffre, Franca Rame, Carlo Bagno, Sylva Koscina, Gastone Moschin, Franca Polesello, Philippe Leroy, Elena Martini, Fabrizio Capucci, Alberto Bonucci, Michele Mercier, Alberto Lionello.

213

Ursula Andress, Christopher Lee,
John Richardson in "She"

Birgitte Federspiel, Preben Lerdorff Rye
in "A Stranger Knocks"

SHE (M-G-M) Producer, Michael Carreras; Director, Robert Day; Screenplay, David Chantler; Based on Novel by H. Rider Haggard; Music, James Bernard; Choreography, Christyne Lawson; Associate Producer, Aida Young; A 7 Arts-Hammer Production in Cinemascope and Technicolor. CAST: Ursula Andress, John Richardson, Peter Cushing, Bernard Cribbins, Rosenda Monteros, Christopher Lee, Andre Morell.

THE SECRET OF BLOOD ISLAND (Universal) Producer, Anthony Nelson Keys; Director, Quentin Lawrence; Screenplay, John Gilling; Music, James Bernard; Director of Photography, Jack Asher; Assistant Director, Peter Price; A Hammer Film in Color. CAST: Barbara Shelley, Jack Hedley, Charles Tingwell, Bill Owen, Peter Welch, Lee Montague, Edwin Richfield, Michael Ripper, Patrick Wymark, Philip Latham, Glyn Houston, Ian Whittaker, John Southworth, David Saire, Peter Craze, Henry Davies.

THE NAKED BRIGADE (Universal) Producer, Albert J. Cohen; Director, Maury Dexter; Assistant Directors, Eric Andreou, George Kosmatos; Screenplay, Albert J. Cohen, A. Sanford Wolf; Based on Story by Irwin Winehouse, A. Sanford Wolf; Music, Theo Fanidi; Associate Producer, A. Sanford Wolf; Director of Photography, A. Karides Fuchs; A Box Office Attractions-Alfa Studios Co-Production. CAST: Shirley Eaton, Ken Scott, Mary Chronopoulou, John Holland, Sonia Zoidou, Eleni Zaferiou, Aris Vlachopoulos, Patrick Kavanaugh, Clive Russell, N. Papaconstantinou, Karl Nurk, Christopher Himaras, Socrates Corres, Zanino Papadopoulos, Gikas Biniaris, Costas Balademas.

A STRANGER KNOCKS (Trans-Lux) Producer-Director, Johan Jacobsen; Screenplay, Finn Methling; Music, Erik Fiehn; A Flamingo Film Production. CAST: Birgitte Federspiel, Preben Lerdorff Rye.

LIFE UPSIDE DOWN (Allied Artists) Producer, Michel Peynet; Directed and Written by Alain Jessua; Assistant Director, Christian De Challonges; Director of Photography, Jacques Robin; Music, Jacques Loussier; Presented by The Landau Company. CAST: Charles Denner, Anna Gaylor, Guy Saint-Jean, Nicole Gueden, Jean Yanne, Yvonne Clech, Robert Bousquet, Francoise Moncey, Jean Dewewer, Gilbert Meunier, Andre Thorent, Bernard Sury, Jenny Orleans, Nane Germon.

ITALIANO BRAVA GENTE (Embassy) Producer, Lionello Santi; Director, Giuseppe De Santis; Screenplay, Ennio De Concini, Augusto Frassineti, Giandomenico Giagni, Serghei Smirnov, Giuseppe De Santis; Story, Ennio De Concini, Giuseppe De Santis; Assistant Director, Romolo Girolami; Director of Photography, Antonio Secchi; Music, Armando Trovaioli; A Mosfilm-Galatea Co-Production. CAST: Arthur Kennedy, Peter Falk, Tatyana Samoilova, Raffaele Pisu, Shanna Prokhorenko, Andrea Checchi, Riccardo Cucciolla, Nino Vingelli, Lev Prygunov, Grigori Mikhailov, Gino Pernice, Valeri Somov, Boris Kozhukhov, Vincenzo Polizzi, Yuri Nazarov.

ONE WAY PENDULUM (Lopert) Executive Producer, Oscar Lewenstein; Producer, Michael Deeley; Director, Peter Yates; Screenplay, N. F. Simpson; Based on his Play of the same name; Associate Producers, Michael Holden, Leigh Aman; Director of Photography, Denys Coop; Music, Richard Rodney Bennett; Assistant Director, Claude Watson; A Woodfall Film Presentation. CAST: Eric Sykes, George Cole, Julia Foster, Jonathan Miller, Peggy Mount, Alison Leggatt, Mona Washbourne, Douglas Wilmer, Kenneth Farringdon, Glyn Houston, Graham Crowden, Walter Horsbruch, Frederick Piper, Vincent Harding, Tommy Bruce.

THE RAVAGERS (Hemisphere) Producer, Kane Lynn; Director, Eddie Romero. CAST: John Saxon, Bronwyn Fitzsimons, Fernando Poe, Jr.

MAN IN THE DARK (Universal) Producer, Tom Blakeley; Director, Lance Comfort; Screenplay, James Kelly, Peter Miller; Story, Vivian Kemble; Director of Photography, Basil Emmott; Choreography, Allen Meachem; Main theme "Concerto" composed by Peter Hart; Songs, Stan Butcher, Syd Cordell; Assistant Directors, John Stoneman, Stephen Christian, Tony Reed; Presented by Mancunian Films. CAST: William Sylvester, Barbara Shelley, Elizabeth Shepherd, Alex Davion, Mark Eden, Ronnie Carroll, Frank Forsyth, Edward Evans, Joy Allen, Unity Grimwood, Wendy Martin.

CODE 7 VICTIM 5 (Universal) Producer, Harry Alan Towers; Director, Robert Lynn; Screenplay, Peter Yeldham; Story, Peter Welbeck; Music, Johnny Douglas; Director of Photography, Nicholas Roeg; A Towers of London Film; In Techniscope and Technicolor. CAST: Lex Barker, Ronald Fraser, Walter Rilla, Dietmar Schonherr, Gert Van Den Bergh, Howard Davies, Percy Sieff, Gustel Gundelach, Sophia Spentzos, Ann Smyrner, Veronique Vendell.

TABOOS OF THE WORLD (American International) Producer, Guido Giambartolomei; Director, Romolo Marcellini; In Color. Narrated by Vincent Price. Presenting men and women of the modern world who still practice some of the ancient rituals of bygone days.

WAR-GODS OF THE DEEP (American International) Producer, George Willoughby; Director, Jacques Tourneur; Screenplay, Louis M. Heyward. CAST: Vincent Price, Tab Hunter, David Tomlinson, Susan Hart, John LeMesurier.

THESE ARE THE DAMNED (Columbia) Producer, Anthony Hinds; Associate Producer, Anthony Nelson Keys; Director, Joseph Losey; Executive Producer, Michael Carreras; Screenplay, Evan Jones; Based on Novel "Children of Light" by H. L. Lawrence; Music, James Bernard; Director of Photography, Arthur Grant; A Hammerscope Film Production. CAST: MacDonald Carey, Shirley Anne Field, Viveca Lindfors, Alexander Knox, Oliver Reed, Walter Gotell, James Villiers, Thomas Kempinski, Kenneth Cope, Brian Oulton, Barbara Everest, Alan McClelland, James Maxwell, Rachel Clay, Caroline Sheldon, Rebecca Dignam, Siobhan Taylor, Nicholas Clay, Kit Williams, Christopher Witty, David Palmer, John Thompson.

214

Shirley Anne Field, Oliver Reed (C), Macdonald
Carey in "These Are The Damned"

Anna Karina, Sami Frey, Claude Brasseur
in "Band Of Outsiders"

OPERATION C.I.A. (Allied Artists) Producer,
Peer J. Oppenheimer; Director, Christian Nyby;
Story, Peer J. Oppenheimer; Bill S. Ballinger;
Music, Leonard (Buzz) Blair; Director of Photography,
Paul Dunlap; Assistant Director, Cyril
Collick; Gowns, Thelma Nyby. CAST: Burt Reynolds,
Kieu Chinh, John Hoyt, Danielle Aubry, Cyril
Collick, Victor Diaz, William Catching, Marsh
Thomson, John Laughinghouse, Frank Estes, Chaiporn,
Michael Schwiner, Robert Gulbranson, Janet
Russell, Santi.

PLANET OF BLOOD (American International)
Producer, Fulvio Lucisano; Director, Mario Bava;
Associate Producer, Salvatore Billitteri; Assistant
Director, Serena Canevari; Director of Photography,
Antonio Rinaldi; Costumes, Gabriele Mayer; Story,
Renato Pestriniero; Screenplay, Ib Melchior, Alberto
Bevilaqua, Callisto Cosulich, Mario Bava, Antonio
Roman, Rafael J. Salvia; In Eastman Color. CAST:
Barry Sullivan, Norma Bengell, Angel Aranda, Evi
Marandi, Fernando Villena, Stelio Candelli, Massimo
Righi, Mario Morales, Franco Andrei, Ivan
Rassimov, Rico Boido, Alberto Cevenini.

GUNFIGHTERS OF CASA GRANDE (M-G-M)
Producer, Lester Welch; Director, Roy Rowland;
Screenplay, Borden and Patricia Chase, Clarke
Reynolds; Story, Borden and Patricia Chase; Music,
Johnny Douglas; Themes, Robert Mellin; Associate
Producer, Sam X. Abarbanel; Directors of Photography,
Jose F. Aguayo, Manuel Merino; Assistant
Director, Manahen Velasco; A Gregor Production
in Association with Tecisa; In Metroscope and
Metrocolor. CAST: Alex Nicol, Jorge Mistral,
Dick Bentley, Steve Rowland, Phil Posner, Mercedes
Alonso, Diana Lorys, Maria Granada, Roberto Rey,
Aldo Sambell, Anthony Fuentes, Angel Solano,
Jose Martin, Jim Gillen, Mike Ekiss, Simon Arriaga,
Fernando Villena, Emilio Rodriquez, Ana Maria
Custodio, Mario Barros, Ivan Tubau, Jose Mayens,
Mike Brendel, Maria Jose Collado.

THE NEW ANGELS (Promenade) Producer, Alfredo
Rini; Director, Ugo Gregoretti; Screenplay,
Ugo Gregoretti, Mino Guerrini; Based on Guerrini's
Stories "The 20-Year-Olds Are Not Madmen"; Director
of Photography, Tonino Delli Colli; A
Titanus-Galates-Arco Production. CAST: Unlisted
non-professionals.

CRAZY PARADISE (Sherpix) Direction and Screenplay,
Gabriel Axel; Based on Novel by Ole Juul;
In Eastman Color. CAST: Dirch Passer, Hans W.
Petersen, Ove Sprogoe, Ghita Norby, Paul Hagen,
Bodil Steen, Karl Stegger, Lone Hertz, Kjeld Petersen,
Gunnar Lemvigh, Arthur Jensen, Elsebeth
Larsen.

RED BEARD (Toho) Producers, Yuko Tanaka,
Ryuzo Kikushima; Director, Akira Kurosawa;
Screenplay, Masato Ide, Hideo Oguni, Ryuzo Kikushima,
Akira Kurosawa; Based on Novel by Shugoro
Yamamoto; Directors of Photography, Asaichi
Nakai, Takao Saito. CAST: Toshiro Mifune, Yuzo
Kayama, Reiko Dan, Kyoko Kagawa, Tsutomu
Yamazaki.

COULD I BUT LIVE (Toho) Executive Producers,
Ichiro Sato, Hideyuki Shiino; Directed and Written
by Zenzo Matsuyama; Music, Masaru Sato; Director
of Photography, Hiroshi Murai; In Tohoscope.
CAST: Keiju Kobayashi, Hideko Takamine.

THE GORGON (Columbia) Producer, Anthony
Nelson Keys; Director, Terence Fisher; Screenplay,
John Gilling; Based on Story by J. Llewellyn
Devine; A Hammer Film Production in Petrifying
Color. CAST: Peter Cushing, Christopher Lee,
Richard Pasco, Michael Goodliffe, Barbara Shelley.

TREASURE OF SILVER LAKE (Columbia) Producer,
Horst Wendlandt; Director, Harald Reinl;
Based on Novel by Karl May; In CinemaScope
and Flaming Arrow Color. CAST: Lex Barker,
Herbert Lom, Gotz George, Pierre Brice.

THE BRIGAND OF KANDAHAR (Columbia)
Producer, Anthony Nelson Keys; Director, John
Gilling; Story and Screenplay, John Gilling; A
Hammer Film Production in ColumbiaColor. CAST:
Ronald Lewis, Oliver Reed, Duncan Lamont,
Yvonne Romain, Catherine Woodville.

THE CURSE OF THE MUMMY'S TOMB (Columbia)
Producer-Director, Michael Carreras;
Screenplay, Henry Younger; A Hammer Film Production
in Techniscope and Technicolor. CAST:
Terence Morgan, Ronald Howard, Fred Clark,
Jeanne Roland, George Pastell, Jack Gwillim,
John Paul.

EAST OF SUDAN (Columbia) Producer, Charles
H. Schneer; Director, Nathan Juran; Screenplay,
Jud Kinberg; In Technicolor and Techniscope.
CAST: Anthony Quayle, Sylvia Sims, Derek
Fowlds, Jenny Agutter, Johnny Sekka.

BAND OF OUTSIDERS (Royal) Written and
Directed by Jean-Luc Godard; Based on Novel
"Fool's Gold" by Dolores Hitchens; Director of
Photography, Raoul Coutard; Music, Michel Legrand;
A Co-Production of Anouchka and Orsay
Films. CAST: Anna Karina, Sami Frey, Claude
Brasseur.

DR. TERROR'S HOUSE OF HORRORS (Paramount)
Producers, Milton Subotsky, Max J. Rosenberg;
Director, Freddie Francis; Screenplay, Milton
Subotsky; Director of Photography, Alan Hume;
Songs, Kenny Lynch; Choreography, Boscoe Holder;
Assistant Director, Bert Batt; In Techniscope and
Technicolor. CAST: Peter Cushing, Christopher
Lee, Roy Castle, Donald Sutherland, Neil McCallum,
Alan Freeman, Max Adrian, Edward
Underdown, Ursula Howells, Peter Madden, Katy
Wild, Ann Bell, Sarah Nicholls, Bernard Lee,
Jeremy Kemp, Kenny Lynch, Harold Lang, Christopher
Carlos, George Mossman, Thomas Baptiste,
Tubby Hayes Quintet, Russ Henderson, Michael
Gough, Isla Blair, Hedger Wallace, Judy Cornwall,
Faith Kent, Brian Hankins, John Martin, Kenneth
Kove, Walter Sparrow, Frank Forsyth, Al Mulock,
Jennifer Jayne, Frank Barry, Irene Richmond,
Laurie Leigh.

**THE WOMAN WHO WOULDN'T DIE (Warner
Bros.)** Producer, Jack Parsons; Director, Gordon
Hessler; Screenplay, Dan Mainwaring; Based on
Novel "Catacombs" by Jay Bennett; Music, Carlo
Martelli; Director of Photography, Arthur Lavis;
Assistant Director, Frank Nesbitt; A Parroch-McCallum
Production. CAST: Gary Merrill, Jane
Morrow, Georgina Cookson, Neil McCallum, Rachel
Thomas, Jack Train, Frederick Piper.

John Saxon, Larry Hagman, Brian Aherne
in "The Cavern"

William Sylvester
in "Devils Of Darkness"

RED DESERT (Rizzoli) Producer, Antonio Cervi; Director, Michelangelo Antonioni; Screenplay, Michelangelo Antonioni, Tonino Guerra; In Technicolor; Italian with English subtitles. CAST: Monica Vitti, Richard Harris, Carlo Chionetti, Xenia Valderi, Rita Renoir, Aldo Grotti, Valero Bartoleschi.

TAFFY AND THE JUNGLE HUNTER (Allied Artists) Executive Producer, Byron Roberts; Producer, William Faris; Director, Terry O. Morse; Associate Producer, Jack Warner, Jr.; Screenplay, Arthur Hoerl; Story, Donald Zimbalist; Music, Shorty Rogers; Director of Photography, Byrdon Baker; Theme Song, Shorty Rogers, Al Zimbalist; Assistant Director, Robert Shannon; Entire Production under Personal Supervision of Alfred Zimbalist; In Technicolor. CAST: Jacques Bergerac, Manuel Padilla, Shary Marshall, Hari Rhodes, Taffy, Margo.

DEVILS OF DARKNESS (20th Century-Fox) Producer, Tom Blakely; Director, Lance Comfort; Story and Screenplay, Lyn Fairhurst; Director of Photography, Reg Wyer; Music, Bernie Fenton; In DeLuxe Color. CAST: William Sylvester, Hubert Noel, Tracy Reed, Carole Gray, Diana Decker, Rona Anderson, Peter Illing, Gerard Heinz, Victor Brooks, Avril Angers, Brian Oulton, Marie Burke, Marianne Stone, Rod McLennan, Geoffrey Kenion, Burnell Tucker.

JOHNNY NOBODY (Medallion) Producer, John R. Sloan; Director, Nigel Patrick; Screenplay, Patrick Kirwin; Based on "The Trial of Johnny Nobody" by Albert Z. Carr. CAST: Nigel Patrick, Yvonne Mitchell, Aldo Ray, William Bendix, Cyril Cusack, Niall MacGinnis, Bernie Winters, Noel Purcell, Eddie Byrne, Jimmy O'Dea, John Welsh, Joe Lynch, Michael Brennan, J. G. Devlin, Christopher Casson, May Craig, Norman Rodway, Michael O'Duffy, Dominic Behan.

PLANET OF THE VAMPIRES (American International) Producer, Fulvio Lucisano; Director, Mario Brava; Associate Producer, Salvatore Billitteri; Screenplay, Ib Melchior, Louis M. Heyward; Director of Photography, Antonio Rinaldi; Costumes, Gabriele Mayer; In Color Scope. CAST: Barry Sullivan, Norma Bengell, Angel Aranda, Evi Marandi, Fernando Villena, Stelio Candelli, Massimo Righi, Mario Morales, Franco Andrei.

THE CAVERN (20th Century-Fox) Producer-Director, Edgar G. Ulmer; Story and Screenplay, Michael Pertwee, Jack Davies; Music, Carlo Rustichelli, Gene Di Novi; Title Song, Caroll Coates; Sung by Bobby Bare. CAST: Rosanna Schiaffino, John Saxon, Brian Aherne, Peter L. Marshall, Larry Hagman, Hans Von Borsody, Nino Castelnuovo, Joachim Hansen.

"Kwaidan"

Gerry Marsden, George A. Cooper, Patricia
Lawrence, Mona Washbourne
in "Ferry Cross The Mersey"

KWAIDAN (Walter Reade-Sterling) Producer, Shigeru Wakatsuki; Director, Masaki Kobayashi; Screenplay, Yoko Mizuki; Story, Lafcadio Hearn; Director of Photography, Giyu Miyajima; Music, Toru Takemitsu; In TohoScope and Eastman Color. CAST: Michiyo Aratama, Misako Watanabe, Rentaro Mikuni, Katsuo Nakamura, Takashi Shimura, Tetsuo Tamba, Yoichi Hayashi, Kanyemon Nakamura, Noboru Nakaya.

FERRY CROSS THE MERSEY (United Artists) Producer, Michael Holden; Director, Jeremy Summers; Executive Producer, Brian Epstein; Screenplay, David Franden; Story, Tony Warren; Songs, Gerry Marsden; Director of Photography, Gilbert Taylor; Associate Producer, Leigh Aman. CAST: Gerry (Marsden) and The Pacemakers, Fred Marsden, Les Chadwick, Les Maguire, Julie Samuel, Cilla Black, The Fourmost, Jimmy Saville, Eric Barker, Deryck Guyler, George A. Cooper, Patricia Lawrence, Mona Washbourne, T. P. McKenna, Mischa De La Motte, Margaret Nolan, Donald Gee, Bernard Sharpe, Keith Smith, Andy Ho.

The Honeycombs
in "Go-Go Mania"

Sara Lezana, Jeffrey Hunter, Arthur Kennedy
in "Murieta"

TO DIE IN MADRID (Altura) Producer, Nichole Stephane; Directed and Written by Frederic Rossif; Music, Maurice Jarre; Original French Text, Madeleine Chapsal; Translated by Helen Scott; Presented by Clem Perry. A feature-length documentary with the voices of Sir John Gielgud, Irene Worth, William Hutt, George Gonneau.

THE MOMENT OF TRUTH (Rizzoli) Producers, Angelo Rizzoli and A.S. Films; Directors, Francesco Rosi, with Antonio Cervi, Pedro Portabella, Ricardo Munoz Suay, Pedro Beltran; Screenplay, Francesco Rosi; In Italian with English subtitles. CAST: Miguel Mateo Miguelin, Pedro Basauri Pedrucho, Jose Gomez Sevillano, Linda Christian.

BLESSINGS OF THE LAND (Lyn) Producer, Manuel de Leon; Director, Manuel Silos; Screenplay, Celso Carunungan; Director of Photography, Remigio Young; Music, Leopaldo Silos; In Philippine Tagalog with English subtitles. CAST: Rosa Rosal, Tony Santos, Le Roy Salvador, Carolos Padilla, Marita Zobel, Carmencita Abad.

WE WILL REMEMBER (Toho) Producer, Sanezumi Fujimoto; Direction and Screenplay, Zenzo Matsuyama; Based on Story by Ikuma Dan; Director of Photography, Asaichi Nakai; Music, Ikuma Dan; in Japanese with English subtitles; Eastman Color CAST: Hisaya Morshige, Chang-Mei-Yao, Keiju Kobayashi, Daisuke Kato, Kon Omura.

DANGEROUS JOURNEY (Casino) Director, Hermann Kugelstadt; Screenplay, Heinz Bothe-Pelzer; A Centropol Film Production in Eastman Color. CAST: Brigitte Corey, Michael Cramer, Michael Kirner, Silva Simon, Robert Mitchell, Gerhard Steinberg, Sandy Bicket.

LOVE ETERNE (Shaw Bros.) Producer, Run Run Shaw; Directed and Written by Li Han-hsiang; In Eastman Color; In Chinese with English subtitles. CAST: Betty Loh Tih, Ivy Ling Po, Jen Chieh, Chen Yen Yen, Li Kwun, Kao Pao-shu, Ching Miao, Yang Chi-ching, Chiang Kwong-chao, Au-yang Sha-fei.

WHEN THE TREES WERE TALL (Artkino) Producer-Director, Lev Kulidzhanov; Screenplay, Nikolai Figurovsky; A Gorky Film Studio Production. CAST: Yuri Nikolin, Inna Gulaya, L. Kuravlev, Y. Mazurova, L. Chursina.

LA TIA TULA (United International) Producer, Nino Quevedo; Director, Miguel Picazo; Screenplay, Luis Enciso; Based on Novel by Miguel de Unamuno. CAST: Aurora Batista, Carlos Estrada, Mari Loli Cabo, Carlos Sanchez Jimenez, Chiro Bermejo, Jose Prada, Manuel Granada, Enriqueta Carballeira.

Pierre Brice, Lex Barker
in "Apache Gold"

Bill Williams, John Lee
in "Space Flight 1C-1"

APACHE GOLD (Columbia) Producer, Horst Wendlandt; Director, Harald Reinl; Screenplay, H. G. Petersen; Based on Novel "Winnetou" by Karl May; Director of Photography, Ernst W. Kalinke; Music, Martin Bottcher; A Co-Production of Rialto Film, Preben Philipsen and Jadran Film; In Cinemascope and Eastman Color. CAST: Lex Barker, Mario Adorf, Pierre Brice, Marie Versini, Ralf Wolter, Walter Barnes, Mavid Popvic, Dunja Rajter, Chris Howland, Husein Cokic, Demeter Bitenc, Niksa Steffanini, Branko Spoljar, Vlado Krstulovic, Ilija Ivezic, Teddy Sotosek, Tomoslav Erak, Hrvoje Evob, Antun Nolis, Vladimir Bosnjak, Kranjcec Ana.

SPACEFLIGHT IC-1 (20th Century-Fox) Producers, Robert L. Lippert, Jack Parsons; Director, Bernard Knowles; Director of Photography, Geoffrey Faithfull; Screenplay, Harry Spalding; Music, Elisabeth Lutyens; Assistant Director, Gordon Gilbert. CAST: Bill Williams, Norma West, John Cairney, Linda Marlowe, Jeremy Longhurst, Kathleen Breck, Donald Churchill, Margo Mayne, John Lee, Tony Doonan, James Terry, Chuck Julian, Mark Lester, Stewart Middleton, Tony Honour.

Akim Tamiroff, Eddie Constantine
in "Alphaville"

Christina Schollin, Jarl Kulle, Edvin Adolphson
in "Swedish Wedding Night"

SYMPHONY FOR A MASSACRE (7 Arts) Producer, Julien Derode; Director, Jacques Deray; Screenplay, Jacques Deray, Jose Giovanni, Claude Sautet; Music, Michel Magne; Director of Photography, Claude Renoir. CAST: Michel Auclair, Claude Dauphin, Jose Giovanni, Michele Mercier, Daniela Rocca, Jean Rochefort, Charles Vanel.

TAXI FOR TOBRUK (7 Arts) Producer-Director, Denys De La Patteliere; Screenplay, Michael Audiard. CAST: Lino Ventura, Charles Aznavour, German Cobos, Maurice Biraud, Hardy Kruger.

THE TOMB OF LIGEIA (American International) Producer-Director, Roger Corman; Screenplay, Robert Towne; Based on Edgar Allan Poe Story; In Wide-Screen and Pathecolor. CAST: Vincent Price, Elizabeth Shepherd, John Westbrook, Oliver Johnston, Derek Francis, Richard Vernon, Ronald Adam, Frank Thornton, Denis Gilmore.

THE GRAND SUBSTITUTION (Frank E. Lee International) Producers, Shaw Brothers; Director, Yen Chun; Screenplay, Chen E-Hsin; Director of Photography, Yu Tsang-Shan; Music, Sian Hua; In Eastman Color and Shawscope. CAST: Li Li-Hua, Ivy Ling Po, Yen Chun, Li Ying, Ching Miao, Tung Di, Chen Yen-Yen.

TOKYO OLYMPIAD (Toho) Producer, Organizing Committee for The XVIII Olympiad; Director, Kon Ichikawa; In Scope-Size and Eastman Color. An on-the-spot feature length documentary of the Olympic Games in Tokyo in 1964.

MURIETA (Warner Bros.) Executive Producer, Jose Sainz de Vicuna; Director, George Sherman; Screenplay, James O'Hanlon; Director of Photography, Miguel F. Mila; Music, Antonio Perez Olea; Songs Composed and Sung by Paco Michel; Assistant Directors, Stanley Torchia, Federico Vaqueda; In EastmanColor. CAST: Jeffrey Hunter, Arthur Kennedy, Diana Lorys, Sara Lezana, Roberto Camardiel, Pedro Osinaga.

FRIEND OF THE FAMILY (International Classics) Producer, Andre Hakim; Directed and Written by Robert Thomas; Based on Play "Patate" by Marcel Achard; Music, Raymond le Senechal; Director of Photography, Robert Lefebvre; Assistant Director, Roberto Bodegas; Costumes, Alex Marcus, Lina Ballet; A Franco-Italian Co-Production in CinemaScope. CAST: Jean Marais, Danielle Darrieux, Anne Vernon, Sylvie Vartan, Pierre Dux, Jane Marken, Noel Roquevert, Hubert Deschamps, Jacques Jouanneau, Henri Virlojeux, Mike Marshall, Laurence Badie, Daniel Ceccaldi, Francois Charet.

Danielle Darrieux, Anne Vernon, Jean Marais,
Sylvie Vartan in "Friend Of The Family"

"Onibaba"

THE RETURN OF MR. MOTO (20th Century-Fox) Producers, Robert L. Lippert, Jack Parsons; Director, Ernest Morris; Screenplay, Fred Eggers; Director of Photography, Basil Emmott; Music, Douglas Gamley; Assistant Director, Gordon Gilbert. CAST: Henry Silva, Terence Longdon, Suzanne Lloyd, Marne Maitland, Martin Wyldeck, Brian Coburn, Stanley Morgan, Peter Zander, Harold Kasket, Anthony Booth, Gordon Tanner, Henry Gilbert, Richard Evans, Dennis Holmes, Ian Fleming, Tracy Connell, Alister Williamson, Sonya Benjamin.

YOU MUST BE JOKING! (Columbia) Producer, Charles H. Schneer; Director, Michael Winner; Screenplay, Alan Hackney; From Story by Alan Hackney and Michael Winner; Assistant Director, Peter Price; Director of Photography, Geoffrey Unsworth; Music, Laurie Johnson; Songs, Buddy Bregman, Hal Shaper. CAST: Michael Callan, Lionel Jeffries, Denholm Elliott, Wilfrid Hyde-White, Bernard Cribbins, Gabriella Licudi, Patricia Viterbo, Terry-Thomas, Lee Montague, Tracy Reed, James Robertson Justice, Leslie Phillips, Irene Handl, Richard Wattis, Miles Malleson, Gwendolyn Watts, Clive Dunn, James Villiers, Graham Stark, Peter Bull, Norman Vaughan.

THE BLUE BEAST (Toho) Producers, Sanezumi Fujimoto, Masakatsu Kaneko; Director, Hiromichi Horikawa; Screenplay, Yoshio Shirasaka; Music, Sei Ikeno. CAST: Tatsuya Nakadai, Yoko Tsukasa, Koreya Senda, Keiko Awaji, Jun Tazaki, Ichiro Nakaya.

CARESSED (Brenner) Producer-Director, Laurence L. Kent. CAST: Robert Howay, Angela Gann, Lannie Beckman, Carol Pastinsky, Bob Silverman.

EVA (Times) A Hakim Production; Director, Joseph Losey. CAST: Jeanne Moreau, Stanley Baker, Virna Lisi, Nona Medici, Francesco Rissone, James Villiers, Alex Revides, Lisa Gastoni, Riccardo Garrone, Giorgio Albertazzi.

GET ON WITH IT! (Governor) Producer, Bertram Ostrer; Director, C. M. Pennington-Richards; Screenplay, Hazel Adair, Hugh Woodhouse. CAST: Bob Monkhouse, Kenneth Connor, Shirley Eaton, Eric Barker, Reginald Beckwith, Richard Wattis, Sheena Marsh.

HYSTERIA (M-G-M) Produced and Written by Jimmy Sangster; Director, Freddie Francis; A Hammer Film. CAST: Robert Webber, Anthony Newlands, Jennifer Jayne, Maurice Denham, Lelia Goldoni, Peter Woodthorpe, Sandra Boize, Sue Lloyd.

IMAGE OF LOVE (Green) Produced, Directed, and Written by Lou Stoumen; Narrated and Title Song sung by Anthony Newley; Director of Photography, Arnold Eagle; Music, Ezra Laderman; In Color. A Documentary that takes a journey through history via art and literature to observe how man's view of woman has changed.

INVASION 1700 (Medallion) Title changed to "Daggers of Blood". Director, Fernando Cerchio; Screenplay, Henry Sienkiewicz; Based on Novel "The Elite of The Crowd"; In Color. CAST: Jeanne Crain, John Drew Barrymore, Pierre Brice, Akim Tamiroff, Gordon Mitchell.

JIG SAW (Beverly) Produced, Directed, and Written by Val Guest. CAST: Jack Warner, Ronald Lewis, Yolande Donlan, Michael Goodliffe.

KING AND COUNTRY (Allied Artists) Director, Joseph Losey; Music Written and Performed by Larry Adler; A Landau-Unger Presentation; Based on Novel and Play. CAST: Dirk Bogarde, Tom Courtenay, Leo McKern, Barry Foster, Peter Copley, James Villiers, Jeremy Spencer, Barry Jutner, Vivian Matalon, Keith Berkley, James Hunter, Jonah Seymour, Larry Taylor, Davis Cook.

ONIBABA (Toho) Directed and Written by Kaneto Shindo; Music, Hikhis Hayashi; In Tohoscope. CAST: Nobuko Otowa, Jitsuko Yoshimura, Kei Sato, Jukichi Uno, Taiji Tonomura.

PARIS SECRET (Cinema V) Producers, Arthur Cohn, Pierre Roustang; Director, Edouard Logerau; Screenplay, Tom Rowe; Director of Photography, Roland Pontoizeau; In Color. A Documentary covering the side streets of Paris where strange people and businesses flourish.

RED LANTERNS (Times) Producers, A. Damaskinos, V. G. Michaelides; Director, Vasilis Georgiadis; Screenplay, Alecos Galanos; Adapted from his Play. CAST: Jenny Karezi, Mary Chronopoulou, Alexandra Ladikou, George Foondas, Phaedon Georgitsis, Manos Katrakis, Despo Diamantidou.

REVENGE OF THE GLADIATORS (Paramount) Producer, Elio Scardamaglia; Director, Michele Lupo; Screenplay, Lionello De Felice, Ernesto Guida; In Color. CAST: Roger Browne, Scilla Gabel, Giacomo Rossi Stuart, Daniele Vargas, Gordon Mitchell, Germano Longo.

SEVEN DWARFS TO THE RESCUE (Childhood) Produced, Directed, and Written by P. W. Tamburella. CAST: Rossana Podesta, Roberto Risso, Georges Marchal, Ave Ninchi, Salvatore Furmari, Francesco Mule, Ulisse Lorenzelli, Mario Mastriantonio, Giovanni Solinas, Arturo Tosi, Domenico Tosi.

THE SKULL (Paramount) Producers, Max J. Rosenberg, Milton Subotsky; Director, Freddie Francis; Screenplay, Milton Subotsky; In Techniscope and Technicolor. CAST: Peter Cushing, Patrick Wymark, Christopher Lee, Nigel Green.

SWEDISH WEDDING NIGHT (Royal) Producers, Tore Sjoberg, Lorens Marmstedt; Director, Ake Falck; Screenplay, Lars Wilding; A Minerva Films Production in Swedish with English subtitles. CAST: Jarl Kulle, Lena Hansson, Christina Schollin, Edvin Adolphson, Isa Quensel, Catrin Westerlund, Tor Isedal, Peter Thelin, Lars Ekborg, Margareta Krook, Yvonne Lombard, Georg Arlin, Ove Tjernberg, Lars Lind, Sigge Fischer, Ulla Edin, Claes Esphagen, John Norman.

HERCULES, SAMSON AND ULYSSES (M-G-M) Producer, Joseph Fryd; Directed and Written by Pietro Francisci; In Eastman Color. CAST: Kirk Morris, Richard Lloyd, Liana Orfel, Enzo Cerusico, Aldo Giuffre.

ALPHAVILLE (Pathe) Producer, Andre Michelin; Directed and Written by Jean-Luc Godard; Music, Paul Misraki; A Chaumiane and Filmstudio Rome Production; In French with titles. CAST: Eddie Constantine, Anna Karina, Akim Tamiroff, Howard Vernon, Laszlo Szabo, Michel Delahaye, Hean-Andre Fieschi, Jean-Louis Comolli.

THE FACE OF FU MANCHU (Seven Arts) Director, Don Sharp; Screenplay, Peter Welbeck; A Hallam Production in Technicolor. CAST: Christopher Lee, Nigel Green, James Robertson Justice, Howard Marion-Crawford, Tsai Chin, Joachim Fuchsberger, Karin Dor, Walter Rilla, Harry Brogan, Poulet Tu, Peter Mossbacher.

COAST OF SKELETONS (Seven Arts) Producer, Oliver A. Unger; Director, Robert Lynn; Screenplay, Anthony Scott Veitch. CAST: Richard Todd, Derrek Nimmo, Dale Robertson, Elga Andersen, Marianne Koch.

HEROINA (Royal) Produced, Directed and Written by Jeronimo Mitchele Melendez; In Spanish with English subtitles. CAST: Kitty De Hoyos, Jaime Sanchez, Otto Sirgo, Jeddu Mascorieto, Marta Casanas, Jose de San Anton, Midia Caro, Felix Monclova.

WHITE VOICES (Rizzoli) Directors, Pasquale Festa Campanile, Massimo Franciosa; Screenplay, Massimo Franciosa, Pasquale Festa Campanile, Luigi Magni; In Italian with English subtitles. CAST: Paolo Ferrari, Sandra Milo, Graziella Granata, Anouk Aimee, Vittorio Caprioli, Jeanne Valerie, Philippe Leroy, Barbara Steele, Leopoldo Trieste, Jacqueline Sassard, Claudio Gora, Jean Tissier.

THE MAD EXECUTIONERS (Paramount) Producer, Arthur Brauner; Director, Edwin Zbonek; Screenplay, R. A. Stemmle; Based on "White Carpet" by Bryan Edgar Wallace. CAST: Hansjorg Felmy, Maria Perschy, Dieter Borsche, Wolfgang Preiss, Chris Howland.

GREED IN THE SUN (M-G-M) Producer, Alain Poire; Director, Henri Verneuil; Screenplay, Michel Audiard; Based on Novel by Claude Veillor; A Gaumont-M-G-M French Production. CAST: Jean-Paul Belmondo, Lino Ventura, Reginald Kerman, Andrea Parisy, Gert Frobe.

SAMURAI ASSASSIN (Toho) Director, Kihachi Okamoto; Screenplay, Shinobu Hashimoto; Based on Story "Samurai Nippon" by Jiroasa Gunji; A Toho-Mifune Production in Japanese with English subtitles. CAST: Toshiro Mifune, Keilu Kabayashi, Yunosuke Ito, Kashiro Matsumoto, Michiyo Aratama, Nao Tamura, Kaoru Yachigusa.

ONLY THE WIND (Casino) Director, Fritz Umgelter; Screenplay, Kurt Nachmann, H. O. Schroeder; A Melodie Film Production in color. CAST: Freddy Quinn, Gustav Knuth, Cordula Trantow, Gottfried Herbe, Gudrun Schmidt, Jelmut Oeser.

EMPRESS WU (Shaw Brothers) Producers, Run Run and Rumme Shaw; Director, Li Han-hsiang; Screenplay, Wang Yueh-ting; In Chinese with English subtitles. CAST: Li Li-hua, Chao Lei, Lo Chi, Chang Chung-wen, Yen Chuan, Lo Wei, Cheung Ying-tsoi, Paul Chang Chung, Ting Ning.

WHY BOTHER TO KNOCK (Seven Arts) Producer, Frank Godwin; Director, Cyril Frankel; Screenplay, Dennis Cannan, Frederick Godfurt, Frederic Raphae; From Novel by Clifford Hanley. CAST: Richard Todd, Nicole Morey, Elke Sommer, June Thorburn, Judith Anderson, Rik Battaglia, Dawn Beret, Scot Finch.

THE CROOKED ROAD (Seven Arts) Producer, David Henley; Director, Don Chaffey; Screenplay, J. Garrison; From Novel by Morris L. West. CAST: Robert Ryan, Stewart Granger, Nadia Gray, Marius Goring, George Coulouris.

Alexandra Stewart, Martin Held
in "And So To Bed"

Jeanne Moreau, Georges Geret
in "Diary Of A Chambermaid"

AND SO TO BED (Medallion) Stadthalle Films Production; Director, Alfred Weidermann. CAST: Lilli Palmer, Hildegard Neff, Peter Van Eyck, Daliah Lavi, Angelo Santi, Paul Hubschmid, Nadja Tiller, Thomas Fritsch, Alexandra Stewart, Martin Held, Peter Parten, Daniele Gaubert.

ATRAGON (American International) A Toho Production; Executive Producer, Yuko Tanaka; Director, Inoshiro Honda; Screenplay, Shinichi Sekizawa; Director of Photography, Hajime Koizumi; Music, Akira Ifukube; In Pathecolor. CAST: Tadao Takashima, Yoko Fujiyama, Yu Fujiki, Kenji Sawara, Akemi Kita, Tetsuko Kobayashi, Akihiko Hirata, Hiroshi Koizumi, Jun Tazaki, Ken Uehara.

THE AVENGER (Medallion) Producer, Giolgio Venturini; Director, Albert Band. CAST: Steve Reeves, Cupia Marlier, John Garko, Liana Orrei.

BEFORE THE REVOLUTION (New Yorker) Directed and Written by Bernardo Bertolucci; A Iride Cinematografica Production. CAST: Adriana Asti, Francesco Barilli, Allen Midgette, Morando Morandini, Cecrope Barilli, Cristina Pariset, Emilia Borghi, Domenico Alpi, Iole Lunardi, Giuseppe Maghenzani.

WILD WILD WORLD (Sokoler) Producer, Alessandro Jacovoni; Director, Robert Sokoler; Music, Roberto Nicolosi; Narrated by Eddie Bracken; In Cinemascope and Color. An exposure of the bizarre and macabre practices that are peculiar to various parts of the world.

DIARY OF A CHAMBERMAID (International Classics) Producers, Serge Silberman, Michel Safra; Director, Luis Bunuel; Screenplay, Luis Bunuel, Jean-Claude Carriere; Based on Novel by Octave Mirbeau; Director of Photography, Roger Fellous; Costumes, Georges Wakhevitch; Assistant Directors, Jean Luis Bunuel, Pierre Lary; A Franco-Italian Co-Production. CAST: Jeanne Moreau, Michel Piccoli, Georges Geret, Francoise Lugagne, Daniel Ivernel, Jean Ozenne, Dominique Sauvage-Dandieux.

BAD GIRLS DON'T CRY (Medallion) Formerly "On Any Street"; Executive Producer, Sante Chimirri; Director, Mauro Bolognini; Story and Screenplay, Pier Paolo Pasolini; Assistant Director, Rinaldo Ricci; Director of Photography, Armando Nannuzzi; Music, Piero Piccioni; A Miller-King Production. CAST: Elsa Martinelli, Antonella Lualdi, Jean Claude Brialy, Laurent Terzieff, Franco Interlenghi, Anna Maria Ferrero.

Elsa Martinelli
in "Bad Girls Don't Cry"

(R) Ian Carmichael, Joan Greenwood
in "The Amorous Mr. Prawn"

GO GO MANIA (American International) Producer, Harry Field; Director, Frederic Goode; Introduced by Jimmy Saville; Choreography, Leo Kharibian; In Techniscope and Technicolor. CAST: Matt Monro, Susan Maughan, The Animals, The Honeycombs, The Rockin' Berries, Herman's Hermits, The Nashville Teens, The Four Pennies, Billy J. Kramer and The Dakotas, The Fourmost, Sounds Incorporated, Peter and Gordon, Tommy Quickly and The Remo Four, Billie Davis, The Spencer Davis Group, The Beatles.

THE AMOROUS MR. PRAWN (Medallion) Formerly "The Playgirl and The War Minister"; Producer, Leslie Gilliat; Director, Anthony Kimmins; Screenplay, Anthony Kimmins, Nicholas Phipps; Director of Photography, Wilkie Cooper; Music, John Barry; Assistant Director, Douglas Hermes; Costumes, Hardy Amies; A Miller-King Production. CAST: Joan Greenwood, Cecil Parker, Ian Carmichael, Robert Beatty, Dennis Price, Liz Fraser, Bridget Armstrong, Derek Nimmo, Harry Locke, Robert Nichols, Roddy McMillan, Patrick Jordan, Godfrey James, Gerald Sim, Geoffrey Bayldon, Eric Woodburn, John Dunbar, Jack Stewart, Sandra Dorne, Finlay Currie, Eric Francis, Reg Lye, Michael Ripper, Drew Russell, Michael Hunt.

BIOGRAPHICAL DATA

(Name, real name, place and date of birth, and school attended)

ADAMS, EDIE: (Edith) Kingston, Pa., Apr. 16, 1931. Juilliard School of Music, Columbia.

ADAMS, JULIE: (Betty May) Waterloo, Iowa, Oct. 17, 1928. Little Rock Jr. College.

ADDAMS, DAWN: Felixstowe, Suffolk, Eng., Sept. 21, 1930. Royal Academy.

ADRIAN, IRIS: (Iris Adrian Hostetter) Los Angeles, May 29, 1913.

AGAR, JOHN: Chicago, Jan. 31, 1921.

AHERNE, BRIAN: Worcestershire, Eng., May 2, 1902. Malvern College, U. of London.

AHN, PHILIP: Los Angeles, Mar. 29, 1911. U. of Calif.

ALBERGHETTI, ANNA MARIA: Pesaro, Italy, May 15, 1936.

ALBERT, EDDIE: (Eddie Albert Heimberger) Rock Island, Ill., Apr. 22, 1908. U. of Minn.

ALBRIGHT, LOLA: Akron, Ohio, July 20, 1925.

ALDA, ROBERT: (Alphonso D'Abruzzo) New York City, Feb. 26, 1914. NYU.

ALEXANDER, BEN: Goldfield, Nev., May 26, 1911. U. of Calif., Stanford.

ALLBRITTON, LOUISE: Oklahoma City, July 3, 1920. U. of Okla.

ALLEN, STEVE: New York City, Dec. 26, 1921.

ALLYSON, JUNE: (Jan) Westchester, N.Y., Oct. 7, 1923.

AMES, LEON: (Leon Wycoff) Portland, Ind., Jan. 20, 1903.

ANDERSON, JUDITH: Adelaide, Australia, Feb. 10, 1898.

ANDERSON, MICHAEL, JR.: London, Eng., 1943.

ANDES, KEITH: Ocean City, N.J., July 12, 1920. Temple U., Oxford.

ANDREWS, DANA: Collins, Miss., Jan. 1, 1912. Sam Houston College.

ANDREWS, HARRY: Tonbridge, Kent, Eng., 1911.

ANGEL, HEATHER: Oxford, Eng., Feb. 9, 1909. Wycombe Abbey School.

ANGELI, PIER: (Anna Maria Pierangeli) Sardinia, June 19, 1932.

ANN-MARGRET: Stockholm, Sweden, Apr. 28, 1941. Northwestern U.

ANSARA, MICHAEL: Lowell, Mass., Apr. 15, 1922. Pasadena Playhouse.

ANTHONY, TONY: Clarksburg, W. Va., Oct. 16, 1937. Carnegie Tech.

ARCHER, JOHN: (Ralph Bowman) Osceola, Neb., May 8, 1915. U. of S. Calif.

ARDEN, EVE: (Eunice Quedens) Mill Valley, Calif.

ARLEN, RICHARD: Charlottesville, Va., Sept. 1, 1900. St. Thomas College.

ARNAZ, DESI: Santiago, Cuba, Mar. 2, 1917. Colegio de Dolores.

ARNESS, JAMES: Minneapolis, Minn., May 26, 1923. Beloit College.

ARTHUR, JEAN: NYC, Oct. 17, 1908.

ARTHUR, ROBERT: (Robert Arthaud) Aberdeen, Wash., June 18. U. of Wash.

ASTAIRE, FRED: Omaha, Neb., May 10, 1900.

ASTOR, MARY: (Lucile V. Langhanke) Quincy, Ill., May 3, 1906. Kenwood-Loring School.

ATTENBOROUGH, RICHARD: Cambridge, Eng., Aug. 29, 1923. Royal Academy of Dramatic Art.

AUMONT, JEAN PIERRE: Paris, Jan. 5, 1913. French Nat'l School of Drama.

AUTRY, GENE: Tioga, Texas, Sept. 29, 1907.

AVALON, FRANKIE: (Francis Thomas Avallone) Philadelphia, Sept. 18, 1940.

AYLMER, FELIX: Corsham, Eng., Feb. 21, 1889. Oxford.

AYRES, LEW: Minneapolis, Minn., Dec. 28, 1908.

BACALL, LAUREN: NYC, Sept. 16, 1924. American Academy of Dramatic Art.

BACKUS, JIM: Cleveland, Ohio, Feb. 25, 1913. American Academy of Dramatic Art.

BADDELEY, HERMIONE: Shropshire, Eng., Nov. 13, 1908. Margaret Morris School.

BAILEY, PEARL: Newport News, Va., March 29.

BAINTER, FAY: Los Angeles, Dec. 7, 1892. Girls' Collegiate School.

BAKER, CARROLL: Johnstown, Pa., May 28, 1931. St. Petersburg Jr. College.

BAKER, STANLEY: Glamorgan, Wales, Feb. 28, 1928.

BALIN, INA: Brooklyn, Nov. 12, 1937. NYU.

BALL, LUCILLE: Jamestown, N.Y., Aug. 6, 1911. Chatauqua Musical Inst.

BANCROFT, ANNE: (Anne Italiano) NYC, Sept. 17, 1931. American Academy of Dramatic Art.

BANKHEAD, TALLULAH: Huntsville, Ala., Jan. 31, 1903. Mary Baldwin School.

BANNEN, IAN: Airdrie, Scot., June 29, 1928.

BARDOT, BRIGITTE: Paris, 1934.

BARKER, LEX: (Alexander Crichlow Barker) Rye, N.Y., May 8, 1919.

BARRY, DONALD: (Donald Barry de Acosta) Houston, Tex. Texas School of Mines.

BARRY, GENE: (Eugene Klass) NYC, June 14, 1921.

BARRYMORE, JOHN DREW: Beverly Hills, Calif., June 4, 1932. St. John's Military Academy.

BARTHOLOMEW, FREDDIE: London, Mar. 28, 1924.

BARTON, JAMES: Gloucester, N.J., Nov. 1, 1890.

BASEHART, RICHARD: Zanesville, Ohio, Aug. 31.

BATES, ALAN: Allestree, Derbyshire, Eng., Feb. 17, 1934. Royal Academy of Dramatic Art.

BATES, BARBARA: Denver, Colo., Aug. 6.

BAXTER, ALAN: East Cleveland, Ohio, Nov. 19, 1911. Williams U.

BAXTER, ANNE: Michigan City, Ind., May 7, 1923. Ervine School of Drama.

BEAL, JOHN: (J. Alexander Bliedung) Joplin, Mo., Aug. 13, 1909. Pa. U.

BEATTY, ROBERT: Hamilton, Ont., Can., Oct. 19, 1909. U. of Toronto.

BEAUMONT, HUGH: Lawrence, Kan., Feb. 16, 1909. U. of Chattanooga, USC.

BECKETT, SCOTTY: Oakland, Calif., Oct. 4, 1920.

BEERY, NOAH, JR.: NYC, Aug. 10, 1916. Harvard Military Academy.

BEGLEY, ED: Hartford, Conn., Mar. 25, 1901. Conn. School for Boys.

BELAFONTE, HARRY: NYC, Mar. 1, 1927.

BEL GEDDES, BARBARA: NYC, Oct. 31, 1922.

BELLAMY, RALPH: Chicago, June 17, 1905.

BENNETT, BRUCE: (Herman Brix) Tacoma, Wash., U. of Wash.

BENNETT, JOAN: Palisades, N.J., Feb. 27, 1910. St. Margaret's School.

BENNY, JACK: (Jack Kubelsky) Waukegan, Ill.

BERGEN, EDGAR: Chicago, Feb. 16, 1903. Northwestern U.

BERGEN, POLLY: Knoxville, Tenn., July 14, 1930. Compton Jr. College.

BERGERAC, JACQUES: Biarritz, France, May 26, 1927. Paris U. of Law.

BERGMAN, INGRID: Stockholm, Sweden, Aug. 29, 1917. Royal Dramatic Theatre School.

BERLE, MILTON: (Milton Berlinger) NYC, July 12, 1908. Professional Children's School.

BERLINGER, WARREN: Brooklyn, Aug. 31, 1937. Columbia University.

BEST, JAMES: Corydon, Ind., July 26, 1926.

BETTGER, LYLE: Philadelphia, Feb. 13, 1915. American Academy of Dramatic Art.

BEYMER, RICHARD: Avoca, Iowa, Feb. 21, 1939.

BISHOP, JULIE: (formerly Jacqueline Wells) Denver, Colo., Aug. 30, 1917. Westlake School.

Sidney Blackmer   Shirley Booth   Horst Buchholz   Billie Burke   John Cassavetes

BLACKMER, SIDNEY: Salisbury, N.C., July 13, 1898. U. of N.C.

BLAINE, VIVIAN: (Vivian Stapleton) Newark, N.J., Nov. 21, 1924.

BLAIR, BETSY: (Betsy Boger) NYC, Dec. 11.

BLAKE, AMANDA: (Beverly Louise Neill) Buffalo, N.Y., Feb. 20.

BLONDELL, JOAN: NYC, Aug. 30, 1909.

BLOOM, CLAIRE: London, Feb. 15, 1931. Badminton School.

BLUE, BEN: Montreal, Can., Sept. 12, 1901.

BLUE, MONTE: Indianapolis, Jan. 11, 1890.

BLYTH, ANN: Mt. Kisco, N.Y., Aug. 16, 1928. New Wayburn Dramatic School.

BOGARDE, DIRK: London, Mar. 28, 1921. Glasgow & Univ. College.

BOLGER, RAY: Dorchester, Mass., Jan. 10, 1906.

BOND, DEREK: Glasgow, Scot., Jan. 26, 1920. Askes School.

BONDI, BEULAH: Chicago, May 3, 1892.

BOONE, PAT: Jacksonville, Fla., June 1, 1934. Columbia U.

BOONE, RICHARD: Los Angeles. Stanford U.

BOOTH, SHIRLEY: NYC, Aug. 30, 1907.

BORGNINE, ERNEST: Hamden, Conn., Jan. 24, 1918. Randall School of Dramatic Art.

BOWMAN, LEE: Cincinnati, Dec. 28, 1914. American Academy of Dramatic Art.

BOYD, STEPHEN: Belfast, Ire., 1928.

BOYER, CHARLES: Figeac, France, Aug. 28, 1899. Sorbonne U.

BRACKEN, EDDIE: NYC, Feb. 7, 1920. Professional Children's School.

BRADY, SCOTT: (Jerry Tierney) Brooklyn, Sept. 13, 1924. Bliss-Hayden Dramatic School.

BRAND, NEVILLE: Kewanee, Ill., Aug. 13, 1921.

BRANDO, JOCELYN: San Francisco, Nov. 18, 1919. Lake Forest College, American Academy.

BRANDO, MARLON: Omaha, Neb., Apr. 3, 1924. New School of Social Research.

BRASSELLE, KEEFE: Elyria, Ohio, Feb. 7.

BRAZZI, ROSSANO: Bologna, Italy, 1916. U. of Florence.

BRENT, GEORGE: Dublin, Ire., Mar. 15, 1904. Dublin U.

BRENT, ROMNEY: (Romulo Larralde) Saltillo, Mex., Jan. 26, 1902.

BRIAN, DAVID: NYC, Aug. 5, 1914. CCNY.

BRIDGES, LLOYD: San Leandro, Calif., Jan. 15, 1913.

BRODIE, STEVE: (Johnny Stevens) Eldorado, Kan., Nov. 25, 1919.

BROMFIELD, JOHN: (Farron Bromfield) South Bend, Ind., June 11, 1922. St. Mary's College.

BROOKS, GERALDINE: (Geraldine Stroock) NYC, Oct. 29, 1925. American Academy of Dramatic Art.

BROWN, JAMES: Desdemona, Tex., Mar. 22, 1920. Baylor U.

BROWN, JOE E.: Helgate, Ohio, July 28, 1892.

BROWN, TOM: NYC, Jan. 6, 1913. Professional Children's School.

BRUCE, VIRGINIA: Minneapolis, Sept. 29, 1910.

BRYNNER, YUL: Sakhalin Island, Japan, June 15, 1915.

BUCHANAN, EDGAR: Humansville, Mo. U. of Oregon.

BUCHHOLZ, HORST: Berlin, Ger., Dec. 4, 1933. Ludwig Dramatic School.

BUETEL, JACK: Dallas, Tex., Sept. 5, 1917.

BURKE, BILLIE: Washington, D.C., Aug. 7, 1885.

BURNET, CAROL: San Antonio, Tex., Apr. 26, 1935. UCLA.

BURNS, GEORGE: (Nathan Birnbaum) NYC.

BURR, RAYMOND: New Westminster, B.C., Can., May 21, 1917. Stanford, U. of Cal., Columbia.

BURTON, RICHARD: (Richard Jenkins) Pontrhydyfen, S. Wales, Nov. 10, 1925. Oxford.

BYGRAVES, MAX: London, Oct. 16, 1922. St. Joseph's School.

BYINGTON, SPRING: Colorado Springs, Oct. 17, 1898.

BYRNES, EDD: NYC, July 30, 1933. Haaren High.

CABOT, BRUCE: (Jacques de Bujac) Carlsbad, N.Mex. U. of South.

CABOT, SUSAN: Boston, July 9, 1927.

CAESAR, SID: Yonkers, N.Y., Sept. 8, 1922.

CAGNEY, JAMES: NYC, July 1, 1904. Columbia.

CAGNEY, JEANNE: NYC, Mar. 25, 1919. Hunter College.

CALHOUN, RORY: (Francis Timothy Durgin) Los Angeles, Aug. 8, 1923.

CALLAN, MICHAEL: (Mickey Calin) Philadelphia, Nov. 22, 1935.

CALVERT, PHYLLIS: London, Feb. 18, 1917. Margaret Morris School.

CALVET, CORINNE: (Corinne Dibos) Paris, Apr. 30. U. of Paris.

CAMERON, ROD: (Rod Cox) Calgary, Alberta, Can., Dec. 7, 1912.

CANALE, GIANNA MARIA: Reggio Calabria, Italy, Sept. 12.

CANOVA, JUDY: Jacksonville, Fla., Nov. 20, 1916.

CAPUCINE: (Germaine Lefebvre) Toulon, France, Jan. 6.

CAREY, HARRY, JR.: Saugus, Calif., May 16. Black Fox Military Academy.

CAREY, MACDONALD: Sioux City, Iowa, Mar. 15, 1913. U. of Wisc., U. of Iowa.

CAREY, PHILIP: Hackensack, N.J., July 15, 1925. U. of Miami.

CARMICHAEL, HOAGY: Bloomington, Ind., Nov. 22, 1899. Ind. U.

CARMICHAEL, IAN: Hull, Eng., June 18, 1920. Scarborough College.

CARNEY, ART: Mt. Vernon, N. Y., Nov. 4, 1918.

CARON, LESLIE: Paris, July 1, 1931. Nat'l Conservatory, Paris.

CARRADINE, JOHN: NYC, Feb. 5, 1906.

CARROLL, JOHN: (Julian La-Faye) New Orleans.

CARROLL, MADELEINE: West Bromwich, Eng., Feb. 26, 1906. Birmingham U.

CARROLL, PAT: Shreveport, La., May 5, 1927. Catholic U.

CARSON, JOHNNY: Corning, Iowa, Oct. 23, 1925. U. of Neb.

CASSAVETES, JOHN: NYC, 1929. Colgate College, Academy of Dramatic Arts.

CASTLE, PEGGIE: Appalachia, Va., Dec. 22, 1927. Mills College.

CAULFIELD, JOAN: Orange, N.J., June 1. Columbia U.

CERVI, GINO: Bologna, Italy, May 3, 1901.

CHAMPION, GOWER: Geneva, Ill., June 22.

CHAMPION, MARGE: Los Angeles, Sept. 2.

CHANDLER, LANE: (Lane Oakes) Culbertson, Mont., June 4, 1899. Ill. U.

CHANEY, LON, JR.: (Creighton Chaney) Oklahoma City, 1915.

CHAPLIN, CHARLES: London, Apr. 16, 1889.

CHARISSE, CYD: (Tula Ellice Finklea) Amarillo, Tex., Mar. 3, 1923. Hollywood Professional School.

CHASE, ILKA: NYC, Apr. 8, 1905.

| Diane Cilento | Montgomery Clift | Arlene Dahl | Sammy Davis, Jr. | Dolores Del Rio |

CHRISTIAN, LINDA: (Blanca Rosa Welter) Tampico, Mex., Nov. 13, 1924.

CHURCHILL, SARAH: London, Oct. 7, 1916.

CILENTO, DIANE: Queensland, Australia, Oct. 5, 1933. American Academy of Dramatic Arts.

CLARK, DANE: NYC, Feb. 18, 1915. Cornell and Johns Hopkins U.

CLARK, DICK: Mt. Vernon, N. Y., Nov. 30, 1929. Syracuse University.

CLARK, FRED: Lincoln, Calif., Mar. 9, 1914. Stanford U.

CLARKE, MAE: Philadelphia, Aug. 16, 1910.

CLEMENTS, STANLEY: Long Island, N.Y., July 16, 1926.

CLIFT, MONTGOMERY: Omaha, Neb., Oct. 17, 1920.

CLOONEY, ROSEMARY: Maysville, Ky., May 23, 1928.

COCA, IMOGENE: Philadelphia, Nov. 18, 1908.

COLBERT, CLAUDETTE: (Claudette Chauchoin) Paris, Sept. 13, 1907. Art Students League.

COLE, GEORGE: London, Apr. 22, 1925.

COLLINS, JOAN: London, May 23. Francis Holland School.

CONNERY, SEAN: Edinburgh, Scot., Aug. 25, 1930.

CONNORS, CHUCK: (Kevin Joseph Connors) Brooklyn, Apr. 10, 1924. Seton Hall College.

CONTE, RICHARD: (Nicholas Conte) NYC, Mar. 24, 1914. Neighborhood Playhouse.

COOGAN, JACKIE: Los Angeles, Oct. 26, 1914. Villanova College.

COOK, ELISHA, JR.: San Francisco, Dec. 26, 1907. St. Albans.

COOPER, BEN: Hartford, Conn., Sept. 30. Columbia U.

COOPER, GLADYS: Lewisham, Eng., Dec. 18, 1891.

COOPER, JACKIE: Los Angeles, Sept. 15, 1921.

COOPER, MELVILLE: Birmingham, Eng., Oct. 15, 1896. King Edward's School.

COOTE, ROBERT: London, Feb. 4, 1909. Hurstpierpont College.

CORCORAN, DONNA: Quincy, Mass., Sept. 29.

CORDAY, MARA: (Marilyn Watts) Santa Monica, Calif., Jan. 3, 1932.

COREY, JEFF: NYC, Aug. 10, 1914. Fagin School.

COREY, WENDELL: Dracut, Mass., Mar. 20, 1914.

CORRI, ADRIENNE: Glasgow, Scot., Nov. 13, 1933. Royal Academy of Dramatic Art.

CORTESA, VALENTINA: Milan, Italy, Jan. 1, 1925.

COTTEN, JOSEPH: Petersburg, Va., May 15, 1905.

COURTENAY, TOM: Hull, Eng., 1937. Royal Academy of Dramatic Arts.

COURTLAND, JEROME: Knoxville, Tenn., Dec. 27, 1926.

COWARD, NOEL: Teddington-on-the-Thames, Eng., Dec. 16, 1899.

COX, WALLY: Detroit, Dec. 6, 1924. CCNY.

CRABBE, BUSTER (LARRY): (Clarence Linden) Oakland, Calif., U. of S. Cal.

CRAIG, JAMES: (James H. Meador) Nashville, Tenn., Feb. 4, 1912. Rice Inst.

CRAIG, MICHAEL: India in 1929.

CRAIN, JEANNE: Barstow, Cal., May 25, 1925.

CRAWFORD, JOAN: (Lucille LeSueur) San Antonio, Tex., Mar. 23, 1908.

CROSBY, BING: (Harry Lillith Crosby) Tacoma, Wash., May 2, 1904. Gonzaga College.

CROWLEY, PAT: Olyphant, Pa., Sept. 17, 1933.

CUMMINGS, CONSTANCE: Seattle, Wash., May 15, 1910.

CUMMINGS, ROBERT: Joplin, Mo., June 9, 1910. Carnegie Tech.

CUMMINS, PEGGY: Prestatyn, N. Wales, Dec. 18, 1926. Alexandra School.

CURRIE, FINLAY: Edinburgh, Scot., Jan. 20, 1878. Watson School.

CURTIS, TONY: (Bernard Schwartz) NYC, June 3, 1925.

CUSHING, PETER: Kenley, Surrey, Eng., May 26, 1913.

CUTTS, PATRICIA: London, July 20, 1927. Royal Academy of Dramatic Arts.

DAHL, ARLENE: Minneapolis, Aug. 11. U. of Minn.

DAMONE, VIC: (Vito Farinola) Brooklyn, June 12.

DANTINE, HELMUT: Vienna, Oct. 7, 1918. U. of Calif.

DANTON, RAY: NYC, Sept. 19, 1931. Carnegie Tech.

DARCEL, DENISE: (Denise Billecard) Paris, Sept. 8, 1925. U. of Dijon.

DARIN, BOBBY: (Robert Walden Cassotto) NYC, May 14, 1936. Hunter College.

DARREN, JAMES: Philadelphia, June 8, 1936. Stella Adler School.

DARRIEUX, DANIELLE: Bordeaux, France, May 1, 1917. Lycée LaTour.

DARVI, BELLA: (Bella Wegier) Sosnoviec, Poland, Oct. 23, 1928.

DA SILVA, HOWARD: Cleveland, Ohio, May 4, 1909. Carnegie Tech.

DAUPHIN, CLAUDE: Corbeil, France, Aug. 19, 1903. Beaux Arts School.

DAVIS, BETTE: Lowell, Mass., Apr. 5, 1908. John Murray Anderson Dramatic School.

DAVIS, SAMMY, JR.: NYC, Dec. 8, 1925.

DAY, DENNIS: (Eugene Dennis McNulty) NYC, May 21, 1917. Manhattan College.

DAY, DORIS: (Doris Kappelhoff) Cincinnati, Apr. 3, 1924.

DAY, LARAINE: (Laraine Johnson) Roosevelt, Utah, Oct. 13, 1920.

DEAN, JIMMY: Plainview, Tex., Aug. 10, 1928.

DE CARLO, YVONNE: Vancouver, B.C., Can., Sept. 1, 1924. Vancouver School of Drama.

DE CORDOVA, ARTURO: Merida, Yucatan, May 8, 1908. Cavin Inst.

DEE, FRANCES: Los Angeles, Nov. 26, 1907. Chicago U.

DEE, JOEY: (Joseph Di Nicola) Passaic, N.J., June 11, 1940. Patterson State College.

DEE, SANDRA: Bayonne, N.J., Apr. 23, 1942.

DE FORE, DON: Cedar Rapids, Iowa, Aug. 25, 1917. U. of Iowa.

DE HAVEN, GLORIA: Los Angeles, July 23, 1926.

DE HAVILLAND, OLIVIA: Tokyo, Japan, July 1, 1916. Notre Dame Convent School.

DEL RIO, DOLORES: (Dolores Ansunsolo) Durango, Mex., Aug. 3, 1905. St. Joseph's Convent.

DENISON, MICHAEL: Doncaster, York, Eng., Nov. 1, 1915. Oxford.

DENNY, REGINALD: Richmond, Surrey, Eng., Nov. 21, 1891. St. Francis Xavier College.

DEREK, JOHN: Hollywood, Aug. 12, 1926.

DE SICA, VITTORIO: Sora, Caserta, Italy, July 7, 1902.

DEVINE, ANDY: Flagstaff, Ariz., Oct. 7, 1905. Ariz. State College.

DE WILDE, BRANDON: Brooklyn, Apr. 9, 1942.

DE WOLFE, BILLY: (William Andrew Jones) Wollaston, Mass., Feb. 18.

DEXTER, ANTHONY: (Walter Reinhold Alfred Fleischmann) Talmadge, Neb., Jan. 19, 1919. U. of Iowa.

Marlene Dietrich   **Vince Edwards**   **Betty Field**   **Albert Finney**   **Ava Gardner**

DICKINSON, ANGIE: Kulm, N. Dak., Sept. 30. Glendale College.

DIETRICH, MARLENE: (Maria Magdalene von Losch) Berlin, Ger., Dec. 27, 1904. Berlin Music Academy.

DILLMAN, BRADFORD: San Francisco, Apr. 14, 1930. Yale.

DOMERGUE, FAITH: New Orleans, June 16, 1925.

DONAHUE, TROY: (Merle Johnson) NYC, Jan. 27. Columbia University.

DONNELL, JEFF: (Jean Donnell) South Windham, Me., July 10, 1921. Yale Drama School.

DONNELLY, RUTH: Trenton, N.J., May 17, 1896.

DORS, DIANA: Swindon, Wilshire, Eng., Oct. 23, 1931. London Academy of Music.

DOUGLAS, KIRK: Amsterdam, N.Y., Dec. 9, 1916. St. Lawrence U.

DOUGLAS, MELVYN: (Melvyn Hesselberg) Macon, Ga., Apr. 5, 1901.

DRAKE, BETSY: Paris, Sept. 11, 1923.

DRAKE, CHARLES: (Charles Ruppert) NYC, Oct. 2, 1914. Nichols College.

DREW, ELLEN: (formerly Terry Ray) Kansas City, Mo., Nov. 23, 1915.

DRISCOLL, BOBBY: Cedar Rapids, Iowa, Mar. 3, 1937.

DRU, JOANNE: (Joanne La-Cock) Logan, W. Va., Jan. 31, 1923. John Robert Powers School.

DUFF, HOWARD: Bremerton, Wash., Nov. 24, 1917.

DUNNE, IRENE: Louisville, Ky., Dec. 20, 1904. Chicago College of Music.

DUNNOCK, MILDRED: Baltimore, Jan. 25. Johns Hopkins and Columbia U.

DURANTE, JIMMY: NYC, Feb. 10, 1893.

DURYEA, DAN: White Plains, N.Y., Jan. 23, 1907. Cornell.

DVORAK, ANN: (Ann McKim) NYC, Aug. 2, 1912.

EASTON, ROBERT: Milwaukee, Nov. 23, 1930. U. of Texas.

EATON, SHIRLEY: London, 1937. Aida Foster School.

EDDY, NELSON: Providence, R.I., June 29, 1901.

EDWARDS, VINCE: NYC, July 9, 1928. American Academy of Dramatic Art.

EGAN, RICHARD: San Francisco, July 29, 1923. Stanford U.

EGGAR, SAMANTHA: London, 1940.

ELLIOTT, DENHOLM: London, May 31, 1922. Malvern College.

ELSOM, ISOBEL: Cambridge, Eng., Mar. 16, 1894.

EMERSON, FAYE: Elizabeth, La., July 8, 1917. San Diego State College.

ERICKSON, LEIF: Alameda, Calif., Oct. 27, 1914. U. of Calif.

ERICSON, JOHN: Dusseldorf, Ger., Sept. 25, 1926. American Academy of Dramatic Art.

ESMOND, CARL: Vienna, June 14, 1906. U. of Vienna.

EVANS, DALE: (Frances Smith) Uvalde, Texas, Oct. 31, 1912.

EVANS, GENE: Holbrook, Ariz., July 11, 1922.

EVANS, MAURICE: Dorchester, Eng., June 3, 1901.

EWELL, TOM: (Yewell Tompkins) Owensboro, Ky., Apr. 29, 1909. U. of Wisc.

FABIAN: (Fabian Forte) Philadelphia, 1940.

FAIRBANKS, DOUGLAS, JR.: NYC, Dec. 9, 1909. Collegiate School.

FARR, FELICIA: Westchester, N.Y., Oct. 4, 1932. Penn State College.

FARRELL, CHARLES: Onset Bay, Mass., Aug. 9, 1901. Boston U.

FARRELL, GLENDA: Enid, Okla., June 30, 1904.

FELLOWS, EDITH: Boston, May 20, 1923.

FELTON, VERNA: Salinas, Calif., July 20, 1890.

FERNANDEL: (Fernand Joseph Desire Constandin) Marseilles, France, 1903.

FERRER, JOSE: Santurce, P.R., Jan. 8, 1912. Princeton U.

FERRER, MEL: Elberon, N.J., Aug. 25, 1917. Princeton U.

FIELD, BETTY: Boston, Feb. 8, 1918. American Academy of Dramatic Art.

FINCH, PETER: London, Sept. 28, 1916.

FINNEY, ALBERT: Salford, Lancashire, Eng., May 9, 1936. Royal Academy of Dramatic Arts.

FISHER, EDDIE: Philadelphia, Aug. 10, 1928.

FITZGERALD, GERALDINE: Dublin, Ire., Nov. 24, 1914. Dublin Art School.

FLEMING, RHONDA: (Marilyn Louis) Los Angeles, Aug. 10.

FLEMYNG, ROBERT: Liverpool, Eng., Jan. 3, 1912. Haileybury College.

FOCH, NINA: Leyden, Holland, Apr. 20, 1924.

FONDA, HENRY: Grand Island, Neb., May 16, 1905. Minn. U.

FONDA, JANE: NYC, Dec. 21, 1937. Vassar.

FONDA, PETER: NYC, Feb. 23, 1939. U. of Omaha.

FONTAINE, JOAN: Tokyo, Japan, Oct. 22, 1917.

FORD, GLENN: (Gwylln Ford) Quebec, Can., May 1.

FORD, PAUL: Baltimore, Nov. 2, 1901. Dartmouth.

FOREST, MARK: (Lou Degni) Brooklyn, Jan. 1933.

FORREST, STEVE: Huntsville, Tex., Sept. 29. UCLA.

FORSYTHE, JOHN: Penn's Grove, N.J., Jan. 29, 1918.

FOSTER, PRESTON: Ocean City, N.J., Aug. 24, 1904.

FRANCES, CONNIE: (Constance Franconero) Newark, N.J., Dec. 12, 1938.

FRANCIOSA, ANTHONY: NYC, Oct. 25.

FRANCIS, ANNE: Ossining, N. Y., Sept. 16.

FRANCIS, ARLENE: (Arlene Kazanjian) Boston, 1908. Finch School.

FRANCIS, KAY: (Katherine Gibbs) Oklahoma City, Jan. 13, 1899. Cathedral School.

FRANZ, ARTHUR: Perth Amboy, N.J., Feb. 29, 1920. Blue Ridge College.

FRANZ, EDUARD: Milwaukee, Wisc., Oct. 31, 1902.

FRAWLEY, WILLIAM: Burlington, Iowa, Feb. 26, 1893.

FREEMAN, MONA: Baltimore, June 9, 1926.

FURNEAUX, YVONNE: Lille, France, 1928. Oxford U.

GABIN, JEAN: Villette, France, May 17, 1904.

GABOR, EVA: Budapest, Hungary, Feb. 11, 1925.

GABOR, ZSA ZSA: (Sari Gabor) Budapest, Hungary, Feb. 6, 1923.

GAM, RITA: Pittsburgh, Apr. 2, 1928.

GARBO, GRETA: (Greta Gustafson) Stockholm, Sweden, Sept. 18, 1906.

GARDINER, REGINALD: Wimbledon, Eng., Feb. 1903. Royal Academy of Dramatic Arts.

GARDNER, AVA: Smithfield, N.C., Dec. 24, 1922. Atlantic Christian College.

GARLAND, JUDY: (Frances Gumm) Grand Rapids, Minn., June 10, 1922.

GARNER, JAMES: Norman, Okla., Apr. 7, 1928. Berghof School.

GARNER, PEGGY ANN: Canton, Ohio, Feb. 3, 1932.

GARRETT, BETTY: St. Joseph, Mo., May 23, 1919. Annie Wright Seminary.

GASSMAN, VITTORIO: Genoa, Italy, Sept. 1, 1922. Rome Academy of Dramatic Art.

| Andy Griffith | Celeste Holm | George Grizzard | Kim Hunter | Robert Horton |

GAVIN, JOHN: Los Angeles, Apr. 8. Stanford U.

GAYNOR, JANET: Philadelphia, Oct. 6, 1906.

GAYNOR, MITZI: Chicago, Sept. 4, 1931.

GENN, LEO: London, Aug. 9, 1905. Cambridge.

GIELGUD, JOHN: London, Apr. 14, 1904. Royal Academy of Dramatic Art.

GILLMORE, MARGOLO: London, May 31, 1897. American Academy of Dramatic Art.

GILMORE, VIRGINIA: (Sherman Poole) Del Monte, Calif., July 26, 1919. U. of Calif.

GISH, DOROTHY: Massillon, Ohio, Mar. 11, 1898.

GISH, LILLIAN: Springfield, Ohio, Oct. 14, 1896.

GLEASON, JACKIE: Brooklyn, Feb. 26, 1916.

GODDARD, PAULETTE: Great Neck, N.Y., June 3, 1911.

GOMEZ, THOMAS: NYC, July 10, 1905.

GORDON, RUTH: Wollaston, Mass., Oct. 30, 1896. American Academy of Dramatic Art.

GOULET, ROBERT: Lawrence, Mass., Nov. 26, 1933. Edmonton School.

GRABLE, BETTY: St. Louis, Mo., Dec. 18, 1916. Hollywood Professional School.

GRAHAME, GLORIA: (Gloria Grahame Hallward) Los Angeles, Nov. 28, 1929.

GRANGER, FARLEY: San Jose, Calif., July 1, 1925.

GRANGER, STEWART: (James Stewart) London, May 6, 1913. Webber-Douglas School of Acting.

GRANT, CARY: (Archibald Alexander Leach) Bristol, Eng., Jan. 18, 1904.

GRANT, KATHRYN: (Kathryn Grandstaff) Houston, Tex., Nov. 25, 1933. UCLA.

GRAVES, PETER: Minneapolis, Mar. 18. U. of Minn.

GRAY, COLEEN: (Doris Jensen) Staplehurst, Neb., Oct. 23, 1922. Hamline U.

GRAYSON, KATHRYN: (Zelma Hedrick) Winston-Salem, N.C., Feb. 9, 1923.

GREENE, RICHARD: Plymouth, Eng., Aug. 25, 1918. Cardinal Vaughn School.

GREENWOOD, JOAN: London, 1919. Royal Academy of Dramatic Arts.

GREER, JANE: Washington, D.C., Sept. 9, 1924.

GREY, VIRGINIA: Los Angeles, Mar. 22, 1923.

GRIFFITH, ANDY: Mt. Airy, N.C., June 1, 1926. U. of N.C.

GRIFFITH, HUGH: Marian Glas, Anglesey, N. Wales, May 30, 1912.

GRIZZARD, GEORGE: Roanoke Rapids, N.C., Apr. 1, 1928. U. of N.C.

GUINNESS, ALEC: London, Apr. 2, 1914. Pembroke Lodge School,

HAAS, HUGO: Czechoslovakia, Feb. 19, 1902. Conservatory of Drama and Music.

HACKETT, BUDDY: Brooklyn, Aug. 31, 1924.

HALE, BARBARA: DeKalb, Ill., Apr. 18, 1922. Chicago Academy of Fine Arts.

HAMILTON, GEORGE: Memphis, Tenn., Aug. 12. Hackley School.

HAMILTON, MARGARET: Cleveland, Ohio, Dec. 9, 1902. Hathaway-Brown School.

HAMILTON, NEIL: Lynn, Mass., Sept. 9, 1899.

HARDING, ANN: (Dorothy Walton Gatley) Fort Sam Houston, Texas, Aug. 17, 1904.

HARRIS, JULIE: Grosse Pointe, Mich., Dec. 2, 1925. Yale Drama School.

HARRISON, REX: Huyton, Cheshire, Eng., Mar. 5, 1908.

HARVEY, LAURENCE: Yonishkis, Lithuania, Oct. 1, 1928. Meyerton College.

HATTON, RAYMOND: Red Oak, Iowa, July 7, 1892.

HAVER, JUNE: Rock Island, Ill., June 10, 1926.

HAVOC, JUNE: (June Hovick) Seattle, Wash., Nov. 1916.

HAWKINS, JACK: London, Sept. 14, 1910. Trinity School.

HAYES, HELEN: (Helen Brown) Washington, D.C., Oct. 10, 1900. Sacred Heart Convent.

HAYES, MARGARET: (Maggie) Baltimore, Dec. 5, 1925.

HAYWARD, SUSAN: (Edythe Marrener) Brooklyn, June 30, 1919.

HAYWORTH, RITA: (Margarita Cansino) NYC, Oct. 17, 1919.

HECKART, EILEEN: Columbus, Ohio, Mar. 29. Ohio State U.

HEDISON, DAVID: Providence, R.I., May 20, 1929. Brown U.

HEFLIN, VAN: Walters, Okla., Dec. 13, 1910.

HENDERSON, MARCIA: Andover, Mass., July 22, 1932. American Academy of Dramatic Art.

HENDRIX, WANDA: Jacksonville, Fla., Nov. 3, 1928.

HENREID, PAUL: Trieste, Jan. 10, 1908.

HEPBURN, AUDREY: Brussels, Belgium, May 4, 1929.

HEPBURN, KATHARINE: Hartford, Conn., Nov. 8, 1909. Bryn Mawr.

HESTON, CHARLTON: Evanston, Ill., Oct. 4, 1924. Northwestern U.

HICKMAN, DARRYL: Hollywood, Calif., July 28, 1933. Loyola U.

HILLER, WENDY: Bramhall, Cheshire, Eng., Aug. 15, 1912. Winceby House School.

HOLLIMAN, EARL: Tennasas Swamp, Delhi, La., Sept. 11. UCLA.

HOLLOWAY, STANLEY: London, Oct. 1, 1890.

HOLM, CELESTE: NYC, Apr. 29, 1919.

HOMEIER, SKIP: (George Vincent Homeier) Chicago, Oct. 5, 1930. UCLA.

HOMOLKA, OSCAR: Vienna, Aug. 12, 1898. Vienna Dramatic Academy.

HOPE, BOB: London, May 26, 1904.

HOPKINS, MIRIAM: Bainbridge, Ga., Oct. 18, 1902. Syracuse U.

HOPPER, DENNIS: Dodge City, Kan., May 17, 1936.

HOPPER, HEDDA: (Elda Furry) Hollidaysburg, Pa., June 2, 1890. Pittsburgh Conservatory of Music.

HORNE, LENA: Brooklyn, June 30, 1917.

HORTON, EDWARD EVERETT: Brooklyn, Mar. 18, 1888. Columbia U.

HORTON, ROBERT: Los Angeles, July 29, 1924. UCLA.

HOWARD, RONALD: Norwood, Eng., Apr. 7, 1918. Jesus College.

HOWARD, TREVOR: Kent Eng., Sept. 29, 1916. Royal Academy of Dramatic Art.

HUDSON, ROCK: (Roy Fitzgerald) Winnetka, Ill., Nov. 17, 1925.

HUNT, MARSHA: Chicago, Oct. 17, 1917.

HUNTER, IAN: Cape Town, S.A., June 13, 1900. St. Andrew's College.

HUNTER, JEFFREY: (Henry H. McKinnies) New Orleans, Nov. 25. Northwestern U.

HUNTER, KIM: (Janet Cole) Detroit, Nov. 12, 1922.

HUNTER, TAB: NYC, July 11, 1931.

HUSSEY, RUTH: Providence, R.I., Oct. 30, 1917. U. of Mich.

HUTTON, BETTY: (Betty Thornberg) Battle Creek, Mich., Feb. 26, 1921.

HUTTON, ROBERT: (Robert Winne) Kingston, N.Y., June 11, 1920. Blair Academy.

HYER, MARTHA: Fort Worth, Tex., Aug. 10, 1930. Northwestern U.

IRELAND, JOHN: Vancouver, B.C., Can., Jan. 30, 1915.

| David Janssen | Jennifer Jones | Jack Lord | Katy Jurado | John Lund |

IVES, BURL: Hunt Township, Ill., June 14, 1909. Charleston Ill. Teachers College.

JAECKEL, RICHARD: Long Beach, N.Y., Oct. 10, 1926.

JAFFE, SAM: NYC, Mar. 8, 1898.

JAGGER, DEAN: Lima, Ohio, Nov. 7, 1903. Wabash College.

JANSSEN, DAVID: Naponee, Neb., Mar. 27, 1930.

JARMAN, CLAUDE, JR.: Nashville, Tenn., Sept. 27, 1934.

JASON, RICK: NYC, May 21, 1926. American Academy of Dramatic Art.

JEAN, GLORIA: (Gloria Jean Schoonover) Buffalo, N.Y., Apr. 14, 1928.

JEFFREYS, ANNE: Goldsboro, N.C., Jan. 26, 1923. Anderson College.

JERGENS, ADELE: Brooklyn, Nov. 26, 1922.

JOHNS, GLYNIS: Durban, S. Africa, Oct. 5, 1923.

JOHNSON, CELIA: Richmond, Surrey, Eng., Dec. 18, 1908. Royal Academy of Dramatic Arts.

JOHNSON, VAN: Newport, R.I., Aug. 28, 1916.

JONES, CAROLYN: Amarillo, Tex., 1933.

JONES, DEAN: Morgan County, Ala., Jan. 25, 1936. Asbury College.

JONES, JENNIFER: (Phyllis Isley) Tulsa, Okla., Mar. 2, 1919. American Academy of Dramatic Art.

JONES, SHIRLEY: Smithton, Pa., March 31.

JOURDAN, LOUIS: Marseilles, France, June 18, 1921.

JURADO, KATY: (Maria Christina Jurado Garcia) Guadalajara, Mex., 1927.

KARLOFF, BORIS: (William Henry Pratt) London, Nov. 23, 1887. Uppingham School.

KASZNAR, KURT: Vienna, Aug. 12, 1913. Gymnasium, Vienna.

KAUFMANN, CHRISTINE: Lansdorf, Graz, Austria, Jan. 11, 1945.

KAYE, DANNY: (David Daniel Kominski) Brooklyn, Jan. 18, 1913.

KAYE, STUBBY: NYC, Nov. 11, 1918.

KEATON, BUSTER: Piqua, Kan., Oct. 4, 1895.

KEEL, HOWARD: (Harold Keel) Gillespie, Ill., Apr. 13, 1919.

KEITH, BRIAN: Bayonne, N.J., Nov. 14, 1921.

KEITH, IAN: Boston, Feb. 27, 1899. American Academy of Dramatic Art.

KEITH, ROBERT: Fowler, Ind., Feb. 10, 1898.

KELLY, GENE: Pittsburgh, Aug. 23, 1912. U. of Pittsburgh.

KELLY, GRACE: Philadelphia, Nov. 12, 1929. American Academy of Dramatic Art.

KELLY, JACK: Astoria, N.Y., Sept. 16, 1927. UCLA.

KELLY, NANCY: Lowell, Mass., Mar. 25, 1921. Bentley School.

KENNEDY, ARTHUR: Worcester, Mass., Feb. 17, 1914. Carnegie Tech.

KERR, DEBORAH: Helensburgh, Scot., Sept. 30, 1921. Smale Ballet School.

KERR, JOHN: NYC, Nov. 15, 1931. Harvard and Columbia.

KITT, EARTHA: North, S.C., Jan. 26, 1928.

KNOWLES, PATRIC: (Reginald Lawrence Knowles) Horsforth, Eng., Nov. 11, 1911.

KNOX, ALEXANDER: Strathroy, Ont., Can., Jan. 16, 1907. Western Ontario U.

KNOX, ELYSE: Hartford, Conn., Dec. 14, 1917. Traphagen School.

KOHNER, SUSAN: Los Angeles, Nov. 11, 1936. U. of Calif.

KORVIN, CHARLES: (Geza Korvin Karpathi) Czechoslovakia, Nov. 21. Sorbonne.

KOSLECK, MARTIN: Barkotzen, Ger., Mar. 24, 1914. Max Reinhardt School.

KREUGER, KURT: St. Moritz, Switz., July 23, 1917. U. of London.

KRUGER, HARDY: Berlin, Ger., Apr. 12, 1928.

KRUGER, OTTO: Toledo, Ohio, Sept. 6, 1885. Michigan and Columbia U.

LAHR, BERT: (Irving Lashrheim) NYC, Aug. 13, 1895.

LAKE, VERONICA: (Constance Keane) Lake Placid, N.Y., Nov. 14, 1919. McGill U.

LAMARR, HEDY: Vienna, 1915.

LAMAS, FERNANDO: Buenos Aires, Jan. 9, 1920.

LAMB, GIL: Minneapolis, June 14, 1906. U. of Minn.

LAMOUR, DOROTHY: Dec. 10, 1914. Spence's School.

LANCASTER, BURT: NYC, Nov. 2, 1913. NYU.

LANCHESTER, ELSA: (Elsa Sullivan) London, Oct. 28, 1902.

LANDIS, JESSIE ROYCE: Chicago, Nov. 25, 1904. Chicago Conservatory.

LANGAN, GLENN: Denver, Colo., July 8, 1917.

LANGE, HOPE: Redding Ridge, Conn., Nov. 28. Reed College.

LANGTON, PAUL: Salt Lake City, Apr. 17, 1913. Travers School of Theatre.

LANSBURY, ANGELA: London, Oct. 16, 1925. London Academy of Music.

LAURIE, PIPER: (Rosetta Jacobs) Detroit, Jan. 22, 1932.

LAWFORD, PETER: London, Sept. 7, 1923.

LAWRENCE, BARBARA: Carnegie, Okla., Feb. 24, 1930. UCLA.

LAWRENCE, CAROL: Melrose Park, Ill., Sept. 5, 1935.

LEDERER, FRANCIS: Karlin, Prague, Czechoslovakia, Nov. 6, 1906.

LEE, CHRISTOPHER: London, May 27, 1922. Wellington College.

LEE, GYPSY ROSE: (Rose Hovick) Seattle, Wash., Feb. 9, 1914.

LEIGH, JANET: (Jeanette Helen Morrison) Merced, Calif., July 6, 1927. College of Pacific.

LEIGH, VIVIEN: (Vivien Mary Hartley) Darjeeling, India, Nov. 5, 1913. Royal Academy of Dramatic Arts.

LEIGHTON, MARGARET: Barnt Green, Worcestershire, Eng., Feb. 26, 1922. Church of England College.

LEMBECK, HARVEY: Brooklyn, Apr. 15, 1923. U. of Ala.

LEMMON, JACK: Boston, Feb. 8, 1925. Harvard.

LESLIE, BETHEL: NYC, Aug. 3, 1929. Breaney School.

LESLIE, JOAN: (Joan Brodell) Detroit, Jan. 26, 1925. St. Benedict's.

LEVENE, SAM: NYC, 1907.

LEWIS, JERRY: Newark, N.J., Mar. 16, 1926.

LINDFORS, VIVECA: Uppsala, Sweden, Dec. 29, 1920. Stockholm Royal Dramatic School.

LIVESEY, ROGER: Barry, Wales, June 25, 1906. Westminster School.

LLOYD, HAROLD: Burchard, Neb., July 28, 1904.

LOCKHART, JUNE: NYC, June 25, 1925. Westlake School.

LOCKWOOD, MARGARET: Karachi, Pakistan, Sept. 15, 1916. Royal Academy of Dramatic Arts.

LOLLOBRIGIDA, GINA: Subiaco, Italy, 1928. Rome Academy of Fine Arts.

LOM, HERBERT: Prague, Czechoslovakia, 1917. Prague U.

LONDON, JULIE: (Julie Peck) Santa Rosa, Calif., Sept. 26, 1926.

LONG, RICHARD: Chicago, Dec. 17, 1927.

LOPEZ, PERRY: NYC, July 22, 1931. NYU.

LORD, JACK: NYC, Dec. 30, 1930. NYU.

| Hedy Lamarr | Jeffrey Lynn | Anna Magnani | Stephen McNally | Mercedes McCambridge |

LOREN, SOPHIA: (Sofia Scicolone) Rome, Italy, Sept. 20, 1934.

LOUISE, ANITA: (Anita Louise Fremault) NYC, 1917. Professional Children's School.

LOY, MYRNA: (Myrna Williams) Helena, Mont., Aug. 2, 1905. Westlake School.

LUKAS, PAUL: Budapest, Hungary, May 26, 1895. Actors Academy of Hungary.

LUND, JOHN: Rochester, N.Y., Feb. 6, 1913.

LUNDIGAN, WILLIAM: Syracuse, N.Y., June 12, 1914. Syracuse U.

LUPINO, IDA: London, Feb. 4, 1918. Royal Academy of Dramatic Arts.

LYNDE, PAUL: Mt. Vernon, Ohio, June 13, 1926. Northwestern U.

LYNLEY, CAROL: NYC, Feb. 13, 1942.

LYNN, DIANA: (Dolly Loehr) Los Angeles, Oct. 7, 1926.

LYNN, JEFFREY: Auburn, Mass., 1910. Bates College.

MacARTHUR, JAMES: Los Angeles, Dec. 8, 1937. Harvard.

MacGINNIS, NIALL: Dublin, Ire., Mar. 29, 1913. Dublin U.

MacLAINE, SHIRLEY: Richmond, Va., Apr. 24, 1934.

MacLANE, BARTON: Columbia, S.C., Dec. 25, 1902. Wesleyan University.

MacMAHON, ALINE: McKeesport, Pa., May 3, 1899. Barnard College.

MacMURRAY, FRED: Kankakee, Ill., Aug. 30, 1908. Carroll College.

MacRAE, GORDON: East Orange, N.J., Mar. 12, 1921.

MADISON, GUY: (Robert Moseley) Bakersfield, Calif., Jan. 19, 1922. Bakersfield Jr. College.

MAGNANI, ANNA: Alexandria, Egypt, Mar. 7, 1908. Rome Academy of Dramatic Art.

MAHARIS, GEORGE: Astoria, L.I., N.Y., Sept. 1, 1928. Actors Studio.

MAHONEY, JOCK: (Jacques O'Mahoney) Chicago, Feb. 7, 1919. U. of Iowa.

MALDEN, KARL: (Malden Sekulovich) Gary, Ind., Mar. 22, 1914.

MALONE, DOROTHY: Chicago, Jan. 30, 1930. S. Methodist U.

MANSFIELD, JAYNE: (Jane Palmer) Byrn Mawr, Pa., Apr. 19, 1933. UCLA.

MARCH, FREDRIC: (Frederick McIntyre Bickel) Racine, Wisc., Aug. 31, 1897. U. of Wisc.

MARGO: (Maria Marguerita Guadalupe Boldao y Castilla) Mexico City, May 10, 1918.

MARGOLIN, JANET: NYC, July 25, 1943. Walden School.

MARLOWE, HUGH: (Hugh Hipple) Philadelphia, Jan. 30, 1914.

MARSHALL, BRENDA: (Ardis Anderson Gaines) Isle of Negros, P.I., Sept. 29, 1915. Texas State College.

MARSHALL, E. G.: Owatonna, Minn., June 18, 1910. U. of Minn.

MARSHALL, HERBERT: London, May 23, 1890. St. Mary's College.

MARTIN, DEAN: Steubenville, Ohio, June 17, 1917.

MARTIN, MARY: Wetherford, Tex., Dec. 1, 1914. Ward-Belmont School.

MARTIN, TONY: Oakland, Cal., Dec. 25, 1913. St. Mary's College.

MARVIN, LEE: NYC, Feb. 19, 1924.

MARX, GROUCHO: (Julius Marx) NYC, Oct. 2, 1895.

MASON, JAMES: Huddersfield, Yorkshire, Eng., May 15, 1909. Cambridge.

MASON, PAMELA: (Pamela Kellino) Westgate, Eng., Mar. 10, 1918.

MASSEN, OSA: Copenhagen, Den., Jan. 13, 1916.

MASSEY, RAYMOND: Toronto, Can., Aug. 30, 1896. Oxford.

MATTHAU, WALTER: NYC, Oct. 1, 1923.

MATURE, VICTOR: Louisville, Ky., Jan. 29, 1916.

MAXWELL, MARILYN: Clarinda, Iowa, Aug. 3, 1922.

MAYEHOFF, EDDIE: Baltimore, July 7. Yale.

MC CALLUM, DAVID: Glasgow, Scot., 1933. Royal Academy of Dramatic Arts.

MC CAMBRIDGE, MERCEDES: Joliet, Ill., March 17. Mundelein College.

MC CARTHY: KEVIN: Seattle, Wash., Feb. 15, 1914. Minn. U.

MC CLORY, SEAN: Dublin, Ire., March 8, 1924. U. of Galway.

MC CREA, JOEL: Los Angeles, Nov. 5, 1905. Pomona College.

MC DERMOTT, HUGH: Edinburgh, Scot., Mar. 20, 1908.

MC DOWALL, RODDY: London, Sept. 17, 1928. St. Joseph's.

MC GAVIN, DARREN: Spokane, Wash., May 7, 1922. College of Pacific.

MC GIVER, JOHN: NYC, Nov. 5, 1915. Fordham, Columbia U.

MC GUIRE, DOROTHY: Omaha, Neb., June 14, 1919. Wellesley.

MC NALLY, STEPHEN: (Horace McNally) NYC, July 29, Fordham U.

MC NAMARA, MAGGIE: NYC, June 18. St. Catherine.

MC QUEEN, STEVE: Indianapolis, Mar. 24.

MEADOWS, AUDREY: Wuchang, China, 1924. St. Margaret's.

MEADOWS, JAYNE: (formerly, Jayne Cotter) Wuchang, China, Sept. 27, 1923. St. Margaret's.

MEDWIN, MICHAEL: London, 1925. Instut Fischer.

MEEKER, RALPH: (Ralph Rathgeber) Minneapolis, Nov. 21, 1920. Northwestern U.

MEREDITH, BURGESS: Cleveland, Ohio, Nov. 16, 1909. Amherst.

MERKEL, UNA: Covington, Ky., Dec. 10, 1903.

MERMAN, ETHEL: (Ethel Zimmerman) Astoria, N.Y., Jan. 16, 1909.

MIFUNE, TOSHIRO: Tsingtao, China, Apr. 1, 1920.

MILES, VERA: Boise City, Okla., Aug. 23.

MILLAND, RAY: (Reginald Truscott-Jones) Neath, Wales, Jan. 3, 1908. King's College.

MILLER, ANN: (Lucille Ann Collier) Houston, Tex., Apr. 12, 1923. Lawler Professional School.

MILLER, MARVIN: St. Louis, July 18, 1913. Washington U.

MILLS, HAYLEY: London, Apr. 18, 1946. Elmhurst School.

MILLS, JOHN: Suffolk, Eng., Feb. 22, 1908.

MIMIEUX, YVETTE: Los Angeles, Jan. 8. Hollywood High.

MINEO, SAL: NYC, Jan. 10, 1939. Lodge School.

MIRANDA, ISA: (Ines Sampietro) Milan, Italy, July 5, 1917.

MITCHELL, CAMERON: Dallastown, Pa., Nov. 1918. NY Theatre School.

MITCHELL, JAMES: Sacramento, Calif., Feb. 29, 1920. LACC.

MITCHUM, ROBERT: Bridgeport, Conn., Aug. 6, 1917.

MONTALBAN, RICARDO: Mexico City, Nov. 25, 1920.

MONTAND, YVES: (Yves Montand Livi) Mansummano, Tuscany, Oct. 13, 1921.

MONTGOMERY, ELIZABETH: Los Angeles, Apr. 15, 1933. American Academy of Dramatic Art.

MONTGOMERY, GEORGE: (George Letz) Brady, Mont., Aug. 29, 1916. U. of Mont.

MONTGOMERY, ROBERT: (Henry, Jr.) Beacon, N.Y., May 21, 1904.

MOORE, CONSTANCE: Sioux City, Iowa, Jan. 18, 1922.

MOORE, DICK: Los Angeles, Sept. 12, 1925.

| George Nader | Merle Oberon | Anthony Newley | Suzy Parker | Claude Rains |

MOORE, KIERON: County Cork, Ire., 1925. St. Mary's College.

MOORE, ROGER: London, Oct. 14. Royal Academy of Dramatic Arts.

MOORE, TERRY: (Helen Koford) Los Angeles, Jan. 7, 1929.

MOOREHEAD, AGNES: Clinton, Mass., Dec. 6, 1906. American Academy of Dramatic Art.

MORE, KENNETH: Gerrards Cross, Eng., Sept. 20, 1914. Victoria College.

MORENO, RITA: Humacao, P.R., Dec. 11, 1931.

MORGAN, DENNIS: (Stanley Morner) Prentice, Wisc., Dec. 10, 1920. Carroll College.

MORGAN, HARRY (HENRY): (Harry Bratsburg) Detroit, Apr. 10, 1915. U. of Chicago.

MORGAN, MICHELE: (Simone Roussel) Paris, Feb. 29, 1920. Paris Dramatic School.

MORISON, PATRICIA: NYC, 1919.

MORLEY, ROBERT: Wiltshire, Eng., May 26, 1908. Royal Academy of Dramatic Arts.

MORRIS, CHESTER: NYC, Feb. 16, 1901. Art Students League.

MORRIS, HOWARD: NYC, Sept. 4, 1919. NYU.

MORROW, VIC: Bronx, N.Y., Feb. 14, 1932. Fla. Southern College.

MORSE, ROBERT: Newton, Mass., May 18, 1931.

MOSTEL, ZERO: Brooklyn, Feb. 28, 1915. CCNY.

MUNI, PAUL: (Muni Weisenfreund) Lemberg, Austria, Sept. 22, 1895.

MURPHY, AUDIE: Kingston, Tex., June 20, 1924.

MURPHY, GEORGE: New Haven, Conn., July 4, 1904. Yale.

MURRAY, DON: Hollywood, July 31, 1929. American Academy of Dramatic Art.

MURRAY, KEN: (Don Court) NYC, July 14, 1903.

NADER, GEORGE: Pasadena, Calif., Oct. 19, 1921. Occidental College.

NAGEL, CONRAD: Keokuk, Iowa, Mar. 16, 1897. Highland Park College.

NAPIER, ALAN: Birmingham, Eng., Jan. 7, 1903. Birmingham University.

NATWICK, MILDRED: Baltimore, June 19, 1908. Bryn Mawr.

NEAL, PATRICIA: Packard, Ky., Jan. 20, 1926. Northwestern U.

NEFF, HILDEGARDE: (Hildegard Knef) Ulm, Ger., Dec. 28, 1925. Berlin Art Academy.

NELSON, DAVID: NYC, Oct. 24, 1936. USC.

NELSON, GENE: (Gene Berg) Seattle, Wash., Mar. 24, 1920.

NELSON, HARRIET HILLIARD: (Peggy Lou Snyder) Des Moines, Iowa, July 18.

NELSON, LORI: (Dixie Kay Nelson) Sante Fe, N.M., Aug. 15, 1933.

NELSON, OZZIE: (Oswald) Jersey City, N.J., Mar. 20, 1907. Rutgers U.

NELSON, RICK: (Eric Hilliard Nelson) Teaneck, N.J., May 8, 1940.

NESBITT, CATHLEEN: Cheshire, Eng., Nov. 24, 1889. Victoria College.

NEWLEY, ANTHONY: Hackney, London, Sept. 21, 1931.

NEWMAN, PAUL: Cleveland, Ohio, Jan. 26, 1925. Yale.

NICOL, ALEX: Ossining, N.Y., Jan. 20, 1919. Actors Studio.

NIELSEN, LESLIE: Regina, Saskatchewan, Can., Feb. 11, 1926. Neighborhood Playhouse.

NIVEN, DAVID: Kirriemuir, Scot., Mar. 1, 1910. Sandhurst College.

NOLAN, LLOYD: San Francisco, Aug. 11, 1902. Stanford U.

NOONAN, TOMMY: Bellingham, Wash., Apr. 29, 1922. NYU.

NORTH, SHEREE: (Dawn Bethel) Los Angeles, Jan. 17, 1933. Hollywood High.

NOVAK, KIM: (Marilyn Novak) Chicago, Feb. 13, 1933. LACC.

NOVARRO, RAMON: (Ramon Samaniegoes) Durango, Mex., Feb. 6, 1905.

NUGENT, ELLIOTT: Dover, Ohio, Sept. 20, 1900. Ohio State U.

NUYEN, FRANCE: Marseilles, France, 1939. Beaux Arts School.

OBERON, MERLE: (Estelle Merle O'Brien Thompson) Tasmania, Feb. 19, 1911.

O'BRIAN, HUGH: (Hugh J. Krampe) Rochester, N.Y., Apr. 19, 1928. Cincinnati U.

O'BRIEN, EDMOND: NYC, Sept. 10, 1915. Fordham, Neighborhood Playhouse.

O'BRIEN, MARGARET: (Angela Maxine O'Brien) Los Angeles, Jan. 15, 1937.

O'BRIEN, PAT: Milwaukee, Nov. 11, 1899. Marquette U.

O'CONNELL, ARTHUR: NYC, Mar. 29, 1908. St. John's.

O'CONNOR, DONALD: Chicago, Aug. 28, 1925.

O'DONNELL, CATHY: (Ann Steely) Siluria, Ala., July 6, 1925. Oklahoma City U.

O'HARA, MAUREEN: (Maureen FitzSimons) Dublin, Ire., Aug. 17, 1921. Abbey School.

O'HERLIHY, DAN: Wexford, Ire., May 1, 1919. National U.

OLIVIER, LAURENCE: Dorking, Eng., May 22, 1907. St. Edward's, Oxford.

O'NEAL, PATRICK: Ocala, Fla., Sept. 26, 1927. U. of Fla.

O'SHEA, MICHAEL: NYC, Mar. 17, 1906.

O'SULLIVAN, MAUREEN: Byle, Ire., May 17, 1911. Sacred Heart Convent.

OWEN, REGINALD: Wheathampstead, Eng., Aug. 5, 1887. Tree's Academy.

PAGE, GERALDINE: Kirksville, Mo., Nov. 22, 1924. Goodman School.

PAGET, DEBRA: (Debralee Griffin) Denver, Aug. 19, 1933.

PAIGE, JANIS: (Donna Mae Jaden) Tacoma, Wash., Sept. 16, 1922.

PALANCE, JACK: Lattimer, Pa., Feb. 18, 1920. U. of N.C.

PALMER, BETSY: East Chicago, Ind., Nov. 1, 1929. DePaul U.

PALMER, GREGG: (Palmer Lee) San Francisco, Jan. 25, 1927. U. of Utah.

PALMER, LILLI: Posen, Austria, May 24, 1914. Ilka Gruning School.

PALMER, MARIA: Vienna, Sept. 5, 1924. College de Bouffement.

PARKER, CECIL: Hastings, Sussex, Eng., Sept. 3, 1897. St. Francis Xavier College.

PARKER, ELEANOR: Cedarville, Ohio, June 26, 1922. Pasadena Playhouse.

PARKER, FESS: Fort Worth, Tex., Aug. 16. USC.

PARKER, JEAN: (Mae Green) Deer Lodge, Mont., Aug. 11, 1918.

PARKER, SUZY: (Cecelia Parker) San Antonio, Tex., Oct. 28.

PARKER, WILLARD: (Worster Van Eps) NYC, Feb. 5, 1912.

PARSONS, LOUELLA: Freeport, Ill., Aug. 6, 1893. Dixon College.

PATRICK, NIGEL: London, May 2, 1913.

PATTERSON, LEE: Vancouver, Can., 1929. Ontario College of Art.

PAVAN, MARISA: (Marisa Pierangeli) Cagliari, Sardinia, June 19, 1932. Torquado Tasso College.

PAYTON, BARBARA: Cloquet, Minn., Nov. 16, 1927.

PEACH, MARY: Durban, S. Africa, 1934.

PEARCE, ALICE: NYC, Oct. 16, 1917. Sarah Lawrence College.

PEARSON, BEATRICE: Denison, Tex., July 27, 1920.

PECK, GREGORY: La Jolla, Calif., Apr. 5, 1916. U. of Calif.

PEPPARD, GEORGE: Detroit, Oct. 1. Carnegie Tech.

PERKINS, ANTHONY: NYC, Apr. 14, 1932. Rollins College.

| Geraldine Page | Ronald Reagan | Martha Raye | Michael Rennie | Rosalind Russell |

PERREAU, GIGI: (Ghislaine) Los Angeles, Feb. 6, 1941.

PETERS, JEAN: (Elizabeth) Canton, Ohio, Oct. 15, 1926. Ohio State U.

PICERNI, PAUL: NYC, Dec. 1, 1922. Loyola U.

PICKENS, SLIM: (Louis Bert Lindley, Jr.) Kingsberg, Calif., June 29, 1919.

PICKFORD, MARY: (Gladys Mary Smith) Toronto, Can., Apr. 8, 1893.

PIDGEON, WALTER: East St. John, N.B., Can., Sept. 23, 1898.

PINE, PHILLIP: Hanford, Calif., July 16, 1925. Actors' Lab.

PLEASENCE, DONALD: Workshop, Eng., Oct. 5, 1919. Sheffield School.

PLESHETTE, SUZANNE: NYC, Jan. 31. Syracuse U.

PLUMMER, CHRISTOPHER: Toronto, Can., 1927.

PODESTA, ROSANA: Tripoli, June 20, 1934.

POITIER, SIDNEY: Miami, Fla., Feb. 20, 1924.

PORTMAN, ERIC: Yorkshire, Eng., July 13, 1903. Rishworth School.

POWELL, JANE: (Suzanne Burce) Portland, Ore., Apr. 1.

POWELL, WILLIAM: Pittsburgh, July 29, 1892. American Academy of Dramatic Art.

POWERS, MALA: (Mary Ellen) San Francisco, Dec. 29, 1921. UCLA.

PRENTISS, PAULA: (Paula Ragusa) San Antonio, Tex., Mar. 4. Northwestern U.

PRESLE, MICHELINE: (Micheline Chassange) Paris, Aug. 22, 1922. Rouleau Drama School.

PRESLEY, ELVIS: Tupelo, Miss., Jan. 8, 1935.

PRESNELL, HARVE: Modesto, Calif., Sept. 14, 1933. USC.

PRESTON, ROBERT: (Robert Preston Meservey) Newton Highlands, Mass., June 8, 1913. Pasadena Playhouse.

PRICE, DENNIS: Twyford, Eng., 1915. Oxford.

PRICE, VINCENT: St. Louis, May 27, 1911. Yale.

PRINCE, WILLIAM: Nicholas, N.Y., Jan. 26, 1913. Cornell U.

PROVINE, DOROTHY: Deadwood, S.D., Jan. 20, 1937. U. of Wash.

PURCELL, NOEL: Dublin, Ire., Dec. 23, 1900. Irish Christian Brothers.

PURDOM, EDMUND: Welwyn Garden City, Eng., Dec. 19. St. Ignatius College.

QUAYLE, ANTHONY: Lancashire, Eng., 1913. Old Vic School.

QUINN, ANTHONY: Chihuahua, Mex., Apr. 21, 1915.

RAFFERTY, FRANCES: Sioux City, Iowa, June 26, 1922. UCLA.

RAINES, ELLA: (Ella Wallace Rains Olds) Snoqualmie Falls, Wash., Aug. 6, 1921. U. of Washington.

RAINS, CLAUDE: London, Nov. 10, 1889.

RANDALL, TONY: Tulsa, Okla., Feb. 26, 1920. Northwestern U.

RANDELL, RON: Sydney, Australia, Oct. 8, 1920. St. Mary's College.

RATHBONE, BASIL: Johannesburg, S. Africa, June 13, 1892. Repton College.

RAY, ALDO: (Aldo DaRe) Pen Argyl, Pa., Sept. 25, 1926. UCLA.

RAYE, MARTHA: (Margie Yvonne Reed) Butte, Mont., Aug. 27, 1916.

RAYMOND, GENE: (Raymond Guion) NYC, Aug. 13, 1908.

REAGAN, RONALD: Tampico, Ill., Feb. 6, 1911. Eureka College.

REASON, REX: Berlin, Ger., Nov. 30, 1928. Pasadena Playhouse.

REDFORD, ROBERT: Santa Monica, Calif., Aug. 18, 1937. American Academy of Dramatic Art.

REDGRAVE, MICHAEL: Bristol, Eng., Mar. 20, 1908. Cambridge.

REDMAN, JOYCE: County Mayo, Ire., 1919. Royal Academy of Dramatic Arts.

REED, DONNA: (Donna Mullenger) Denison, Iowa, Jan. 27, 1921. LACC.

REEVES, STEVE: Glasgow, Mont., Jan. 21, 1926.

REINER, CARL: NYC, Mar. 20, 1923.

REMICK, LEE: Quincy, Mass., Dec. 14, 1935. Barnard College.

RENNIE, MICHAEL: Bradford, Eng., Aug. 25, 1909. Cambridge.

RETTIG, TOMMY: Jackson Heights, N.Y., Dec. 10, 1941.

REYNOLDS, DEBBIE: (Mary Frances Reynolds) El Paso, Tex., Apr. 1, 1932.

REYNOLDS, MARJORIE: Buhl, Idaho, Aug. 12, 1921.

RICH, IRENE: Buffalo, N.Y., Oct. 13, 1897. St. Margaret's School.

RICHARDS, JEFF: (Richard Mansfield Taylor) Portland, Ore., Nov. 1. USC.

RICHARDSON, RALPH: Cheltenham, Eng., Dec. 19, 1902.

RITTER, THELMA: Brooklyn, Feb. 14, 1905. American Academy of Dramatic Art.

ROBARDS, JASON: Chicago, July 26, 1922. American Academy of Dramatic Art.

ROBERTSON, CLIFF: La Jolla, Calif., Sept. 9, 1925. Antioch College.

ROBINSON, EDWARD G.: (Emanuel Goldenberg) Bucharest, Rum., Dec. 12, 1893. Columbia U.

ROBSON, FLORA: South Shields, Eng., Mar. 28, 1902. Royal Academy of Dramatic Arts.

ROCHESTER: (Eddie Anderson) Oakland, Calif., Sept. 18, 1905.

ROGERS, CHARLES "BUDDY": Olathe, Kan., Aug. 13, 1904. U. of Kan.

ROGERS, GINGER: (Virginia Katherine McMath) Independence, Mo., July 16, 1911.

ROGERS, ROY: (Leonard Slye) Cincinnati, Nov. 5, 1912.

ROLAND, GILBERT: (Luis Antonio Damasco De Alonso) Juarez, Mex., Dec. 11, 1905.

ROMAN, RUTH: Boston, Dec. 23. Bishop Lee Dramatic School.

ROMERO, CESAR: NYC, Feb. 15, 1907. Collegiate School.

ROONEY, MICKEY: (Joe Yule, Jr.) Brooklyn, Sept. 23, 1922.

ROTH, LILLIAN: Boston, Dec. 13, 1910.

RUGGLES, CHARLES: Los Angeles, Feb. 8, 1892.

RULE, JANICE: Cincinnati, Aug. 15, 1931.

RUSH, BARBARA: Denver, Colo., Jan. 4. U. of Calif.

RUSSELL, JANE: Bemidji, Minn., June 21, 1921. Max Reinhardt School.

RUSSELL, JOHN: Los Angeles, Jan. 3, 1921. U. of Calif.

RUSSELL, ROSALIND: Waterbury, Conn., June 4, 1912. American Academy of Dramatic Arts.

RUTHERFORD, ANN: Toronto, Can., 1924.

RUTHERFORD, MARGARET: London, May 11, 1892. Wimbledon Hill School.

RYAN, ROBERT: Chicago, Nov. 11, 1913. Dartmouth.

SAINT, EVA MARIE: Newark, N.J., July 4, 1924. Bowling Green State U.

ST. JOHN, BETTA: Hawthorne, Calif., Nov. 26, 1929.

SANDERS, GEORGE: St. Petersburg, Russia, 1906. Brighton College.

SANDS, TOMMY: Chicago, Aug. 27, 1937.

SAN JUAN, OLGA: NYC, Mar. 16, 1927.

SAXON, JOHN: Brooklyn, Aug. 5, 1935.

SCALA, GIA: Liverpool, Eng., Mar. 3, 1936. Stella Adler School.

SCHELL, MARIA: Vienna, Jan. 15, 1926.

| Robert Sterling | Kim Stanley | Mark Stevens | Gene Tierney | David Wayne |

SCHELL, MAXIMILIAN: Vienna, Dec. 8, 1930.

SCHNEIDER, ROMY: Vienna, Sept. 23, 1938.

SCOFIELD, PAUL: Hurstpierpont, Eng., Jan. 21, 1922. London Mask Theatre School.

SCOTT, GEORGE C., Wise, Va., Oct. 18, 1927. U. of Mo.

SCOTT, GORDON: (Gordon M. Werschkul) Portland, Ore., Aug. 3, 1927. Oregon U.

SCOTT, MARTHA: Jamesport, Mo., Sept. 22, 1914. U. of Mich.

SCOTT, RANDOLPH: Orange County, Va., Jan. 23, 1903. U. of N.C.

SEARS, HEATHER: London, 1935.

SEBERG, JEAN: Marshalltown, Iowa, Nov. 13, 1938. Iowa U.

SELLERS, PETER: Southsea, Eng., Sept. 8, 1925. Aloysius College.

SELWART, TONIO: Wartenberg, Ger., June 9, 1906. Munich U.

SEYLER, ATHENE: (Athene Hannen) London, May 31, 1889.

SEYMOUR, ANNE: NYC, Sept. 11, 1909. American Laboratory Theatre.

SHATNER, WILLIAM: Montreal, Can., Mar. 22, 1931. McGill U.

SHAW, SEBASTIAN: Holt, Eng., May 29, 1905. Gresham School.

SHAWLEE, JOAN: Forest Hills, N.Y., Mar. 5, 1929.

SHAWN, DICK: (Richard Schulefand) Buffalo, N.Y., Dec. 1. U. of Miami.

SHEARER, MOIRA: Dunfermline, Scot., Jan 17, 1926. London Theatre School.

SHEARER, NORMA: Montreal, Can., Aug. 10, 1904.

SHEFFIELD, JOHN: Pasadena, Calif., Apr. 11, 1931. UCLA.

SHERIDAN, ANN: Denton, Tex., Feb. 21, 1915. N. Tex. State Teachers College.

SHORE, DINAH: (Frances Rose Shore) Winchester, Tenn., Mar. 1, 1917. Vanderbilt U.

SHOWALTER, MAX: (Formerly Casey Adams) Caldwell, Kan., June 2, 1917. Pasadena Playhouse.

SIDNEY, SYLVIA: NYC, Aug. 8, 1910. Theatre Guild School.

SIGNORET, SIMONE: (Simone Kaminker) Wiesbaden, Ger., Mar. 25, 1921. Solange Sicard School.

SILVERS, PHIL: (Philip Silversmith) Brooklyn, May 11, 1912.

SIM, ALASTAIR: Edinburgh, Scot., 1900.

SIMMONS, JEAN: London, Jan. 31, 1929. Aida Foster School.

SIMON, SIMONE: Marseilles, France, Apr. 23, 1914.

SINATRA, FRANK: Hoboken, N.J., Dec. 12, 1915.

SKELTON, RED: (Richard Skelton) Vincennes, Ind., July 18, 1913.

SLEZAK, WALTER: Vienna, Austria, May 3, 1902.

SMITH, ALEXIS: Penticton, Can., June 8, 1921. LACC.

SMITH, JOHN: (Robert E. Van Orden) Los Angeles, Mar. 6, 1931. UCLA.

SMITH, KATE: (Kathryn Elizabeth) Greenville, Va., May 1, 1909.

SMITH, KENT: NYC, Mar. 19, 1907. Harvard U.

SMITH, ROGER: South Gate, Calif., Dec. 18, 1932. U. of Ariz.

SOMMER, ELKE: Germany, 1941.

SOTHERN, ANN: (Harriet Lake) Valley City, N.D., Jan. 22, 1911. Washington U.

STACK, ROBERT: Los Angeles, Jan. 13, 1919. USC.

STANG, ARNOLD: Chelsea, Mass., Sept. 28, 1925.

STANLEY, KIM: (Patricia Reid) Tularosa, N.M., Feb. 11, 1925. U. of Tex.

STANWYCK, BARBARA: (Ruby Stevens) Brooklyn, July 16, 1907.

STAPLETON, MAUREEN: Troy, N.Y., June 21, 1925.

STEEL, ANTHONY: London, May 21, 1920. Cambridge.

STEELE, BOB: (Robert Bradbury) Pendleton, Ore., Jan. 23, 1907.

STEELE, TOMMY: London, Dec. 17, 1936.

STEIGER, ROD: Westhampton, N.Y., Apr. 14, 1925.

STERLING, JAN: (Jane Sterling Adriance) NYC, Apr. 3, 1923. Fay Compton School.

STERLING, ROBERT: (Robert Sterling Hart) Newcastle, Pa., Nov. 13, 1917. U. of Pittsburgh.

STEVENS, CONNIE: (Concetta Ann Ingolie) Brooklyn, Aug. 8, 1938. Hollywood Professional School.

STEVENS, INGER: (Inger Stensland) Stockholm, Sweden, Oct. 18. Columbia U.

STEVENS, MARK: (Richard) Cleveland, Ohio, Dec. 13, 1922.

STEWART, ELAINE: Montclair, N.J., May 31, 1929.

STEWART, JAMES: Indiana, Pa., May 20, 1908. Princeton.

STEWART, MARTHA: (Martha Haworth) Bardwell, Ky., Oct. 7, 1922.

STORM, GALE: (Josephine Cottle) Bloominton, Tex., Apr. 5, 1922.

STRASBERG, SUSAN: NYC, May 22, 1938.

STRAUSS, ROBERT: NYC, Nov. 8, 1913.

STRUDWICK, SHEPPERD: Hillsboro, N.C., Sept. 22, 1907. U. of N.C.

SULLIVAN, BARRY: (Patrick Barry) NYC, Aug. 29, 1912. NYU.

SULLY, FRANK: (Frank Sullivan) St. Louis, 1910. St. Teresa's College.

SWANSON, GLORIA: (Josephine Swenson) Chicago, Mar. 27, 1898. Chicago Art Inst.

SWINBURNE, NORA: Bath, Eng., July 24, 1902. Royal Academy of Dramatic Arts.

SYLVESTER, WILLIAM: Oakland, Calif., Jan. 31, 1922. Royal Academy of Dramatic Arts.

SYMS, SYLVIA: London, 1934. Convent School.

TALBOT, LYLE: (Lysle Hollywood) Pittsburgh, Feb. 8, 1904.

TALBOT, NITA: NYC, Aug. 8, 1930. Irvine Studio School.

TAMBLYN, RUSS: Los Angeles, Dec. 30.

TANDY, JESSICA: London, June 7, 1909. Dame Owens' School.

TAYLOR, DON: Freeport, Pa., Dec. 13, 1920. Penn State U.

TAYLOR, ELIZABETH: London, Feb. 27, 1932. Byron House School.

TAYLOR, KENT: (Louis Weiss) Nashua, Iowa, May 11, 1907.

TAYLOR, ROBERT: (S. Arlington Brugh) Filley, Neb., Aug. 5, 1911. Pomona College.

TEAL, RAY: Grand Rapids, Mich., Jan. 12, 1902. Pasadena Playhouse.

TEMPLE, SHIRLEY JANE: Santa Monica, Calif., Apr. 23, 1928.

TERRY-THOMAS: (Thomas Terry Hoar Stevens) Finchley, London, July 14, 1911. Ardingly College.

THATCHER, TORIN: Bombay, India, Jan. 15, 1905. Royal Academy of Dramatic Arts.

THAXTER, PHYLLIS: Portland, Me., Nov. 20, 1921. St. Genevieve School.

THOMAS, DANNY: (Amos Jacobs) Deerfield, Mich., Jan. 6, 1914.

THOMPSON, MARSHALL: Peoria, Ill., Nov. 27, 1925. Occidental College.

THORNDIKE, SYBIL: Gainsborough, Eng., Oct. 24, 1882. Guild Hall School of Music.

TIERNEY, GENE: Brooklyn, Nov. 20, 1920. Miss Farmer's School.

TIERNEY, LAWRENCE: Brooklyn, Mar. 15, 1919. Manhattan College.

Ethel Waters   **Clifton Webb**   **Teresa Wright**   **Robert Young**   **Mai Zetterling**

TODD, RICHARD: Dublin, Ire., June 11, 1919. Shrewsbury School.

TONE, FRANCHOT: Niagara Falls, N.Y., Feb. 27, 1905. Cornell U.

TRACY, LEE: Atlanta, Ga., Apr. 11, 1898. Union College.

TRACY, SPENCER: Milwaukee, Apr. 5, 1900. Marquette U., American Academy of Dramatic Art.

TRACY, WILLIAM: Pittsburgh, Dec. 1, 1917. American Academy of Dramatic Art.

TRAVERS, BILL: Newcastle-on-Tyne, Eng., Jan. 3, 1922.

TRAVIS, RICHARD: (William Justice) Carlsbad, N.M., Apr. 17, 1913.

TREMAYNE, LES: London, Apr. 16, 1913. Northwestern, Columbia, UCLA.

TRUEX, ERNEST: Kansas City, Mo., Sept. 19, 1890.

TRYON, TOM: Hartford, Conn., Jan. 14, 1926. Yale.

TUCKER, FORREST: Plainfield, Ind., Feb. 12, 1919. George Washington U.

TURNER, LANA: (Julia Jean Turner) Wallace, Idaho, Feb. 8, 1920.

TYLER, BEVERLY: (Beverly Jean Saul) Scranton, Pa., July 5, 1928.

ULRIC, LENORE: New Ulm, Minn., July 21, 1894.

USTINOV, PETER: London, Apr. 16, 1921. Westminster School.

VALLEE, RUDY: (Hubert) Island Pond, Vt., July 28, 1901. Yale.

VALLI, ALIDA: Pola, Italy, May 31, 1921. Rome Academy of Drama.

VAN DOREN, MAMIE: (Joan Lucile Olander) Rowena, S.D., Feb. 6, 1933.

VAN ROOTEN, LUIS: Mexico City, Nov. 29, 1906. U. of Pa.

VENUTA, BENAY: San Francisco, Jan. 27, 1911.

VERDON, GWEN: Culver City, Calif., Jan. 13, 1925.

VITALE, MILLY: Rome, Italy, July 16, 1938. Lycée Chateaubriand.

VYE, MURVYN: Quincy, Mass., July 15, 1913. Yale.

WAGNER, ROBERT: Detroit, Feb. 10, 1930.

WALBROOK, ANTON: Vienna, Nov. 19, 1900.

WALBURN, RAYMOND: Plymouth, Ind., Sept. 9, 1887.

WALKER, CLINT: Hartford, Ill., May 30, 1927. USC.

WALKER, NANCY: (Ann Myrtle Swoyer) Philadelphia, May 10, 1921.

WALLACH, ELI: Brooklyn, Dec. 7, 1915. CCNY, U. of Tex.

WALSTON, RAY: New Orleans, Nov. 22, 1918. Cleveland Playhouse.

WARDEN, JACK: Newark, N.J., Sept. 18, 1920.

WASHBOURNE, MONA: Birmingham, Eng., Nov. 27, 1903.

WATERS, ETHEL: Chester, Pa., Oct. 31, 1900.

WATLING, JACK: London, Jan. 13, 1923. Italia Conti School.

WAYNE, DAVID: (Wayne McKeehan) Travers City, Mich., Jan. 30, 1916. Western Michigan State U.

WAYNE, JOHN: (Marion Michael Morrison) Winterset, Iowa, May 26, 1907. USC.

WEAVER, MARJORIE: Crossville, Tenn., Mar. 2, 1913. Indiana U.

WEBB, ALAN: York, Eng., July 2, 1906. Dartmouth.

WEBB, CLIFTON: (Webb Parmelee Hollenbeck) Indianapolis, Nov. 9, 1896.

WEBB, JACK: Santa Monica, Calif., Apr. 2, 1920.

WELD, TUESDAY: (Susan) NYC, Aug. 27, 1943. Hollywood Professional School.

WELDON, JOAN: San Francisco, Aug. 5, 1933. San Francisco Conservatory.

WELLES, ORSON: Kenosha, Wisc., May 6, 1915. Todd School.

WERNER, OSKAR: Vienna, Nov. 13, 1922.

WEST, MAE: Brooklyn, Aug. 17, 1892.

WHITE, JESSE: Buffalo, N.Y., Jan. 3, 1919.

WHITE, WILFRID HYDE: Gloucestershire, Eng., May 12, 1903. Royal Academy of Dramatic Arts.

WHITMAN, STUART: San Francisco, Feb. 1. CCLA.

WHORF, RICHARD: Winthrop, Mass., June 4, 1906.

WIDMARK, RICHARD: Sunrise, Minn., Dec. 26, 1914. Lake Forest U.

WILCOXON, HENRY: British West Indies, Sept. 8, 1905.

WILDE, CORNELL: NYC, Oct. 13, 1915. CCNY, Columbia.

WILDING, MICHAEL: Westcliff, Eng., July 23, 1912. Christ's Hospital.

WILLIAMS, EMLYN: Mostyn, Wales, Nov. 26, 1905. Oxford.

WILLIAMS, ESTHER: Los Angeles, Aug. 8, 1923.

WILLIAMS, GRANT: NYC, Aug. 18, 1930. Queens College.

WILLIAMS, JOHN: Chalfont, Eng., Apr. 15, 1903. Lancing College.

WILSON, MARIE: Anaheim, Calif., Dec. 30, 1917. Cumnock School.

WINDSOR, MARIE: (Emily Marie Bertelson) Marysvale, Utah, Dec. 11, 1924. Brigham Young University.

WINTERS, JONATHAN: Dayton, Ohio, Nov. 11, 1925. Kenyon College.

WINTERS, ROLAND: Boston, Nov. 22, 1904.

WINTERS, SHELLEY: (Shirley Schrift) St. Louis, Aug. 18, 1922. Wayne U.

WINWOOD, ESTELLE: Kent, Eng., Jan. 24, 1883. Lyric Stage Academy.

WITHERS, GOOGIE: Karachi, India, Mar. 12, 1917. Italia Conti School.

WOLFIT, DONALD: Newark-on-Trent, Eng., Apr. 20, 1902. Magnus School.

WOOD, NATALIE: (Natasha Gurdin) San Francisco, July 20, 1938.

WOOD, PEGGY: Brooklyn, Feb. 9, 1894.

WOODWARD, JOANNE: Thomasville, Ga., Feb. 27, 1931. Neighborhood Playhouse.

WOOLAND, NORMAN: Dusseldorf, Ger., Mar. 16, 1910. Edward VI School.

WRAY, FAY: Alberta, Can., Sept. 10, 1907.

WRIGHT, TERESA: NYC, Oct. 27, 1918.

WYATT, JANE: Campgaw, N.J., Aug. 10, 1912. Barnard College.

WYMAN, JANE: (Sarah Jane Fulks) St. Joseph, Mo., Jan. 4, 1914.

WYMORE, PATRICE: Miltonvale, Kan., Dec. 17, 1927.

WYNN, ED: (Edwin Leopold) Philadelphia, Nov. 9, 1886.

WYNN, KEENAN: NYC, July 27, 1916. St. John's.

WYNN, MAY: (Donna Lee Hickey) NYC, Jan. 8, 1930.

YORK, DICK: (Richard Allen York) Fort Wayne, Ind., Sept. 4, 1928. DePaul U.

YORK, SUSANNAH: London, 1942.

YOUNG, ALAN: (Angus) North Shield, Eng., Nov. 19, 1919.

YOUNG, GIG: (Byron Barr) St. Cloud, Minn., Nov. 4, 1917. Pasadena Playhouse.

YOUNG, LORETTA: (Gretchen) Salt Lake City, Jan. 6, 1913. Immaculate Heart College.

YOUNG, ROBERT: Chicago, Feb. 22, 1907.

ZETTERLING, MAI: Sweden, May 27, 1925. Ordtuery Theatre School.

ZIMBALIST, EFREM, JR.: NYC, Nov. 30, 1923. Yale.

Judy Holliday
1924-1965

OBITUARIES

BACHER, WILLIAM A., 67, Rumanian-born producer, director, and writer, died of a stroke April 20, 1965 on a film set in London while preparing a feature to be shot there. He practiced dentistry before turning to producing radio shows in 1929, and films in 1943 when he moved to Hollywood. Among his credits are "Leave Her To Heaven," "A Wing and A Prayer," "Carnival In Costa Rica," and "The Foxes of Harrow." A wife and daughter survive.

BARRISCALE, BESSIE, 81, stage and silent screen actress, died June 30, 1965 in Kentfield, Calif. She had been in retirement for 20 years. Howard C. Hickman, her actor-playwright-director husband died in 1950. She is survived by a son. In addition to her many silent films she appeared in "Show People," "Above The Clouds," and "Beloved" in 1934.

BENNETT, CONSTANCE, 59, screen and stage actress, died July 24, 1965 in Walson Army Hospital, Fort Dix, N.J., of a cerebral hemorrhage. Her career which spanned 40 years, began with a small film role in "Cytherea" in 1924, and ended with the 1965 production of "Madam X." She was the daughter of actor Richard Bennett and actress Adrienne Morrison, and sister of actresses Joan and Barbara Bennett. After a series of successful films, she became the industry's highest paid star. After the successful 1937 "Topper" with Cary Grant, she made several other "Topper" films before tiring of the role. Among her other films were "The Goose Hangs High," "My Son," "Common Clay," "Sally, Irene and Mary," "Tailspin," "This Thing Called Love," "Three Faces East," "Our Betters," "Smart Woman," and "Madame Spy." Her romances were as well publicized as her films. She was married 5 times. Surviving are her husband Gen. John T. Coulter, two daughters by actor Gilbert Roland who was her fourth husband, an adopted son, and her sister Joan. Burial was in Arlington National Cemetery, Washington.

BERLIN, ABBY, 58, veteran comedy director, died in his sleep in Hollywood on Aug. 19. He gained prominence by directing 10 "Blondie" films, and "Double Deal," "Father Is A Bachelor," "Target," and "Leave It To A Blonde." He switched to TV and directed such series as "Amos 'n' Andy," "Beulah," "Life of Riley," "The Ann Sothern Show," and "Casey Jones." His wife, actress Iris Meredith, and a daughter survive.

BLUM, DANIEL, 65, founder and editor of 16 volumes of SCREEN WORLD, died of a heart attack in New York's Mt. Sinai Hospital on Feb. 24, 1965. He was widely known for his pictorial books on the movies, theatre, television, and opera. He edited 20 volumes of THEATRE WORLD, an annual record of the theatrical season, A PICTORIAL HISTORY OF THE SILENT SCREEN, A PICTORIAL HISTORY OF THE TALKIES, A PICTORIAL HISTORY OF THE AMERICAN THEATRE, A PICTORIAL HISTORY OF TELEVISION, and GREAT STARS OF THE AMERICAN STAGE. Interment was in the family mausoleum in Chicago's Rosehill Cemetery. Three sisters survive.

BOLAND, MARY, 83, veteran Broadway and Hollywood film comedienne, died in her sleep at the Essex House in New York on June 23, 1965. During her career of more than 60 years she became famous for her portrayals of fluttery dowagers and zanily doting mothers. She was born in Philadelphia, and made her New York stage debut in 1905. Her film credits include "Ruggles of Red Gap," "A Son Comes Home," "Marry The Girl," "Love At Work," "There Goes The Groom," "Mama Runs Wild," "Boy Trouble," "Three-Cornered Moon," "Pursuit of Happiness," "The Women," "New Moon," "Pride and Prejudice," "In Our Time," "Nothing But Trouble," and "Forever Yours." She was never married and left no immediate survivors. Interment was in Forest Lawn Memorial Park, Calif.

Constance Bennett

Mary Boland

Clara Bow

Nancy Carroll

Helen Chandler

Sydney Chaplin

BOW, CLARA, 60, red-haired sex symbol of the '20's as the "It" girl, died Sept. 27, 1965, at her home in West Los Angeles of a heart attack. From 1927 to 1930 she was one of the top boxoffice stars. Several courtroom scandals, and mental illness blighted the rest of her life, and except for her appearance as "Mrs. Hush" on radio in 1947 she remained a recluse, attended by a nurse who was with her when she died. Her first movie was "Down To The Sea In Ships" in 1925 after winning a Coney Island beauty contest. Her best pictures were "Kiss Me Again," "Black Oxen," "Dancing Mothers," "It," "The Plastic Age," "The Fleet's In," "Ladies of The Mob," "Mantrap," "Wings," "Rough House Rosie," and "Kid Boots." Her private life and loves were even more public and news-worthy than her films. After several torrid affairs, she married her long-time boy friend and cowboy actor, Rex Bell. They separated but never divorced. He died in 1962 after a campaign speech for governor of Nevada. Two sons survive.

BROWNE, IRENE, 72, British stage and screen actress, died in London of cancer on July 24, 1965. She made many successful stage appearances in the U. S., and in Hollywood films "Cavalcade," "The Letter" and "Berkeley Square."

BUTTERFIELD, ALFRED C., 49, producer of documentary films, died April 1, 1965 in Weston, Conn. Included in his credits are "Helen Keller In Her Story," "Secrets Of The Reef," "Fifty Years Before Your Eyes," and "Horizons of Science." He was also producer of films for "The March of Time." A wife and three sons survive.

CARROLL, NANCY, 60, screen and stage actress, was found dead from natural causes in her New York apartment on Aug. 6, 1965, when she failed to appear for a stage performance. Born Ann Veronica LaHiff on New York's West Side, her flaming red hair and cupid's bow mouth helped her in becoming a top romantic screen star. After appearing in a play on the West Coast, she was signed for films and remained in Hollywood for many years, appearing in such films as "Abie's Irish Rose," "Illusion," "The Sin Sister," "Sweetie," "The Dance of Life," "That Certain Age," "There Goes My Heart," "Shopworn Angel," "Child of Manhattan," "Honey," "The Wolf of Wall Street," "Springtime For Henry," "I'll Love You Always," "After The Dance," and "Follow Thru." For a while she appeared on TV as the mother in "The Aldrich Family." At one time, she received more fan mail than any other actor. Three times married and divorced, she is survived by a daughter by her first marriage, actress Patricia Kirkland Bevan.

CHANDET, LOUIS W., 81, pioneer director, died May 10, 1965 in Burbank, Calif. He entered the industry in 1913 and directed over 100 silent films, such stars as Henry Walthall, Monte Blue, Irene Rich, and Marion Davies, and the two-reel series "Adventures of Kathleen" with Kathleen Williams, and "Mr. and Mrs. Carter de Haven." Surviving are his wife and two sons.

CHANDLER, HELEN, 59, screen and stage actress, died as a result of surgery in a Hollywood hospital on Apr. 30, 1965. After a successful career on Broadway, she went to Hollywood where she appeared in such films as "Salute," "Mother's Boy," "Outward Bound," and "Worst Woman In Paris." Her husband, Walter Piascik, survives.

CHAPLIN, SYDNEY, 80, film comedian, and manager of his brother Charlie Chaplin, died April 16, 1965 in Nice, France after an illness of several months. Born in Johannesburg, he moved to London with his mother. Charles brought him to the U.S. to work for Mack Sennett where he frequently appeared as a foil for his brother in the Keystone Kop series. He later appeared in "The Better Ole," "The Missing Link," "The Fortune Hunter," "Man In The Box," "Her Temporary Husband," "Oh, What A Nurse!," "Charley's Aunt" (his best known), "A Bit Of Fluff," and his last "The Great Dictator" again with his brother. His wife survives.

COCHRAN, STEVE, 48, stage and screen actor, died June 15, 1965 of an acute lung infection aboard his yacht in the Pacific Ocean off the coast of Guatemala, where he was filming for his independent company. He was born in Eureka, Calif., and appeared on the stage before going into films. His credits include "The Chase," "The Damned Don't Cry," "Storm Warning," "Carnival Story," "Tomorrow Is Another Day," "Highway 301," "Operation Secret," "Come Next Spring," "Il Grido," "The Big Operator," "The Beat Generation," "The Deadly Companions," and "Tell Me In Sunlight." He was married and divorced three times, and has a daughter by his second wife singer Fay McKenzie.

COLE, NAT KING, 45, top recording star, night club, radio and TV performer, and film actor, died Feb. 15, 1965 in St. John's Hospital, Santa Monica, Calif. after undergoing surgery for lung cancer. He had singing and acting roles in "Small Town Girl," "The Blue Gardenia," "Istanbul," "China Gate," "St. Louis Blues," "The Nat King Cole Story," and "Cat Ballou." Surviving are his wife, singer Marie Ellington, a son and four daughters. Burial was in Forest Lawn Memorial Park.

COLLINS, RAY, 77, veteran stage, radio, film, and television actor, died July 11, 1965 in St. John's Hospital, Santa Monica of emphysema. A native of Sacramento, he made his reputation in New York, then went to Hollywood with Orson Welles' group. He appeared in over 75 films, including "Citizen Kane," "The Magnificent Ambersons," "The Hitler Gang," "Francis," "Ma and Pa Kettle On Vacation," "The Human Comedy," "Leave Her To Heaven," "The Solid Gold Cadillac," "A Double Life," "The Fountainhead," "Rose Marie," "Desperate Hours," and "Never Say Goodbye." He is best known as Detective Lt. Tragg in the "Perry Mason" TV series which he played for 8 years.

COLLINS, RUSSELL, 65, veteran character actor, was found dead Nov. 14, 1965 in his Hollywood apartment. He was born in New Orleans, reared in Indiana, and attended Carnegie Tech. He appeared in more than 40 Broadway productions, and a score of films which include "Bad Day At Black Rock," "Sadie Thompson," "Raintree County," "The Enemy Below," and "Fail Safe." He also appeared in many TV productions. A sister survives.

CRAIG, NELL, 74, pioneer film actress, died in Hollywood, Jan. 5, 1965. For several years she was starred in Lubin and Essanay films. Her best-known roles were in "Abraham Lincoln," "Cimarron," and "Consolation Marriage."

DANDRIDGE, DOROTHY, 41, top night club singer and film actress, was found dead in her Hollywood apartment on Sept. 8, 1965. An autopsy revealed that particles of bone marrow in her bloodstream from a fracture in her foot had caused embolism. It was later determined that she died of barbiturate poisoning. Born in Cleveland, she was taken to Hollywood at 4 where she appeared in several films. Her cafe work later brought her to the attention of film producers, and she appeared in "Carmen Jones" for which she received an Academy Award nomination, "Porgy and Bess," "Island In The Sun," "The Happy Road," and "Tamango." She was twice married and divorced, and a daughter by her first marriage survives.

DANE, CLEMENCE, 77, novelist, playwright, and scenarist, died March 28, 1965 in London. She rewrote her famous novel "Legend" into the play and film "Bill Of Divorcement." She wrote for films both in Hollywood and London. Her best known is "Anna Karenina" which starred Garbo.

DARNELL, LINDA, 43, actress, died April 10, 1965 in Cook County Hospital, Chicago, as a result of burns received in a fire in the home of friends she was visiting in Glenview. She was trapped when she tried to rescue the daughter of her friends. A native of Texas, she entered films at 15, and appeared in numerous productions including "Hotel For Women," "Daytime Wife," "Star Dust," "Brigham Young," "Blood and Sand," "Summer Storm," "Forever Amber," "No Way Out," "A Letter To Three Wives," "Zero Hour," and her last "Black Spurs." She also appeared in one Broadway play, and several summer stock productions. She was married and divorced 3 times. A brother and adopted daughter survive. She was cremated.

Steve Cochrane

Nat King Cole

Russell Collins

Dorothy Dandridge

Linda Darnell

Louise Dresser

DONNER, VYVYAN, 69, filmmaker and fashion commentator, died June 27, 1965 of a heart ailment. For 30 years she did capsule comments on fashion for Fox Movietone News. She also produced and directed short subjects on music, art, and travel, and designed costumes and sets. She retired in 1963.

DRESSER, LOUISE, 86, retired stage and screen actress, died Apr. 24, 1965 in Woodland Hills, Calif., after surgery for an intestinal ailment. Her career spanned a half century, beginning in vaudeville, then in Broadway musicals. Her film career began in 1923, and her greatest success was in 7 films with Will Rogers. She was born Louise Kerlin in Evansville, Ind. She retired in 1937 and devoted her time to the Motion Picture Country House and Hospital where she died. Film credits include "State Fair," "Lightnin'," "David Harum," "When My Ship Comes In," "Mammy," "Doctor Bull," "Cradle Song," "The Scarlet Empress," "The Girl of The Limberlost," "The County Chairman," "Lone Eagle," "Air Circus," "Madonna Of Avenue A," and "Mother Knows Best."

DUMONT, MARGARET, 75, versatile screen, stage, and television actress-singer, died March 6, 1965 of a heart attack in her Hollywood home. On stage with the Marx Brothers, and then in their 7 films, she was the reserved statuesque society matron unperturbed by the low-comedy antics around her. Recently she had appeared on TV, and only a few days before her death had taped a skit with Groucho Marx. Her films include "A Day At The Races," "Duck Soup," "A Night At The Opera," "Anything Goes," "The Horn Blows At Midnight," "Up In Arms," "Diamond Horseshoe," "Three For Bedroom C," "Stop You're Killing Me."

ELLIOTT, WILLIAM "WILD BILL," 62, cowboy star of more than 60 films, died Nov. 26, 1965 of cancer in Las Vegas, Nev. He became "Wild Bill" after playing Wild Bill Hickock in a 1939 serial. He also appeared in a Red Ryder series in 1943. Born near Pattonsburg, Mo., he moved at an early age with his family to Kansas City. He studied at the Pasadena Playhouse and early in his career appeared in non-Western dramatic films. Picture credits include "In Old Sacramento," "The Plainsman and The Lady," "Wyoming," "The Fabulous Texan," and "Old Los Angeles." Surviving are his widow the former Dolly Moore, and a daughter by his first marriage which ended in divorce.

ENRIGHT, RAY, 69, director, died of a heart attack in Hollywood April 3, 1965 after a long illness. For many years he directed the Rin-Tin-Tin pictures. His other features include "Golddiggers In Paris," "The Spoilers," "Gung Ho," "Montana," "South of St. Louis," and his last "Man From Cairo." He was a founder of The Masquers. His widow survives.

GIROSI, MARCELLO, 62, producer-importer, died in Rome Jan. 9, 1965 after a long illness. An American of Italian descent, his production credits include "Europa," "Terminal Station," "Bread, Love and Dreams," "Bread, Love and Jealousy," "Black Orchid," "Heller With A Gun," and "Breath of Scandal." His wife survives.

GLASS, GASTON, 66, film and TV executive and actor, died Nov. 11, 1965 in Santa Monica, Calif., after a long illness. Paris born, he came to America as Sarah Bernhardt's leading man in 1917. Was signed for films and made numerous ones until the advent of talkies when his heavy accent forced him into the business side of the profession. Appeared in "Behind Closed Doors," "Humoresque," "The Faker," "Tiger Rose," "She Got What She Wanted," "I Am The Law," "The Spider and The Rose," "The Hero," "Mothers-in-Law," "The Red Mark," "Name The Woman," and "Geraldine." Surviving are his former-actress wife, Bo Peep Karlin, and two sons.

GREEN, HOWARD J., 72, first president of the Screen Writers Guild, died at a Guild meeting on Sept. 2, 1965. After working as a reporter, and writer for revues, he began writing for films in the 1930's and had more than 60 screenplays to his credit. Among them are "Patent Leather Kid," "Private Life of Helen of Troy," "I Am A Fugitive From A Chain Gang," and "Morning Glory." He is survived by his widow, and a son and daughter.

GRIBBON, EDDIE T., 75, one of the original Keystone Kops, and veteran of 49 years in films, died in Hollywood on Sept. 28, 1965 after a long illness. He arrived from New York and vaudeville in 1916 and went to work for Mack Sennett. He appeared in "Tell It To The Marines," "The Callahans and The Murphys," "United States Smith," and a series of war films with Slim Summerville. His wife survives.

HALE, CREIGHTON, 83, star of silent films, died Aug. 9, 1965 in South Pasadena, Calif. hospital. Born in County Cork, Ireland, he came to New York at an early age. He starred in many silent films, but his roles became minor with the advent of talkies. He appeared in "Annie Laurie," "The Iron Claw," "The Clutching Hand," "The Marriage Circle," "The Cat and The Canary," "The Circle," "The Perils of Pauline," "The Great Divide," "Way Down East," and "What's Your Racket." He was twice married, and 2 sons by his first marriage survive.

HANSON, LARS, 78, one of Sweden's most prominent dramatic actors on stage and screen, died April 8, 1965 in Stockholm after a brief illness. He appeared in both Swedish and American films in the late 1920's. In 1936 he introduced Ingrid Bergman to the U.S. with "Paa Solsidan," a Swedish film.

HARTE, BETTY, 82, self-styled Hollywood's first movie queen, died Jan. 3, 1965 in a Sunland, Calif. rest home. Her career began in 1909 as the first leading lady of the Selig Polyscope Co. Her real name was Daisy Mae Light. She appeared in many silent films co-starring with Hobart Bosworth. She was married in 1917 and retired from the movies. Among her best known films were "The Roman," and "The Pride of Jennico." A sister survives.

HOLLIDAY, JUDY, 42, stage and film actress-singer, died of cancer June 7, 1965 in New York's Mt. Sinai Hospital. After her Broadway success in "Born Yesterday," she went to Hollywood to re-create her role in the film version for which she received an "Oscar" in 1950. She was born Judith Tuvim in New York City, and never stayed away from the metropolis for long. Following her triumph in her first film, she was in great demand, but made only 5 others: "Something For The Boys," "The Solid Gold Cadillac," "Adam's Rib," "The Marrying Kind," and "Phfft!" She was divorced from musician David Oppenheim. Surviving are her mother and one son.

HOWARD, ESTHER, 72, veteran character actress, died in Hollywood of a heart attack on March 8, 1965. Appeared on Broadway before going to Hollywood where she appeared in numerous supporting roles for over 20 years in such films as "Vice Squad," "Murder, My Sweet," "Champion," and "All That I Have." A brother survives.

HUGHES, GARETH, 71, Welsh-born retired stage and screen actor, died Oct. 1, 1965 at the Motion Picture Country House, Woodland, Calif., where he had lived since 1958. He had been hospitalized for over a year. Prior to Hollywood, he played juvenile leads on Broadway. His best-known films were "Sentimental Tommy," "The Little Minister," "Enemies of Women," "Silent Sentinel," "Comrades," "Whirlwind of Youth," "Sky Rider," "Mister Antonio," and "Broken-Hearted." He renounced acting in 1944 to become a lay missionary among the Piute Indians in Nevada. He lived among them as Brother David until ill health forced his return to Hollywood.

JOHNSON, RITA, 52, stage and screen actress, died Oct. 31, 1965 in Hollywood's County General Hospital after a brain hemorrhage. Born in Worcester, Mass., she appeared on Broadway and regular radio programs before going to California where she had over 35 films to her credit. They include "My Friend Flicka," "Edison, The Man," "Appointment For Love," "Here Comes Mr. Jordan," "Susan Slept Here," "Second Face," "General Hospital," "The Major and The Minor," "They Won't Believe Me," "Sleep, My Love," and "The Big Clock." She married and divorced L. Stanley Kahn, a New York businessman. There were no children. Her mother survives.

Margaret Dumont

Creighton Hale

Lars Hanson

Rita Johnson

Stan Laurel

Jeanette MacDonald

JORDAN, BOBBY, 42, one of the "Dead End Kids," died of sclerosis of liver on Sept. 10, 1965 at Sawtelle Veterans Hospital in Los Angeles. He had spent his later years in comparative obscurity after being starred in "Dead End" in 1937 and the subsequent "Bowery Boys" series. He also appeared in "A Slight Case of Murder," "My Bill," and "Crime School." A son survives.

KALMUS, NATALIE M., 73, who with her late ex-husband, Dr. Herbert T. Kalmus, devised the Technicolor process for films, died Nov. 15, 1965 in Boston. She not only was a laboratory expert, but was also the first female photographer in Technicolor. Born in Norfolk, Va., she moved with her family to Boston, where she retired after many years in Hollywood.

KULKY, HENRY, 43, film and television character actor, died Feb. 12, 1965 of a heart attack in an Oceanside, Calif., club while studying a TV script. Best-known for his role as Chief Max Bronsky in the TV series "Hennessey," he appeared in more than 500 movie and TV roles, including such films as "Call Northside 777," "A Global Affair," "The Robe," and "Up Periscope." Surviving are his parents and a brother.

LARKIN, JOHN, 52, film, radio, and TV actor, died of a heart attack Jan. 29, 1965 in Hollywood. Began his career in radio, switched to TV soap-operas in the mid-1950's, and then went to Hollywood where his TV and film credits include "The Detectives," "Saints and Sinners," "12 O'Clock High," "Seven Days In May," "Those Callaways," and "The Satan Bug." His wife, son, and three daughters survive.

LARKIN, JOHN, newspaperman, playwright, screenwriter, director, film and TV producer, died Jan. 6, 1965 of a heart ailment. His credits include "Rose of Washington Square," "The Dolly Sisters," "Carnival In Costa Rica," "Two Weeks With Love," "Circumstantial Evidence," "Fabian of Scotland Yard," "M Squad," and "Riverboat." A wife and son survive.

LAUREL, STAN, 74, the skinny, sad-faced half of the famed Laurel and Hardy comedy team, died Feb. 23, 1965 of a heart attack in his home in Santa Monica, Calif., 8 years after the death of Oliver Hardy with whom he had appeared in over 300 slapstick films. He had been in retirement since 1955. They were often acclaimed as the most successful comedy team in movie history. In 1933 the pair won an "Oscar" for their short film "The Music Box," and in 1961 the Academy gave Laurel a special award for "creative pioneering in the field of cinema comedy." Born in England, he came to New York in 1910 with a song and dance act. His first film was in 1917, and in 1926 he was cast with Hardy. He was married to 4 women 8 times. His last wife and a daughter survive. Burial was in Forest Lawn Memorial Park.

MacDONALD, JEANETTE, 57, singer-actress, died Jan. 14, 1965 of a heart attack in Houston, Texas, after having been admitted 2 days previous for heart surgery. After a successful career in Broadway musicals, she was signed for films in 1931. She is best remembered for a series of musicals with Maurice Chevalier and Nelson Eddy. After leaving films in 1942, she made concert tours, recordings, radio, and TV appearances, and sang several roles in grand opera. Among her best-known films are "One Hour With You." "Love Me Tonight," "The Merry Widow," "Naughty Marietta," "Rose Marie," "Maytime." "Girl Of The Golden West." "Sweethearts," "New Moon," and "Bittersweet." She was married to Gene Raymond who was at her side when she died. Interment was in Forest Lawn Memorial Park.

MANNING, BRUCE, 65, veteran screen writer, died Aug. 3, 1965 in Hollywood following his retirement because of a heart condition. His screen credits include "Back Street," "Jubilee Trail," "Three Smart Girls," "Hoodlum Empire," "100 Men and A Girl," "Mad About Music," "Broadway," and "That Certain Age." Surviving is his wife, novelist Gwen Bristow.

MARION, SID, 65, veteran stage and screen actor, died of a heart attack in The Masquers Club in Hollywood on June 29, 1965. He had appeared in many Broadway productions before going to Hollywood where he had roles in over 100 films including "Lady of Burlesque," "Call Me Madam," and "Oh, You Beautiful Doll." His wife survives.

MAUGHAM, WILLIAM SOMERSET, 91, prolific author of novels, short stories, and plays, died Dec. 16, 1965 in his villa in Nice, France, an hour after leaving the Anglo-American Hospital where he was taken on Dec. 11, after suffering a fall and stroke. He was born in the British Embassy in Paris where his father was solicitor. He became one of the most financially successful writers of all time, and had a working career longer than any other British author. He retired, with reservations, in 1962. He was translated into nearly every language, and many of his works were adapted for the films. His most successful were "Of Human Bondage," "Theater," "The Narrow Corner," "The Razor's Edge," "The Moon and Sixpence," "The Painted Veil," and "Rain." He was married and divorced from Lady Wellcome. A daughter, Lady John Hope, survives. Cremation was followed by burial in the grounds of Canterbury Cathedral.

McDONALD, MARIE, 42, singer and actress, was found dead from an overdose of pills on Oct. 21, 1965 in her Calabasas, Calif. home by her film-producer husband Donald Taylor. Former showgirl, model, and band-singer from Burgin, Ky., she began her Hollywood career as a contract starlet appearing in minor roles. She got her first break in 1944 in "Guest In The House" and her press agent nicknamed her "The Body," and the tag stayed with her. Other film roles were in "It Started With Eve," "You're Telling Me," "Pardon My Sarong," "Lucky Jordan," "Living In A Big Way," and "Hit Parade of 1951," with which her screen career ended, except for "Promises, Promises" in 1963. However, she never dropped out of the news and gossip columns. She had 5 other husbands besides Mr. Taylor. Three children survive. Burial was in Forest Lawn Memorial Park.

MICHAEL, GERTRUDE, 53, stage and film star of the 1930's, died Jan. 1, 1965 in her Beverly Hills home. She had been in ill health for several months. She was perhaps best known to movie audiences as the heroine of the "Sophie Lang" series in which she played an international jewel thief. Born in Talladega, Ala., she appeared on Broadway until 1933 when she went to Hollywood for "Unashamed," followed by "Cleopatra," "Sailor Be Good," "A Bedtime Story," "I'm No Angel," "Cradle Song," "Bolero," "Night of Terror," "Ann Vickers," "Murder At The Vanities," "Menace," "George White's Scandals," "Woman Trap," "The Last Outpost," "Till We Meet Again," "Forgotten Faces," "Second Wife," "The Farmer's Daughter," "Women In Bondage," "Flamingo Road," "Bugles In The Afternoon," and "Caged." A brother survives.

MUDIE, LEONARD, 82, English-born screen and stage actor, died April 14, 1965 in Hollywood of a heart ailment. He went to California in 1933 to appear in "Voltaire," followed by "The Magnificent Obsession," "Adventures of Robin Hood," "Kidnapped," "Suez," "Dark Victory," "Don't Gamble With Strangers," "Song Of My Heart," and his last "The Greatest Story Ever Told." A wife and son survive.

MURRAY, MAE, 75, first dancing star of the screen, and one of Hollywood's most glamorous star personalities of the past, died of a heart ailment March 23, 1965 in the Motion Picture Country House, Woodland Hills, Calif. Born in Portsmouth, Va., she became one of Ziegfeld's stars in 1908. In 1915 she was signed for films and embarked on one of the most lucrative and colorful screen careers in history. She was a top star until talking pictures when she was forced to abandon her career. Several comeback film appearances failed, and she died penniless and almost friendless She was married four times. Her most memorable film was "The Merry Widow" in 1925; others were "To Have And To Hold," "Sweet Kitty Bellairs," "Peacock Alley," "The Delicious Little Devil," "Fascination," "Broadway Rose," "Gilded Lily," "Jazz Mania," and "Bachelor Apartment." Surviving is a son by her marriage to Prince David M'Divani. Burial was in Valhalla Memorial Park, North Hollywood.

Marie McDonald

Mae Murray

Nance O'Neil

Catherine Dale Owen

James Rennie

Zachary Scott

NUGENT, FRANK S., 57, screen writer, and former film critic for The New York Times, died of a coronary attack, Dec. 29, 1965, after suffering from heart trouble for 5 years. Born in New York City, and graduated from Columbia College, he joined The Times in 1929 as a reporter. In 1934 he was assigned to the screen department. His reviews were noted for their wit as well as their sarcasm. In 1940 he accepted an offer to join 20th Century-Fox as a screenplay "doctor," but left there in 1944 to freelance, and became associated with producer-director John Ford. Among the many scripts he wrote alone, or in collaboration, were "Fort Apache," "Three Godfathers," "She Wore A Yellow Ribbon," "Wagonmaster," "The Quiet Man" and "Mister Roberts" (for both he received the year's best script award), "The Searchers," "Rising of The Moon," "The Last Hurrah." He is survived by his second wife, Jean Lavell, and a stepson.

O'NEIL, NANCE, 90, retired stage and screen tragedienne, died Feb. 7, 1965 at the Actors Fund Home in Englewood, N.J. Born Gertrude Lamson in Oakland, Calif., she attained world-wide acclaim for her stage performances in tragedies. In 1929 she began a prolific film career that did not prove as successful. Her better known movies were "Ladies of Leisure," "Cimarron," "The Lady of Scandal," "Eyes Of The World," "Call of The Flesh," "Westward Passage," "The Rogue Song," "The Queen's Husband," "A Woman of Experience," "The Transgression," and "Resurrection." She was the widow of British actor Alfred Hickman. She retired in 1935. There were no immediate survivors.

OWEN, CATHERINE DALE, 62, stage and film actress, died in New York on Sept. 7, 1965. Born in Louisville, Ky., in 1925 she was named as one of the 10 most beautiful women in the world. After a successful Broadway career, she turned to films in 1929 and appeared in "His Glorious Night" with John Gilbert, "The Rogue Song" with Lawrence Tibbett, "Born Reckless," "Forbidden Woman," "The Circle," "Today," "Behind Office Doors," "In Defense Of The Law," and "Such Men Are Dangerous." Her husband and son survive.

QUIMBY, FRED, 79, pioneer film cartoon producer, and 8-time Academy Award winner, died Sept. 15, 1965 in Santa Monica, Calif., following surgery. After serving as manager of short subjects for 20th Century-Fox, he joined Metro where he headed its short subjects department until his retirement in 1956. His "Colonel Heeza Liar" films were the first cartoon series. Surviving are his wife, a son and daughter.

REICHER, FRANK, 89, pioneer film actor and director, died Jan. 19, 1965 in Playa del Rey, Calif. After coming from his native Germany in 1899, he appeared on Broadway and directed for the Theatre Guild until Cecil B. DeMille brought him to Hollywood. His screen credits include more than 100 films, such as "King Kong," "The Secret Life of Walter Mitty," "Kiss Tomorrow Goodbye," and "Country Doctor." He is survived by a brother and two sisters, actresses Hedwiga and Elly Reicher.

RENNIE, JAMES, 76, former Broadway leading man, and film actor, died July 31, 1965 in New York. After several legitimate successes, he made his film debut in 1921. His most recent roles were in "Tales of Manhattan," "Now, Voyager," "Wilson," and "A Bell For Adano." His marriage to Dorothy Gish, with whom he appeared in several films, ended in divorce in 1935. He is survived by his second wife.

RITZ, AL, 62, oldest of the three zany Ritz Brothers comedy team, died Dec. 22, 1965 in New Orleans' Touro Infirmary. The Brothers were playing a two-week engagement at the Roosevelt Hotel. Born in Newark with the surname of Joaquim, reared in Brooklyn, the brothers, persuaded by Al, made their stage debut as a team in 1925, and have been clowning for audiences ever since. After several Broadway successes, they made their film debut in 1936 in "Sing, Baby, Sing," and were immediately successful. Other films were "One In A Million," "On The Avenue," "You Can't Have Everything," "Life Begins In College," "The Goldwyn Follies," "Kentucky Moonshine," "Straight, Place and Show," "The Three Musketeers," "The Gorilla," "Pack Up Your Troubles," "Argentine Nights," "Behind The Eight Ball," and "Hi-Ya Chum." After their television debut in 1952, they confined themselves to nightclub appearances. Al is survived by his wife, two brothers, Harry and Jimmy. Interment was in Calif.

ROSSE, HERMAN, 78, who created more than 200 sets for the stage and films, died April 13, 1965 in Nyack, N.Y. following a heart attack. He won an "Oscar" in 1930 for his set designs for "King of Jazz." A wife, 4 sons and 5 daughters survive.

SCOTT, ZACHARY, 51, stage and screen actor, died Oct. 3, 1965 at his home in Austin, Texas of a malignant brain tumor. He had been bedridden following brain surgery in July in New York. In his screen roles he was most often cast as the smooth, tough, but charming heel. After several Broadway appearances, he made his film debut in 1943 in "The Mask of Demetrios," followed by "Mildred Pierce," "Cass Timberlaine," "Appointment In Honduras," "Her Kind of Man," "The Southerner," "Born To Be Bad," and "The Young One." His first marriage to Elaine Anderson, by whom he had two daughters who survive, ended in divorce. His second wife, actress Ruth Ford, was with him when he died.

SELZNICK, DAVID O., 63, film producer, died June 22, 1965 in Hollywood's Mt. Sinai Hospital of acute coronary occlusion. He was the son of Lewis J. Selznick, an early producer. His greatest feature film was "Gone With The Wind." After working for Metro, Paramount, and RKO, he formed his own Selznick International Co. He had been inactive in recent years. He was married and divorced from Irene Mayer by whom he had two sons, and then married to actress Jennifer Jones by whom he has a daughter. His films include "Duel In The Sun," "Since You Went Away," "Four Feathers," "King Kong," "Topaze," "Bird of Paradise," "Animal Kingdom," "Viva Villa," "Anna Karenina," "David Copperfield," "Tale of Two Cities," "Dinner At Eight," "Dancing Lady," "A Star Is Born" (1937), "Prisoner of Zenda," "A Farewell To Arms," "Nothing Sacred," and "Tom Sawyer." Burial was in Forest Lawn Memorial Park.

SLOANE, EVERETT, 55, one of the screen's busiest character actors, was found dead from barbiturates by his wife on Aug. 6, 1965 in his Brentwood home, an apparent suicide. Reportedly, he was worried over his failing eyesight. A native New Yorker, he had a distinguished career on Broadway and radio, before he went to Hollywood where he appeared in "Citizen Kane," "Journey Into Fear," "The Lady From Shanghai," "Patterns," "The Magnificent Ambersons," "Prince of Foxes," "The Men," "Bird of Paradise," "The Enforcer," "Sirocco," "Blue Veil," "Desert Fox," "Sellout," "The Prince Who Was A Thief," "Way Of A Gaucho," "The Big Knife," "Somebody Up There Likes Me," and "Home From The Hill." Surviving is his actress wife, Luba Herman, and son and daughter.

TANNEN, JULIUS, 84, vaudeville monologuist and film comedian, died Jan. 3, 1965 at the Motion Picture Country Hospital, Woodland Hills, Calif. With the decline of vaudeville in which he was a headliner, he went to Hollywood and appeared in numerous films, including "Collegiate," "The Great Moment," and "The Miracle of Morgan's Creek." Surviving are two sons, William, an actor, and Charles, a TV series writer.

TIERNEY, HARRY, 74, songwriter, died March 22, 1965, of a heart attack in New York. He wrote music for the "Ziegfeld Follies" and other Broadway musicals. For films, he wrote "Rio Rita," "Irene," "Cross My Heart," "Kid Boots," "Up She Goes," "I've Got A Million Girls Around Me," "Dixiana," "Half Shot At Sunrise," and "Follow Me." He was one of the founders of the American Society of Composers, Authors and Publishers. A wife and son survive.

VEILLER, ANTHONY, 62, film writer and producer, died of cancer June 27, 1965 in Hollywood. Son of playwright Bayard Veiller and actress Margaret Wycherly, he went to Hollywood as a writer in 1934 and subsequently worked for most of the major studios. His screenplays include "State of The Union," "Moulin Rouge," "A Woman Rebels," "Winterset," "The Stranger," "The Killers," and "Night of The Iguana." He produced "Force of Arms," "Fort Worth," "Victory," and "Along The Great Divide." Surviving are his wife, a son and daughter, and a step-son.

WAGNER, JACK, 68, stage and screen actor, died Feb. 6, 1965 in Hollywood. He appeared in such films as "Paris In The Spring," "Girl Crazy," "The Only Girl," and "The Fortune Teller."

David O. Selznick

Everett Sloane

WATERS, JOHN S., 71, pioneer director, died in Hollywood May 4, 1965 after an illness of many years. He went to California in the mid-1920's where he directed many Zane Grey films. He also directed "Viva Villa" for which he received an "Oscar" in 1935. His wife survives.

WATSON, BOBBY (Robert Watson Knucher), 77, stage and screen comedian, died May 22, 1965 in Hollywood. After touring in vaudeville and legitimate shows, he went to California where he became best known for his portrayals of Hitler in such films as "The Devil With Hitler," "Hitler, Dead Or Alive," and "The Hitler Gang." Other films were "Going Hollywood," "Adventurous Blonde," "Miracle of Morgan's Creek," "Practically Yours," and "Duffy's Tavern."

WATSON, MINOR, 75, veteran character actor of stage and screen, died July 28, 1965 in Alton, Ill. where he had been in retirement for several years. He had been an actor for more than 45 years, and his was one of the more familiar faces in such films as "The Jackie Robinson Story," "Guadalcanal Diary," "The Big Shot," "As Young As You Feel," "My Son John," "Mr. District Attorney," and his last "Trapeze" in 1956. His wife and daughter survive.

WESSEL, RICHARD, 52, screen and stage actor, died of a heart attack April 20, 1965 in his Hollywood home. After a lengthy stage career, he appeared in such films as "Pocket Full of Miracles," and "Wives and Lovers." He also starred in television series "River Boat" and "Tycoon." A wife and daughter survive.

INDEX

248

249

250

251

252

255